Toulouse Lautrec

Henri Perruchot

Must Have Books
503 Deerfield Place
Victoria, BC
V9B 6G5
Canada

ISBN: 9781773238388

Copyright 2022 – Must Have Books

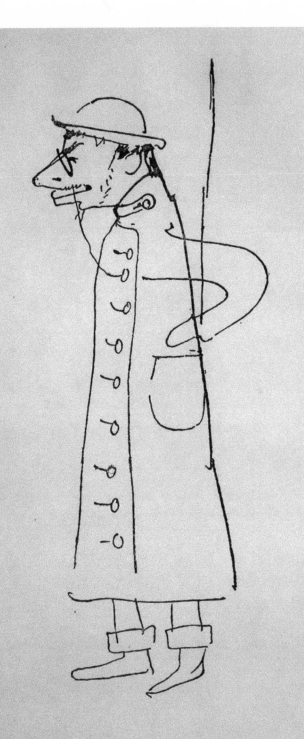

Foreword & Acknowledgements

TOULOUSE-LAUTREC has often been the victim of legend, and this was true even in his own lifetime. In this biography, I have attempted to discover his real personality but it has not been easy. Although, at first sight, Lautrec's life may seem perfectly familiar, it is not enough, as has too often been done, simply to place him against the gaudy décor of Montmartre and imagine that all has been said. The bright lights of the Butte have concealed Lautrec more often than they have served to illuminate him. Moreover, as far as he was concerned, Montmartre was far from being merely a décor. It was not only the picturesque he found there, but naked humanity. He knew, better than anyone, the bitterness that lay behind the laughter. He was never deceived about men, things or himself. His life was short, dramatic and tragic. Few men can ever have been more clearly aware of their destiny, nor lived it with greater lucidity than did Lautrec.

It is this destiny I have done my best to relate in this book. My aim has been to keep as close as possible to facts, to be as precise and accurate as I can. I have spared no effort to attain this end. I have read and collated everything that has been written about Lautrec; I have collected all the unpublished documents and evidence I have been able to discover; I have asked the few survivors who knew the painter for their recollections; I have searched for memories of him in the various places in which he lived; and I have taken similar pains over the lives of the people who were mixed up in his short and turbulent career.

I could not have written this book without help in my research from very many people. Thanks to them, I have been able to cast light on several periods of Lautrec's life which had hitherto been obscure, reinterpret it on many points, establish facts which are often of essential importance and, in general, acquire a more intimate knowledge of my subject than has previously been possible.

Concerning the painter's family, childhood and youth, his relative, Mademoiselle Mary Tapié de Céleyran, whose books form an inestimable source for everything to do with Lautrec's early years, has furnished me with invaluable information; and I had the advantage of her sensitive and erudite guidance on my visit to the Château du Bosc. M. Robert de Montcabrier, also a relative of the painter, and who was moreover his pupil for a time, has kindly replied to my questions in writing and at length. M. de Cercy d'Erville (Sylvain Bonmariage) has also given me invaluable information by generously placing at my disposal the records of the conversations he has had at various times with many of those who knew Lautrec, in particular Jane Avril, Romain Coolus, Degas, Maxime Dethomas, Alfred Edwards, Félix Fénéon, Footit, Mme Hayem, Maurice Joyant, Charles-Édouard Lucas, L. O. Raquin, Ambroise Vollard, etc. M. Michel-Ange Bernard has considerately placed the archives of his father, Émile Bernard, at my disposal. MM. Francis Jourdain, Édmond Heuzé and Doctor Louis Chouquet, Adolphe Albert's son-in-law, have been kind enough to give me their reminiscences of Lautrec and some of his friends. M. and Mme Maurice Exsteens have given me interesting information concerning Gustave Pellet and other friends of the artist. M. Émile Pottier, mayor of Villiers-sur-Morin, has assisted my search for traces of the painter in that locality. Doctor Gaston Lévy has helped me to a better understanding of the nature of the disease which determined Lautrec's life. M. Jean Adhémar, Deputy Keeper of the Cabinet des Estampes, whose works on Lautrec provide an abundant documentation, has very kindly given me his help, as has Mme Tulard, archivist at the Préfecture de Police. The researches of Mme Marcelle Duchemin, of the Inspectorate of Asylums, have added enormously to my information about Lautrec's stay in Doctor Semelaigne's private asylum at Neuilly. M. Romi has given me access to the treasures of his collection of documents and suggested valuable sources of information. Finally, my grateful thanks are due also to Mme du Ferron-Anquetin, Louis Anquetin's daughter-in-law, to Professor Henri Mondor and to Professor Logre, to Doctors Semelaigne (junior), Pierre Vallery-Radot and R. Chantemesse, to MM. Charles Laurent, André Devèche, Maurice Lambilliotte, Armand Got and Lucien Nöel, who have all in one way or another helped to enrich my documentation or facilitate my task. I would like to express my gratitude to them all.

H. P.

Contents

PART THREE
Women (1893–1897)

PART FOUR
The Dog in Spectacles (1897–1901)

Illustrations

As a pictorial biography of Lautrec the illustrations in this book are unique. For over a year the publishers have sought out every available photograph of the artist and they appear together for the first time in these pages. The photographs, many of which have not previously been published, are arranged as nearly as possible in chronological order.

Many have been reproduced from badly faded or damaged prints and in some cases, such as the frontispiece, they have been enlarged considerably. The publishers extend their thanks to the many people who have made this material available, and especially to the descendants of the Lautrec family and the Musée Toulouse-Lautrec. Wherever possible, the source of each picture and the name of the photographer is given in the list of illustrations.

LINE DRAWINGS IN THE TEXT

Unless otherwise mentioned the drawings in the text are
by Lautrec and are self-portraits

PHOTOGRAPHS

Frontispiece

Henri de Toulouse-Lautrec (c. 1890) Paris

A previously unpublished Daguerrotype, (approx. 2 in. × 3 in.) Toulouse-Lautrec collection, Palais de la Berbie, Albi. Photographer unknown

Toulouse-Lautrec

PROLOGUE

[1864—1879]

PROLOGUE

The Little Treasure
(1864–1879)

Schlägst du erst diese Welt zu Trümmorn,
Die andre mag darnach entstehn.
                              GOETHE: *Faust*

THERE was a storm over Albi that night. It was one of the usual
violent thunderstorms of autumn. Lightning flickered over the roofs,
illuminating the red brick houses of the town and the fortified
cathedral close by: farther off, in the hollow of the valley, the
waters of the Tarn were in spate. In the old Hôtel du Bosc, which
backed on to one of the ancient towers of the city's ramparts, the
Countess Adèle de Toulouse-Lautrec Montfa was in childbirth. The
date was November 24, 1864.

It was a difficult and prolonged birth.

The Countess had been married in May of the previous year to
Count Alphonse, her first cousin, then serving in the army. His uniform
had attracted her, for she was only twenty-one. Now, awaiting her
first child, she hoped it would be a son worthy of the name to which
so many ancestors had given lustre.

And everyone about her was hoping for a boy too: her mother
and her mother-in-law, who were sisters and about to become grandmothers for the first time; the 'Black Prince,' her father-in-law, that
austere, autocratic lord who lived in retreat in his Château du Bosc at

23

Rouergue; and her husband who, somewhat inclined to live in a dream-world, was already thinking of the time—and the sooner the better—when his son would be old enough to ride out hawking with him over the family estates.

All was ready for the heir's arrival: cradle and linen, muslin and lace; ivory, silver and gold rattles; a christening robe worthy of a prince, embroidered with lilies; and a little gold-embroidered bonnet, in the shape of a crown, that he would wear when the bells of the cathedral of Sainte-Cécile rang out in his honour.

All was ready. His christian names had been chosen. He was to be called Marie and Raymond, but first Henri, after the Count de Chambord who, as the last descendant of the elder branch of the Bourbons was, in the view of the diehard legitimist Count Alphonse, the only possible pretender to the throne of France, now so shamefully occupied by the nephew of the Usurper.

It was a terrible night, one the Countess Adèle was to remember until her dying day. Now she awaited the birth of her child in suffering and fear. If only it were a son! May God will* that it be a son, who would later become all that a Toulouse-Lautrec should be: a man who lived outside this unworthy century, who was well versed in the noble arts, a proud horseman, a great sportsman, clever with hawk and hound, a son who would never prostitute his great name and the centuries' old traditions of his race to sordid ambition. It must be a son. 'Believe me,' Count Alphonse had said, 'it is better to be a male toad than a female Christian.'

And finally, while the storm continued to rage, Countess Adèle gave birth to a boy.

*   *   *

Young Henri was a charming child, bright-eyed and round-cheeked, very smart in the fashionable baby's clothes of the time, a tartan cape and dress (for the fashion was very British).

He was the first child of his generation to be born to the Toulouse-

---

* *Diex lo volt*, 'God wills it', is given as the motto of the family and the arms surmounted by the crown of a sovereign count are Quarterly; 1 and 4. Gules, a cross clechy voided throughout and hommety or, for Toulouse; 2 and 3. Gules, a lion rampant armed and langued or, for Lautrec.

Lautrecs who, with their numerous relations, were a large family, and a great quantity of love was bestowed on him. Proudly, fondly he was called—in the Rouergat patois—*Bébé lou poulit* (pretty baby); or *petit bijou* (the Little Treasure), as one of his grandparents named him with indulgent admiration.

The Little Treasure began to take note of life amid the admiring circle that formed about him wherever he might be. For his family moved frequently. Sometimes he was at Albi, in the old town house, hung with ancient tapestries, in which he had been born; sometimes at the huge Céleyran estate, in Languedoc; but most often at the Château du Bosc above the valley of the Viaur, where the 'Black Prince' reigned. A fine old house with its big round tower, tiled roofs and high ivy-clad walls.

From dawn onwards every morning the Château du Bosc was in a state of bustle. Horses pawed the ground in the courtyard, the pack gave tongue; while his grandfather, tightly buttoned into his hunting clothes, curvetted on his thoroughbred before giving the signal to move off.

Still at the height of his powers, being only a little over fifty, taciturn, haughty, abrupt, with a long face, a thick black beard, a heavy moustache and bushy eyebrows beneath which gleamed piercing eyes, the 'Black Prince' dominated his sons, Alphonse, Charles and Odon, his grooms, his kennelmen, and Pierre Grèzes, his huntsman.

'At bay,' 'the death,' 'a good scent,' 'a check,' 'a heel line': these were the words Henri heard every day of his life from the first moment he could lisp. Even before he could speak he knew the horses, the hounds, and the hawks with their sharp eyes and steely beaks which the Martins, peasants of Rabastens, were specially commissioned to train for Count Alphonse. He was a wild child and, whenever he could escape supervision, hurried to the stables, where he revelled in the strong smells of hay, bedding and horses. Sometimes he trotted off to the huge kennels, and crouched among the big tufters or the running hounds. He was slowly discovering his kingdom.

'In our family,' said Count Alphonse, 'we christen a child at once,

and then put him on a horse!' Henri promised well. He had been found
tasting the horses' water and eating the black bread that was specially
cooked for the hounds.

The first years of Henri's life at Le Bosc went by in a dream. In the
evening, after dinner, before being taken to bed, he was allowed to
spend a few minutes in the drawing-room with the grown-ups. Here,
after the physical exertions of the day, it was the time for more peaceful pastimes. Sitting in their easy chairs, silk shawls about their shoulders,
the women embroidered, the Abbé Peyre, the Château's chaplain,
smoked his pipe, and the men discussed the day's sport, filled cartridges,
read, drew or modelled in wax.

These artistic predelictions were part of the tradition of the Toulouse-
Lautrecs. The family had portraits executed at the beginning of the
century by the 'Black Prince's' own father. Count Alphonse, Henri's
father, was given to modelling little statuettes of horses and hounds
and had a considerable facility for turning out a sketch with a few
strokes of pencil or pen. He shared his tastes with his younger brothers,
Odon and, in particular, Charles, who showed a lively liking for
art.

'When my sons shoot a woodcock,' said grandmother Gabrielle, 'it
gives them three pleasures: shooting, drawing and eating.'

Standing beside one of his uncles, Henri would gaze in fascination
at his moving hand drawing lines, joining one to another, till suddenly
a huntsman, a stag at bay, or a wild boar surrounded by hounds
emerged from the paper. Then lying flat on his stomach by the hearth,
where huge logs were burning, Henri would pull out a burnt stick
and set about drawing lines and circles on the big drawing-room
carpet.

He was not quite three years old when, on August 28, 1867, a
brother, Richard, was born. 'I like his Christian name,' his grandmother wrote; 'a previous one of that name married the sister of
Richard of England.' On the day of the christening in Albi cathedral,
Henri was placed in charge of a canoness, who was scandalised by his
short socks and bare legs. After the ceremony, she took him in the
procession to the sacristy where the parish register was to be signed. 'I
want to sign too,' he said in his childish way. 'But you don't yet know

how to write,' said the canoness. 'Very well,' he replied, 'I'll draw an ox!'

*   *   *

All was not well with Count Alphonse's marriage. Countess Adèle was far from happy, to say the least. Sweet-natured, tactful, intelligent and fastidious, she had inherited from her ancestors, the Tapié de Céleyrans, virtues that might perhaps be called *bourgeoises*. Natives of Azille-en-Minervois, a village some forty kilometres from Carcassonne, the Tapiés, who had become de Céleyran only at the very end of the eighteenth century, had been under the Ancien Régime magistrates, treasurer-generals and canons, spread widely over the Narbonne countryside. Shrewd people, clever in business and with an eye to the main chance, they had added lands to their vineyards and town houses to their country properties. In 1798, Esprit-Jean-Jacques-Toussaint-Tapié, Henri's great-grandfather, had been adopted by a cousin, Jacques Mengau, Councillor of the Sovereign Court of Accounts, Taxes and Finance of Montpellier, second lord of Céleyran. The adopted heir inherited both the title and estates, in particular the magnificent domain of Céleyran, which included a fine house and three thousand, five hundred acres, mostly of vineyards.

Countess Adèle, whose inclinations lay towards a peaceful, retired life, had certainly no idea on her wedding day of the fate that awaited her on marrying her cousin. For the blood of the Toulouse-Lautrecs was very dissimilar to that of the Tapié de Céleyrans.

The wild spirit of their forebears lived on unquenched in the Toulouse-Lautrecs, whose ancestors had been Counts of Toulouse and Viscounts of Lautrec, and whose story was part of history. Ardent, violent and splendidly audacious, they had indulged throughout the centuries in the wildest escapades and excesses. Nothing could cast them down. Staunch in adversity, they belonged to a race that would never admit defeat. Possessed by a frenzied need for action, they had spent their natural turbulence in deeds and misdeeds, in crusades to the Holy Land, in wars of religion and in battles in foreign parts. While Raymond IV had been among the first to enter Jerusalem in 1099, his descendants, involved in the appalling struggle of the Albigensian war, were excommunicated by the Popes ten times. They were not, however, the sort of men to be unduly perturbed by that; and retaliated by hanging the legate, who so impudently brought them His Holiness's writ.

'Ah, Monseigneur,' Count Alphonse once exclaimed nostalgically to an archbishop over the dinner-table, 'the days are gone when the Counts of Toulouse could violate a monk and hang him afterwards if it so pleased them.' They were not beyond similar violence towards their own family. In 1214, Baudoin, who had been so ill-advised as to join the party of Simon de Montfort, was sentenced to death by Raymond VI, his brother, who watched the hanging.* This was the traditional behaviour of Henri's ancestors on his father's side.

Accustomed by heredity to conduct themselves as absolute masters, closely related to the royal families of France, England and Aragon, and marrying the brothers, sisters, sons, and daughters of monarchs, they knew no law but their own. Their vitality was inexhaustible. And the chronicle was by no means limited to their feats of arms; it recorded also the excesses into which some of them had been led by the heat of their southern blood: the debauches of a Pierre-Joseph de Toulouse-Lautrec, Count of Foix, in 1790; or the aberrations of that Adélaide de Toulouse, whose unbridled lust, it was said, 'no man, servant, lord, burgess or peasant could satisfy.' 'Citizen Duchess,' superbly declared Pierre-Joseph de Toulouse-Lautrec to the Duchess de la Trémoille, 'let us not confuse love with matters of copulation.'

Anathematising the revolutionaries of 1789, the republicans, the freemasons, the Orléanists and the Bonapartists, Count Alphonse, who though a little on the short side was physically strong and extremely energetic, expended his superabundant vitality as best he could.

Until his marriage at the age of twenty-five, he had served as a second-lieutenant in the 6th Regiment of Lancers, after passing through the military college of Saint-Cyr. He was devoted to all forms of horsemanship, racing, jumping, steeplechasing, paper-chasing, and was famed for being exceptionally good on a horse. Indeed, his ability was the despair of his rivals. He was the 'glory of the

---

* The Toulouse-Lautrec-Montfa branch of the family was descended from this Baudoin who, in 1196, married the Viscountess Alix de Lautrec, heiress to the lordships of Montfa.

regiment'. As inexhaustible as he was courageous, he had been known to tire out three horses in a single day; and then, fresh and unwearied, spend the night dancing and enjoying himself in the highest of spirits.

Count Alphonse had known his cousin Adèle since childhood. The two young people seemed to like and understand each other. They imagined they were in love: they yielded to the 'impetuosity of impulse.'* But from the very first weeks of their life together, the unhappy and disappointed Countess discovered that her husband was very different from what she had imagined. They had nothing in common; indeed, their temperaments were utterly at variance.

A character out of the Middle Ages rather than of 1868, Count Alphonse had been born into a world that gave him horses and hunting as the only outlets for his energy. He had no aims in life, and merely obeyed his impulses. And, indeed, what was there to prevent him? Money? The Toulouse-Lautrecs kept a great chest which was filled by their stewards and from which each took what he required. Public opinion? Count Alphonse was utterly unaware of it. He was completely unaffected by the restraints imposed by society and had no fear of appearing ridiculous. He lived in a world of his own, doing precisely as he pleased, and his wild, totally uncontrolled temperament led him into the strangest eccentricities. There was no doubt, in the opinion of everyone who knew him, that he was very odd indeed.

In summer, he would walk through the streets of Albi with his shirt tails flying and a hawk on his wrist. Stopping from time to time, he would feed the bird pieces of raw meat. In order not to deprive his hawks of the benefits of religion, he gave them holy water to drink.

He was fond of dressing-up and often found it agreeable or convenient to turn himself into a cowboy, a Circassian, a Scottish Highlander, or to wear a Crusader's hauberk. Nor did the various pieces of these disguises necessarily correspond: he once came down to family luncheon wearing a plaid and a dancer's tutu. In his rooms, amid trophies of the chase, old books on falconry, out of date calendars and worm-eaten documents, he kept quantities of arms and horse furniture from all over the world. There were Samurai daggers, Kirghiz saddles and Red Indian wigwams. He was particularly

* Count Alphonse's phrase in a letter to René Princeteau, September 18, 1901.

attracted by everything that originated in the Near or Middle East. Persia fascinated him. He collected everything he could lay his hands on from the peoples of western Asia: harness, medicines, cooking recipes. 'I'm delighted with my new Caucasian helmet, which is shaped like the towers of Le Bosc,' he wrote to his mother, adding a rapid sketch of it for her. 'I wear it in the Bois with a crest of red cloth that floats in the wind when I gallop.'

This was the Bois de Boulogne. He was far too restless ever to remain in one place for long. He was constantly travelling all over France, from time to time 'forgetting' his wife on a station platform. Left penniless, she would have to persuade the railway company to send her home.

For Count Alphonse was also very absent-minded: a few days after his wedding, he went to Paris and rejoined his boon companions from the regiment, having completely 'forgotten' that he had just got married.

He hunted in the south at Le Bosc, at his Château de Montfa, near Castres in Sologne (where he intended letting loose two lions), and also near Orléans, in the forests by Loury. In the Canton of Neuville-aux-Bois, he kept a portable hunting-box, which he took with him from place to place, according to his fancy or the exigencies of his sport.

It was at Loury in August, 1868 (when Henri was three and a half), that the Toulouse-Lautrec marriage came finally to grief. Countess Adèle's dignity had already suffered severely from her husband's many eccentricities. But now there were more serious differences. She had dreamed of love and quiet happiness, and she could no longer put up with the continual infidelities into which Count Alphonse's hot blood led him. Like his distant ancestor, Adélaide de Toulouse, everything was grist to his mill, shepherdesses, cabaret dancers, prostitutes. Countess Adèle could stand it no longer.

Her second son, Richard, had just died at Loury, on August 27, at the age of one year less a day. Half out of her mind with grief, she quitted the Orléanais for Le Bosc, taking Henri with her, and determined to have no further relationship with Count Alphonse except that of a cousin.

Her life was over. From now on, Henri was her sole consolation.

*   *   *

Henri's education began under the direction of his mother, the Abbé Peyre and a distant unmarried cousin, Armandine d'Alichoux de Sénégra. He had a quick brain and made rapid progress. But he was also a difficult pupil. Lively, noisy, and curious about everything that went on round him, he was never still for a moment: just like a ball, his mother said. He was wilful and generally got his own way. He was affectionate, demonstrative and cajoling; but as soon as anyone resisted him, he retaliated. 'I want to pee! Yes, here!' he said one day in the Cathedral of Saint-Cécile, and oblivious to the horrified protests of his nurse, the dear Adeline, he proceeded to do so on the cathedral's mosaic floor.

In stables and pantry, in drawing-room and kennels, the spoilt, un-disciplined child behaved like a tyrant, imposing his will and abusing his power. He was also a tease. Never slow to grasp the vivid or comic side of people and things, he subjected everyone to his raillery: the cooks whose sauces he gravely and pompously tasted, the grooms to whom he would jabber English and the kind chaplain whom he tried to caricature. His mother shut her eyes to it, scolding tenderly. She was delighted by his lively naughtiness.

She was indeed very proud of her son. She never grew weary of teaching him the history of his family, its illustrious relationships (Henri was also a great-nephew of La Fayette), and the princely marriages by which royal blood flowed in the veins of the Toulouse-Lautrecs. 'In that case,' cried the boy, 'I can say that kings are my cousins!'

Nevertheless, from time to time, Countess Adèle felt a slight disquiet. Though not exactly sickly, Henri did not seem to be very strong. His fontanel was not closing. He had, too, a curious defect in his speech; he lisped a little.

But all this would pass as he grew older, she reassured herself. How could her son fail to inherit the characteristics of the men of his family, of his rugged grandfather, and of his father who would wade into lakes in the middle of winter or sit up all night for game, and whose rare letters (when he was away from his family, which was more often than not) consisted of nothing but accounts of hunting, and ended with the laconic formula: 'I'm dropping with sleep and quite well'?*

During these years Count Alphonse paid little attention to his son. So long as the boy was too young to ride a thoroughbred, he took no interest in him. The education of children was a woman's business. It was only later on that really serious matters began, and these had nothing whatever to do with Latin and arithmetic. To a friend, who was giving his heir riding lessons, Count Alphonse said: 'Teach him also to use a lasso; it'll be useful to him later to capture women, whereas Latin . . .' There was one thing, however, that Henri did learn from his father: 'To turn the melancholy profile of Napoleon III on a big penny into that of a pig by using two fingers.'†

In the year 1870 the Second Empire was drawing to a close. On July 19, Napolean III declared war against Prussia; at the beginning of September, he surrendered at Sedan, and on the 17th the Prussians besieged Paris. These events caught Count Alphonse at Loury. While he was adapting himself as best he could to the occupation of his hunting country by the enemy, his brothers joined the army of the Loire, Odon riding his beautiful mare Bavolette.

---

* Mary Tapié de Céleyran quotes from one of these letters, dated from Loury, December 29, 1869: 'My dearest, I have not had time to write because we have been dividing the hounds into two categories: Odon is keeping ten hounds, to be used exclusively for roe-deer, and is completely handing over to me eighteen hounds for wild boar. I have had to look for a new horse and I've at last found a little mare who goes perfectly in harness. I was able to take the hounds out yesterday. The woods had been very well done. I laid the hounds on at once,and in two hours they had brought to bay and killed a boar which gave us a very good hunt. The next day, my mare was staked in the foreleg and she'll need ten days rest. Odon, who had gone out with the roe-deer hounds had a fall with Paroli, who is also lame. A few days later, we drew blank (the wood had been badly done). Nevertheless, I attacked a two-year-old boar, which went away and was brought to bay after an hour's run! The hounds were unhurt: only Lucifer and Blucher were slightly scratched. Loury is becoming a good centre. My twenty hounds give tongue well, as much as French hounds do. I'm hunting tomorrow with the Prince de Montholon who will lend me his Vautrait. Etc.' Count Alphonse gave six pages of similar details, before concluding abruptly with the formula mentioned above. As Mary Tapié de Céleyran remarks, on reading such a love letter as this one is irresistibly reminded of: 'Madame, it's blowing hard and I've killed six wolves.'

† Thadée Natanson.

The artist's mother, Adèle Tapié de
eyran, Comtesse de Toulouse-
trec Montfa

The artist's father, Le Comte
honse de Toulouse-Lautrec Montfa,
young man

e Comte Alphonse as a Saracen.

e Comte Alphonse as a Highland
ef

2.

4.

Lautrec's nursery at the Château du Bosc   (*below*) Château du Bosc

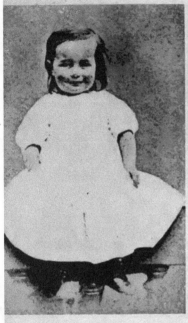

'Bébé Lou Poulit'

Aged two

Aged two

Aged five

LAUTREC AS A CHILD

HENRI-MARIE-RAYMOND DE TOULOUSE-LAUTREC MONTFA
aged fourteen (1878)

On January 28, 1871, Paris capitulated to the Prussian forces. On March 18, the Commune insurrection broke out, for which Count Alphonse could never find words bad enough. Of the four revolutions which had torn France asunder in less than a century, the Commune seemed to him the most disgraceful. When would the Count de Chambord mount the throne of France?

These years of war ended for the Toulouse-Lautrecs with a tragic accident. On the morning of December 23, 1871, Henri's grandfather, the 'Black Prince,' accompanied by his huntsman and his pack of hounds, rode away from the Château as usual. The weather was very cold, the countryside was frozen. The 'Black Prince' put up a hare and hunted it for some time. At noon he sent his huntsman back to Le Bosc. He would continue the hunt alone. No one was to wait luncheon for him.

The hours went by. The short December day began to fade. As night fell over the Château, the women became increasingly anxious.

The hounds returned, but without their master, and the household searched the neighbourhood of Le Bosc all night. Henri kept trying to persuade his mother to go down into the valley of the Viaur, but no one would listen to him. Yet it was there by the river that at dawn they found the fierce old sportsman's broken and frozen body.

The 'Black Prince' had suffered the same fate as his father, who had been killed out hunting at the age of thirty-seven. There seemed no doubt that he had been thrown from his horse and fallen from rock to rock down the steep slope above the Viaur. Wounded to death, he must have tried to blow his horn, which lay blood-stained beside him.

It was a sad Christmas. The knell tolled amid the bells ringing out for the Nativity.

*   *   *

'Monsieur l'Abbé is prayed by his dung-eating pupil to tell him whether one writes Γνωτι σεαυτου or Γνωθι σεαυτου.

All my respects.

'HENRI DE TOULOUSE-LAUTREC.'

The 'dung-eating pupil' was not yet quite eight years old. There was no doubt about his intelligence and precocity. He was already learning the rudiments of Latin and beginning Greek.

B

Whether at Le Bosc, at Albi or at Céleyran, life seemed to him more
and more enchanted. Cousins of both sexes had now been born; from
the first he took resolute charge of them. He was never weary of
inventing new games.

But there was an extraordinary contrast between his vitality and
his physical appearance. In spite of living an open air life and eating
abundantly and well (the boy had the 'legendary Lautrec stomach,')*
he remained puny and delicate in health. Countess Adèle watched him
anxiously, concerned at his sloping shoulders, narrow chest and skinny
legs. And yet it was clearly time he went to school. It was 1872 and
term was beginning. Should she still wait a little?

As it happened, Count Alphonse wanted to live in Paris, from where
he could hunt more easily in Orléanais and Sologne. He would also
be better placed to follow the doings of the horsey world. A decision
was made, and one morning in early autumn Henri left the Château
du Bosc with his mother.

Count Alphonse was living in Paris on the ground floor of an
aristocratic lodging-house, the Hôtel Pérey, at 5 Cité du Retiro. The
Cité du Retiro was one of the many places in the capital with a romantic
charm and a redolence of the past. It was reached through No. 30,
Rue du Faubourg-Saint-Honoré; on the left, a few steps away from
the entrance, was the Hôtel Pérey; farther on, at the end of the street,
were some fine eighteenth century façades; then the street on which
the Cité was built made a right-angle turn and led out through No. 35,
Rue Boissy d'Anglas. The ground plan, which at first seemed peculiar,
was easily explained. In the days of the Ancien Régime the Cité du
Retiro had been the mews in which the Court carriages were housed.

From now on Henri lived in the Hôtel Pérey with his parents,
though their marriage existed only in appearance, and indeed consisted
of no more than 'courtesy and indifference.'† But the child's welfare
had to be considered. 'Over his little brown head, husband and wife
still held each other's hands, though their wedding-rings were loose.'‡
The Toulouse-Lautrecs sent their son as a day-boy to the eighth
preparatory class of the Lycée Fontanes§ in the Rue du Havre, where

* † ‡ Mary Tapié de Céleyran
§ Now the Lycée Condorcet.

one of his cousins on his mother's side, Louis Pascal, was already a pupil.

The boy did not leave everything that had made up his former life without reluctance. When the moment came to go, he felt like bursting into tears. But he controlled himself: a gentleman never cried. Nevertheless, he clung to his mother as they got into the carriage and asked: 'Mama, shall we come back one day?' But instead of '*jour*' he said '*zour*,' for Henri was not, alas, losing his childish lisp.

But this early sorrow quickly vanished. A new life was opening before him and, since he was always interested in what was going on round him, he adapted himself to school life very quickly. He naturally made close friends with his cousin, Louis Pascal, who was a boarder (his father, who was in the Prefectorial service, worked outside Paris), and also with Maurice Joyant, the son of a rich bourgeois family, who was about his own age. These two became inseparable companions. They competed in their studies, and were always very close together at the top of the class. In some subjects, French grammar for instance, Lautrec was the better; but in others, such as Latin grammar, Joyant beat him.

The master of the eighth preparatory class, M. Mantoy, had reason to be pleased with his pupil. But he would have been even more so had Lautrec not encouraged the others in mischief by his example.

But 'how can he be punished severely? He works so well!' exclaimed Countess Adèle, who was all the more forbearing since her son's health was causing her increasing anxiety. 'He's growing only very slowly and has already been nicknamed "little man" at school.'

Would riding set him up? Countess Adèle hoped so, and Henri went every day with his father for a lesson at the Duphot Riding School. He loved movement; and he never grew tired of looking at horses. Like his father, he instinctively took to animals that had achieved an individual and peculiar perfection. He loved the subtle play of a horse's muscles, the conformation of a well-bred animal precisely adapted to the exigencies of the racecourse.

All forms of horsemanship were very fashionable at the time. The Allée des Poteaux in the Bois de Boulogne was crowded with horsemen and horsewomen every morning and, during the afternoon, in the Allée des Acacias, the *monde* and the *demi-monde* came to show off their dresses and luxurious turn-outs in a ceaseless procession of phaetons, hansoms, landaus, victorias, dog-carts, broughams and coupés, as well as four-in-hands with postilions wearing powdered hair. The fashionable world met at the races, at Chantilly or Long-champ (a new course was being laid out at Auteuil). And the Derby, the Horse Show and the Grand Prix, as well as the point-to-points, were among the great events it was impossible to miss.

Count Alphonse, who when necessary could dress like a dandy and wear a London-made top-hat, did not much care for the frivolous and entirely artificial existence led by the people of his rank in life. Devoted to 'sport' (that English word, then new to France, which meant above all riding), he enjoyed fashionable gatherings only to the extent that they afforded him the opportunity of indulging his personal tastes. If he frequented the clubs it was mainly to see hunting and steeple-chasing friends. Trying out a new horse or leisurely inspecting a hawk or a great eagle-owl were his real pleasures. On the ground floor of the Hôtel Pérey, where he had arranged a small studio (he did a little sculpting and modelling), he had set up some hives so as to study the flight of bees. He often took his son to race-meetings or to the Bois de Boulogne, for he was now educating him as a future sportsman. He taught him to judge the quality of a horse with a naturalist's minute attention to detail, to observe and analyse what made it what it was. The boy liked looking at horses; his father taught him to see them.

Undoubtedly, Henri admired his father. Nor did his father's eccentricities particularly astonish him; he was used to them. That Count Alphonse should wash his shirts in the gutter of the Rue Royale on the pretext that the Paris laundresses did not know their business (did anyone in France know how to wash linen 'since Louis XVI's head had been cut off?'*); that he should ride to the Bois on a mare in milk, saddled and bridled in Caucausian fashion, and milk his mount for breakfast when he reached the Cascade; that, in the Bois again, he should put in his own peculiar form of personal appearance by driving a long-haired Shetland pony in a Norwegian trap or,

* Francis Jourdain.

alternatively, be seen riding there in Kirghiz costume—what, after all, was so surprising about these things? Were they so very much more unusual than the horn-blowing by which Uncle de Céleyran hastily summoned his household at the approach of a thunderstorm? Assembled in the hall of the Château, they had to sit on chairs insulated from the ground by panes of glass, and recite prayers till the sky cleared.

Count Alphonse's complete indifference to what people said or did no doubt contributed to the fascination he held for Henri. They had many similar characteristics. The boy saw his father as a model. His bearing, his courage, his strength and his good horsemanship were an example to him. One day, Count Alphonse bet a member of the Jockey Club two hundred louis that he would jump his horse over a covered cab; and he won. Henri was lost in admiration.

On his side, Count Alphonse was delighted by his son's passion for animals. He could see himself in the boy who so eagerly shared this taste. For Count Alphonse loved animals; indeed, he loved them more then he was prepared to admit. He not only loved his horses, hounds and hawks, but he also loved the quarry he hunted. He hated wanton killing. On several occasions, he had called off hunts that were not being conducted in accordance with the rules, and were therefore not giving the stag, roe-deer or boar a fair chance.

He was always trying to create new difficulties to make the conditions of his sporting activities harder. M. de Montesquieu used to tell a story in the clubs about a day when Count Alphonse had invited him to shoot in Sologne. They had walked for miles. The weather was very hot, and M. de Montesquieu was exhausted. Eventually, the two men reached a lake, which was to be the scene of operations. Numbers of duck and teal rose off the water. Forgetting his fatigue, M. de Montesquieu quickly loaded his gun. Upon which his host restrained him with some embarrassment and said: 'My dear fellow, please don't shoot. These birds are the delight of my eyes and if you shoot you'll frighten them, they might never come back.'

But Count Alphonse did not take his son only to see horses. He often took him to the studio of a painter friend of his, René Princeteau, who lived in a sort of artists' colony at the top of the Rue du Faubourg-

Saint-Honoré, at No. 233. The studios were behind a gate on either side of a blind alley and there was a pleasant country atmosphere about the place.

Princeteau was a curious man. The son of a Libourne wine-merchant, he had been born a deaf mute, but this had not prevented his acquiring a good education. First his mother and then various specialists had taught him to speak: he talked in a rather hoarse, broken, throaty voice which, though it had something artificial about it, was fluent enough, and since he had also learnt to lip-read he was able to carry on a conversation comparatively easily. He had taken lessons in a wide variety of subjects, including gymnastics and horsemanship, and had at first intended to become a sculptor. Before coming to Paris, he had studied in Bordeaux at the Imperial School of Fine Arts. And it was there he had turned to painting.

By the time he was thirty, René Princeteau had acquired a certain reputation as a painter. He exhibited at the Arts Club in the Rue Volney, and at the Salon, where his paintings and sculptures attracted favourable notice and were occasionally bought by the State. Always elegantly turned out in frock-coat and top-hat, he went a good deal into society and even attended balls. He could 'hear the music in his stomach,' he said.* A good horseman himself, he devoted his talents mainly to painting horses, hounds, and the vicissitudes of steeple-chasing.

He was somewhat worldly—'I never paint horses worth less than 20,000 francs,'—but his work was very conscientious. When he painted a horse or a hound, he did his best to make the portrait a true one, precisely as if he were painting a human being.

Princeteau took a few pupils; five or six rich amateurs, all sportsmen from the Cité du Retiro, had chosen him for master and attended his lessons, among them Count Alphonse.† Now Henri also acquired the habit of going regularly to the studio in the Rue du Faubourg-Saint-Honoré, where he never tired of watching the artist draw and paint.

---

* Quoted by Robert Martrinchard.
   † The museum at Libourne has a canvas by Princeteau, *La Banquette irlandaise*, in which Count Alphonse is shown jumping a bank on his horse Paroli together with other gentlemen riders.

Princeteau rarely drew an animal in repose. He was above all a painter
of movement, and this delighted the boy, who also enjoyed Princeteau's mocking wit, directed against the ridiculous and the absurd. Had
he not a similar tendency himself?

'The child,' as Princeteau called him, drew ceaselessly. He did so
from no mere boyish desire to imitate his elders, but because of an
innate gift that enabled him to find in drawing a second—indeed, one
might almost say, a first—calligraphy. When he needed to express an
emotion or impression, he turned spontaneously to drawing. He
discovered with amazement the resources of this other language,
whose elements were not learnt like words, but whose signs he had
to invent as he went along. His delight in this game was mingled with
astonishment as he began to discover what his fingers could do.

The margins of his notebooks and exercises were covered with
sketches, particularly of horses and horsemen, hounds and birds.
But he also exercised his powers of observation on his school-friends,
whose likenesses he could catch in a few lines, frequently in caricature,
and often clumsily, but not without zest and life.*

But Henri's health was still far from satisfactory and he often had
to stay away from school for months at a time. In the winter of 1873,
he went back to school only in December, and yet in spite of these
interruptions he made excellent progress, and at the prize-giving in
July 1874, he was, to judge from the number of his prizes, one of the
most successful boys in the eighth class.†

Altogether the year had been a very successful one and Countess
Adèle had a right to be proud of him. Nevertheless, her chief concern
was not so much for his studies as for his health. He was now nearly
ten, but seemed to grow no stronger. His bones were still fragile.
Words, such as tuberculosis and coxalgia, which no family in those
days could mention without anguish, were beginning to haunt
Countess Adèle's mind. Her marriage had brought her very little
happiness. Was she destined to regret it still more by the thought

---

* The earliest of Lautrec's drawings we possess date from this period (1873).
† He got first prizes for Latin prose, Latin translation, French grammar and
English grammar, second honourable mention for recitation, third honourable
mention for history and geography, and fifth honourable mention for arithmetic.

that she and Alphonse ought, before marrying, to have considered more carefully the consequences of consanguinity?

In October 1874, when term began, Henri, who was now in the seventh class, could not go back to school. It was November 23 before he was well enough and, on January 9, his schooling was interrupted again, and this time for good, for his mother carried him off to the Pyrénées Orientales to take the cure at Amélie-les-Bains.

*   *   *

The cousins at Le Bosc and Céleyran had grown. From now on, Henri was to be brought up among them. His life in the country or in Albi would now be broken from time to time only by a visit to a spa or to Nice.

Count Alphonse's sister had married Countess Adèle's brother: they were to have fourteen children, who were doubly first cousins to Henri. All these boys and girls with their parents, tutors, governesses, nurses and the servants formed one of those large family societies of which there were many in the French countryside of those days.

Henri was perfectly happy and contented in this family society. There was nothing of the solitary child about him. He liked the human warmth of groups and he was delighted to get back to the woods and vineyards. As leader of the lively, noisy band of cousins, he was a stimulating influence, never at a loss for new games, practical jokes, and amusements of all kinds.

'Henri sings from morning till night,' wrote his grandmother. 'He's like a cricket and gladdens the whole house. His departure always leaves a great gap, for he takes the place of twenty people.' Even in chapel, Henri found it hard to behave, and his irreverent laughter, which would soon infect his cousins, was apt to be heard at the comic passages in certain Languedoc hymns:

> *A l'enfant divin*
> *J'ai donné*
> *Un saucisson*
> *Dans un cornet.*

In those days Henri seemed to be everywhere at once. He was down by the lake where he was rearing cormorants and had a flotilla of model ships which, as he said: 'Capsize but never sink'; or he was playing with his toy theatre, manipulating, with appropriate changes of voice, puppets for whom he invented endless farcical situations; or he was at the kitchen-range where, since he was naturally greedy, he looked into everything, had no hesitation in giving advice, and was already contriving little dishes on his own. For which he was nicknamed: 'Henri the cook.'

This greed was a family characteristic. The Toulouse-Lautrecs had always paid particular attention to the pleasures of the table. Game, fowl, foies gras and truffles poured into the kitchens where exquisite dishes simmered. The family was passionately fond of its food, and not only traditional food at that. They loved innovation. One of Henri's great-great-uncles, to the horror of the ladies, had one day served up a fat monkey with its little hands dabbling in the sauce. Count Alphonse, who was as eccentric in cookery as in everything else, would eat truffles soaked in milk or a beefsteak with Roquefort or an omelette with apricots, when not experimenting with some oriental recipe.

On the Le Bosc lawns, Henri had laid out 'a miniature Bois de Boulogne,'* where he and his cousins played with their toy carriages, smart turn-outs they had ordered from England, giving precise specifications for what they required, which led to long exchanges of correspondence.

Imperious, and used to getting his own way, Henri was furious when things did not go as he wished. 'My dear Raoul,' he wrote to one of his cousins, 'Augé told me he would send me a brougham and a dog-cart . . . And now you're talking about a landau. Write to him bluntly that, if he doesn't send these carriages, I don't want any others (unless you can find me some light carriage with two wheels), and if there isn't one, with four: with a horse that can be unharnessed; I want black and yellow harness and a dog-cart. But remember . . . two wheels, if possible. Tell my godmother to take charge of my order. Send your carriages as models and let me know what your landaus are like.'

*   *   *

* Mary Tapié de Céleyran.

By Henri's room at Château Le Bosc, in the passage near the bathrooms, the mothers had a habit of marking their children's height on
the wall with a line, a Christian name and a date, and Henri was often
bidden to stand against the wall.

For he was growing very slowly, and some of his younger cousins
were already nearly as tall as he.

In fact he was puny. His physical capacities were not commensurate
with his ardent spirit. Though he longed to hunt, he could take no
part in violent games. Impatiently cracking his little crop, he awaited
his hour, for he thought of nothing but hunting. But in the meantime,
he had to continue his education under tutors and the general direction
of his mother, who was not only an extremely cultivated woman
but an excellent Latin scholar. He was working hard at Latin, Greek,
German and English. He spoke English more or less fluently, and
wanted to perfect himself in it. To this end, he undertook to translate
a whole book, a work by Salvin on falconry.*

Count Alphonse must have been delighted at the choice. On
January 1, 1876, he gave his eleven-year-old son a treatise called *La
Fauconnerie ancienne et moderne.*† The book had the following dedication:

'Remember, my son, that an outdoor life in the fresh air is the
only healthy one; everything deprived of freedom wilts and soon dies.

'This little book on falconry will teach you to appreciate the life of
the open spaces; and should you, one day, encounter the bitterness
of life, first the horse, then the hound and the hawk will be precious
companions and help you to forget things a little.'

                    *   *   *

'Forget things a little': there is a deal of melancholy in those words
of Count Alphonse—'Old Sachem,' as his son now sometimes called
him, having read Fenimore Cooper's *The Last of the Mohicans*.

'Wherever Papa is, you stand no chance of being the most remarkable

---

* It is not known whether this was *Falconry in the British Isles* by Salvin and
Brodwick, or *Falconry; its Claims, History and Practice* by Freeman and Salvin.

† This manual of practical falconry, by J. C. Chenu and O. des Murs, had been
published by Hachette a few years before, in 1862. This in itself is evidence
against the assertion, which has so often been made by Lautrec's biographers, that
Count Alphonse was the last man to practise hawking in France. There are still
falconers in France.

person present,' the boy said a little mockingly. Yet, Count Alphonse had great qualities in Henri's eyes. There was, indeed, considerable fascination about a man who, when wanting to try out some stallions, set off bare-back across country at six o'clock in the morning almost entirely naked; who would be found by the servants looking for mushrooms at night, with a candle in one hand and a hat-box in the other; and who, at Montfa, had ordered his peasants to lay out an avenue, insisting that they should work with wooden spades, for iron, he told them, was 'an ignoble metal, and poisonous into the bargain.' One day, he took it into his head to have a camel-hair tent erected in front of Albi cathedral, and went to live in it, together with a few hounds and hawks, so as to be able to gaze his fill at the church which had been 'built by his forefathers.' As the years went by the Count's peculiarities increased. When he was living under the same roof as his wife—(he was inclined to arrive without warning and stay for an indefinite period, two days, two months or two years)— Countess Adèle, whose only wish was to see him depart, lived in fear of his committing one of his wilder eccentricities, which were amusing enough for onlookers, but infinitely wearying to herself.

'Forget things a little.' It is more than probable that Count Alphonse was not a happy man. He was doubtless less indifferent to his marriage's failure than he seemed. He often gazed at his son with sadness and compassion, and, very probably, with a certain contempt. Would the boy ever be able to follow in his footsteps? He seemed curiously weak, he even used a stick to walk with. A Toulouse-Lautrec with a stick!

Henri's grandmother, too, often expressed the family's anxieties in her letters. And yet, as she once exclaimed: 'How can one be anxious about such a jolly fellow!' For the object of their concern had lost none of his gaiety and high spirits.

> *C'est l'amant d'A*
> *C'est l'amant d'A*
> *C'est l'amant d'Amanda.*

Le Bosc echoed to Henri's singing of that popular tune of the moment. Every day, weather permitting—for wet weather was not considered good for him—he had his riding-lesson. Mounted on one or other of his favourite horses, Usurpateur or Volga, he went off, in charge of the huntsman, for a ride that he made last as long as possible. 'You really cannot tell which of the two is the prouder, the teacher or the pupil,' remarked his grandmother in a moment of optimism.

Henri was convinced that horses would be his life; they were to him what they were to his father. And the time could not be far distant now when he would be allowed to go hunting with his father and uncles. Indeed why should that time be deferred, why should he not follow hounds today? He was sure of himself. 'His courage and skill,' said his grandmother, 'would be bound to lead him on to take jumps that were much too big for him.' They had some difficulty in pacifying him. His impatience was becoming more lively every day.

Though he was not yet permitted the pleasure of shooting, he could at least enjoy the pleasures of drawing and eating. When the weather was too bad to allow him to ride, the boy stayed indoors in the Château; he drew and painted in water-colours with his Uncle Charles, who had taken his artistic education in hand. He made a whole series of water-colours of game: red partridges, landrails, hares and roe-deer.

Whenever he took up pen or pencil, he started to draw. He could scarcely open an exercise book without sketching: horses, carriages, horsemen, hounds, birds, and then still more horses, still more hounds and still more horses. He drew the things he loved, and animals took first place. Nor did he limit himself to the stables and kennels. He observed with no less interest the poultry in the farmyard, or the monkeys and baboons his grandmother kept for company (she was often to be seen out walking with a she-monkey on her shoulder). Like his master Princeteau, who sometimes came on a visit, Henri never seemed at a loss when expressing movement. With eloquent economy, he could render the effort of a horse drawing a waggon. His sketches had vitality and gusto. It was evident, too, that he had an eye for capturing the significant characteristics of his subject.

In Paris, in January 1878, at the Lycée Fontanes, Louis Pascal, who had dreams of becoming a journalist, founded with another schoolboy, Portalis, a magazine pompously entitled *L'Écho français*. He immediately asked for a contribution from his cousin at Albi. The magazine was to have only an ephemeral existence, but Henri had time to send its editors a story called *L'Histoire du Pélican et de l'Anguille*, 'universally declared to be very witty.'

Henri was now just over thirteen. He was growing a little. The wall in the passage at Le Bosc bears witness to it. If it were not that he had to walk with a stick everything would be going pretty well.

Soon now the gorges of the Viaur would echo to the sound of his horse's galloping hooves.

The boy was happy to be alive, and confident in the future. And then disaster suddenly overtook him.

On May 30 of that year, 1878, Henri was at Albi with his mother. His grandmother was unwell and the family doctor had been called in. While the doctor was busy prescribing, Henri tried to get out of a low chair with the help of his stick. He tripped and fell. His bones gave way.

'A fracture of the left femur,' the doctor diagnosed.

*   *   *

With his leg in plaster, Henri was obliged to do what he loathed most in the world: keep still. But this would not have mattered much if the consequences of the accident—in itself so commonplace—had not been so serious. For there was great difficulty in getting the bones to knit. They were too fragile. It was clear that the boy would not quickly recover from the consequences of his fall—that 'insignificant fall,' as his father sadly said.

At Le Bosc, where he was soon taken, he went out for drives in a carriage. Once the plaster had been removed, a normal boy would have quickly recovered after a period of convalescence. But it was not so with Henri.

His mother was dismayed and distraught, and never left his side. She did not know what to think, consulted doctor after doctor, experimented with remedy after remedy, and alternated between hope and fear. What was this mysterious disease from which her son was suffering? In general, her fears had the upper hand.

The others went off riding, while he walked the gravelled paths as best he could with the help of his crutches. The day when Usurpateur and Volga would take him out hunting roe-deer had now to be postponed indefinitely.

Henri showed no regrets and never uttered a complaint. He seemed as gay and unconcerned as ever. He was always serene though he must have suffered from being reduced to such a limited existence. In no circumstances would he either pity himself or allow others to pity him. He tried to console his relations by blaming himself. 'You don't need to be sorry for me,' he said, 'I don't deserve it, I was just clumsy.'

As soon as the condition of her 'little cripple' allowed it, Countess Adèle set off for the spas. After a cure at Amélie-les-Bains, she took him to Barèges, and then on to Nice, where they spent the winter in an English pension.

Henri liked Nice. The Mediterranean delighted him. He spent his time making boats. At Barèges, that summer, he had met an invalid boy, a little older than himself, Etienne Devismes, from whom he asked advice about naval construction. He read, he drew, and spent his time in indoor occupations. He also began painting.

(Inspired by Princeteau's methods,) he painted a few canvases of horses and sailors. Taking carriage exercise or being pushed in a wheelchair, he had no 'very varied menu.' He painted the carriages on the Promenade des Anglais and two American men-of-war, the *Trentham* and the *Devastation*, which were at anchor in the bay. He liked the southern countryside, though landscapes were not his strong point. 'I am quite incapable of doing them, even the shadow,' he admitted to Devismes. 'My trees look like spinach and my sea like heaven knows what.' The Mediterranean was beautiful enough. But it was 'the devil to paint, precisely because it is so beautiful.' A landscape, even a seascape, was immobile; and though he was now compelled to content himself with inactivity, Henri remained, if not in body, at least in mind and character, what he had always been: a being of movement. Thinking of the happy past, he painted a *Souvenir de Chantilly*, in which he depicted himself coming back from the races in a victoria with (Princeteau and Louis Pascal.)

Towards the end of winter, Countess Adèle and her son returned to Le Bosc. Here they found irrefutable proof of their fears: Henri had almost completely stopped growing since his accident. The last measurement on the wall of the passage was dated September. Since then he had grown no more than half a centimetre. But the effects of his illness were not limited to this alone. Puberty was bringing strange changes. His features were growing heavier; his lips becoming thick and protuberant; while his head was beginning to look too large on a body that had almost ceased to develop.

Nevertheless, the last celebrated physician consulted had been optimistic, declaring that it was merely a matter of 'growing pains'. With an 'active regimen' and long stays in the south, they would succeed in making of the 'dear child' a 'straight and robust boy.' 'It would be a long process and demand much patient and intelligent perseverance,' but when Henri had overcome this crisis, his constitution would re-assert itself, 'and his retarded growth would then recover its impulse.'

It so happened that the army this year was holding manoeuvres near Le Bosc. Comforted by the doctor's prognosis, Henri waited hopefully to get well. Now that he could walk a little more easily, he often went to watch the soldiers. He took the opportunity to paint a few scenes of military life: an artilleryman saddling his horse, a battery of guns, a despatch-rider at the trot.

During the summer, his mother took him once again to Barèges. These thermal cures were bound to hasten his convalescence. For, indeed, the accident had taken place fifteen months ago. The most important thing was that Henri's leg was improving and mother and son were now able to stroll in the neighbouring countryside. And then, one disastrous day in August, when they were walking not far from the military hospital, the boy suddenly slipped and fell into a dry ditch.

It was not very deep. No more than four or five feet at most. But it was enough. As had happened at Albi, fifteen months before, his bones gave way. This time it was the right femur.

While his mother ran to get help from the hospital, Henri sat in the ditch.

He made no complaint, shed no tears. Sitting on the grass, he merely held his thigh as tightly as he could.

'Tréclau'

PART ONE
[1880—1886]

CHAPTER ONE

Monsieur Bonnat

'Painting for me is merely a means of forgetting life. It is a
cry in the night. A sob broken off. A strangled laugh.'

ROUAULT

The winter at Nice in the year 1880 was particularly mild.

The season, as always at this time, was at its height. Rich foreigners
were arriving from all over the world. The Prince of Wales and the
Russian grand-dukes were there. On the Promenade des Anglais
beautifully dressed women were driving to parties in smart turn-outs,
leaving a wave of scent behind them.

Henri de Toulouse-Lautrec and his mother watched the procession
of carriages on the Promenade, where his father would appear at any
moment driving a four-in-hand at high speed. He watched and listened.
He drew deep breaths of the mild winter air with its tang of salt.
He walked painfully, leaning on a stick, and with a waddle that was
rather like that of a duck.

He was fifteen and a cripple.

His mother did her best to be calm and consoling. She still hoped.
But his two accidents had sounded the knell of those happy times
when he could believe himself to be a boy like other boys.

What was there to hope for now? After forty days of lying immobile
in plaster he had left Barèges for Le Bosc, before going on to Nice.
At Le Bosc, he had once again placed his 'miserable body' against
the wall where his many cousins went so happily to measure how much
they had grown. In a year, he had grown one centimetre at most. He
could never go by that wall without a shudder—the 'wailing wall,'
as the compassionate servants called it.

Indeed, he had no need now to go to the wall. It was enough to
look at his arms and legs, which were both very short. His torso was
more or less normal, but his limbs refused to grow, and month by

month lent his body an increasingly grotesque appearance. What sort of caricature of himself was going to emerge eventually from this transformation? He was growing uglier every day. His nose was broadening, his lips were swelling and becoming puffy, forming a sort of roll above his retreating chin. The words that issued from his pendulous lips were deformed by a lisp and a curious rolling of the 'r's, and fell over each other, while many of the syllables were drowned in a flood of saliva. His whole body seemed to be swelling, thickening, growing rickety and out of proportion. His tiny forearms ended in hugely fingered hands. Who would ever dare to refer to him as Little Treasure now? Only his eyes retained a vivacious and luminous quality; they had a dark, clear beauty.* His spirit was still alive;

* There has been much discussion about the nature of Lautrec's illness. Dr G. Séjournet (see the Bibliography at the end of the book) has suggested a late achondroplasia; Professor Maurice Lamy osteogenesis imperfecta. Though a retrospective diagnosis is always difficult, it would seem, nevertheless, that Dr Gaston Lévy's theory corresponds most closely to the known facts. According to this doctor, he was stricken by an illness belonging to the group of epiphysial dysplasias, perhaps, to be even more precise, by the epiphysial dystrophy of Clément.

In these conditions 'the bony tissue around the epiphyses is friable and the epiphyses themselves are diseased.' It is, indeed, true that Lautrec's fractures did not present as simple fractures. 'It can be suggested,' writes Dr Lévy, 'that the fractures took place through the neck of the femur which had *coxa vara* deformity and was extremely friable, or as the result of a subluxation (i.e. partial dislocation) leading to a fall and, as a result, fractures of the femur. But the hypothesis of subluxation leading to complete dislocation cannot be excluded.'

In any case, contrary to what a superficial examination of the biographical data has often led people to think, Lautrec's fractures were not the *cause* of his arrest of growth. His growth, indeed, had never been really satisfactory. These fractures were a *consequence*, 'the dramatic fulfilment of an earlier development process' caused by a pathological bony factor. Furthermore, there is nothing surprising in the fact that the two accidents to Lautrec occurred at the time of puberty. If abnormal processes of this sort manifest themselves some years after their onset (the diagnosis was after all impossible in Lautrec's time because radiography was not in existence), they become more serious during periods of rapid growth and at puberty.

Perhaps this is the place to remember that our biological destiny closes on us like an 'inexorable door,' as Jean Rostand said, on the day we are conceived? It is a merciless determinism of which Lautrec was a distressing example.

(From information gathered by Dr Lévy, one of Lautrec's female cousins was a dwarf.)

it was merely that his body had ceased to obey its injunctions. At
the slightest effort, his limbs became desperately weary. All his dreams
of horses and hunting were destroyed. He could never be what he
had wished to become. And now at the age when his blood was singing,
and the ardour of his race was stirring within him, he could do no
more than contemplate in his looking-glass the horror that a wry fate
had made of him.

There was a poignancy about that winter in Nice. The previous
summer, at Barèges, while he lay with his leg in plaster, Lautrec
had often been visited in the evening by one of his cousins, Jeanne
d'Armagnac. 'I'm very much alone all day,' he wrote. 'I read a little
but, in the long run, it gives me a headache. I draw and paint as much
as I can, indeed till my hand grows tired, and when night begins to
fall I hope Jeanne d'Armagnac will come to my bedside. She does
sometimes, and cheers me up and plays with me, and I listen to her
talk, without daring to look at her. She is so tall and so beautiful!
And I am neither tall nor beautiful.'

Lautrec felt himself balanced on the edge of an abyss. While other
boys of his age were beginning to dream of love, he had to repudiate
its temptations. He could now understand better what it meant to be a
Toulouse-Lautrec, how the passions could set the blood coursing
through your veins in an impulse of sensuality, excessive and abnormal.*

As a child he had enjoyed being caressed by his mother and his
aunts. He had great powers of affection. His heart was on the point
of opening; now he must close it forever. Beauty could never again
be for him an invitation to the imagination, a stimulus to the sensibility. His intelligence was too lucid and precise for him not to realise
that he was excluded from the world. What could he ever read in the
eyes of girls except repulsion or, worse still, pity?

Pity was the most intolerable thing of all and he turned it aside with
a joke and a laugh. 'Look at this figure so utterly lacking in elegance
with its wide behind and a nose like a potato; it's far from pretty.'
Lautrec knew he was vulnerable. He forestalled mockery by insisting

---

* Intimate though the fact may be it has its importance and must be mentioned:
Lautrec had monstrously developed sexual organs. He often compared himself
to a 'coffee pot with a big spout.'

on his ludicrous appearance. His self-mockery was a defence. Wounded to the heart by the disaster of his mutilated life, Lautrec nevertheless accepted it as a challenge.

Though life seemed to be denying him, he refused to allow himself to be exiled from it. He painted and drew continually. Not as a drug, but as a drowning man clutches desperately at a plank. As he said himself, the 'furia' of painting seized on him. 'My room is full of things that don't even deserve the name of daubs,' he wrote to Devismes. A pastime, a refuge and a means of assuaging his hunger for life— painting was all these things to him. Above all, it was a way of asserting his existence both to others and to himself. To become a mere inert cripple looked after by others was an intolerable prospect.

His favourite subjects were still the same. Animals, carriages and boats were the principal items on his 'menu.' And the work he did at this time is full of movement. In his sketch books, he returned ceaselessly to horses, whose every movement he analysed with the enthusiastic concentration of a connoisseur. 'I'll make splendid and beautiful ones,' he said to his father. 'Yes, just in daubs!' replied Count Alphonse.

It was a cruel thing to say, but Count Alphonse was unconsciously thinking of himself rather than of his son. It was not for his son that he was sorry. Indeed, his son's misfortune afflicted him only in the sense that he felt himself frustrated by it. He had hoped for a hunting companion and he had not even an heir. He let it be understood that neither money nor pains were to be spared in the endeavour to improve the cripple's condition. But, that said, he took no further interest in him whatever. It was as if he had never had a son. In his disappointment, he became more and more solitary; a solitude peopled with wild hawks and phantoms from the past.

> *De chiens, d'oiseaux, d'armes, d'amours*
> *Pour une joie, cent doulours . . .*
> *Méfiez-vous de la tempête*
> *Et des femmes comme la peste . . .*
> *Pour un peu de plaisir, mille douleurs*
> *Ont les amoureux et les chasseurs.**

---

* Device of the Irish eighth Earl of MacMahon, at the Court of King Patrick. Count Alphonse had it put on the shutters of his falcon house in 1913.

At the age of fifteen Lautrec had become an outsider—and he knew it—even in his own family circle. He was no more than a rotten branch; the unworthy scion of an illustrious and vigorous race. Count Alphonse emphasised the fact by excluding him from the entail in favour of his younger sister Alix.

Lautrec sometimes stared at his parents with 'intensity.'* He felt moments of rebellion against his father and mother who had made him what he was. But though he quickly suppressed such feelings, he would mock a little at times. 'No one can be more virtuous than my mother!' he exclaimed. 'But she couldn't resist a pair of red trousers.'

Wherever he was, he painted. After Nice, he was taken back to the various family houses, to Albi, Céleyran and Le Bosc—where, on November 4, the 'wailing wall' recorded the usual derisory centimetre as the amount he had grown during the past year. But he worked ceaselessly. During the year 1880 he made three hundred drawings and fifty paintings.

At Céleyran, he tried landscape painting again. At Albi, he painted the viaduct of Castelviel as seen from the balcony of the Hôtel du Bosc. But while every work in which he represented movement had a convincing strength, and his portraits had both power and truth, his landscapes remained uninspired. There is an insipid quality about the great still woods and the inert vines which he painted in the torrid heat of August. He did not care for nature. 'Nature has betrayed me,' he said.

He loved everything that reminded him of the world he had lost, and all humans and animals that had some positive distinguishing characteristic. Both his southern temperament and his education had taught him to appreciate the individual. Singularity attracted him. It gave him a fellow-feeling, made him feel more normal: every man in one form or another was a sort of monster, a mixture of the absurd and the marvellous, the sublime and the abject. Drawing became for him a reason for living. It was another sort of hunt that was beginning.

During his various journeys, he was in the habit of keeping little journals, half written and half drawn. When he left Céleyran in January 1881 and went back to Nice for the winter, he composed a

* Mary Tapié de Céleyran.

Cahier de Zigzags, which he dedicated to his cousin, Madeleine Tapié, 'with the laudable object of distracting her a little from the lessons of Mme Vergnettes.' It is full of spontaneous satire and amusingly malicious irony directed at the people he met on the road or in hotels. His sense of humour, sharpened by his need to fall back on his own thoughts, quickly discovered the oddities and absurdities of human beings. 'There are two young Englishmen in the next rooms to ours who are superb; their two sisters, looking like umbrellas, are here too, dressed in pink, with a little friend in blue with red hair. She is a type I have tried to draw on horseback but have not succeeded.'

But Lautrec's efforts were not limited to the use of pencil, pen or brush. With obstinate energy, he submitted his limbs to the discipline of physical exercise. He walked, swam and rowed. The sea was a friend to him. He swam, so he said, 'like a toad, but fast and well.' He concentrated day after day on developing his faculties; he even succeeded in diving from a boat.

By the time his stay at Nice came to an end—it had been prolonged by the illness of an aunt—he had bathed no less than fifty times. He was delighted with this result which proved, he said with evident satisfaction, that his 'locomotor extremities had made real progress.'

*   *   *

From Nice Lautrec went with his mother to Paris where, in July, he was to take the first part of his *baccalauréat*.

How much time did he spend on his studies? Much less than on his painting, no doubt. In Paris he found 'with wild joy' his friend Princeteau. The affection linking the sixteen-year-old cripple to the deafmute of thirty-seven was stronger than ever. Their respective infirmities served to increase their friendship. They saw each other every day. Lautrec called Princeteau his 'master'; Princeteau called Lautrec his 'studio foster-child.'

The animal painter loved Lautrec 'paternally.' He was saddened by the 'distortion' of his protegé, as he called it in his peculiar language. He was also very surprised by the evidence of the boy's talent. What he himself had taken years to discover and learn, Lautrec assimilated with disconcerting speed.

Indeed, Lautrec imitated him 'like a monkey.' He copied his methods, his brushwork and his technique which had both solidity and fluency and was much concerned with the management of light. Under the indirect and diffused influence of the abhorred Impressionism, which was then fighting for recognition (the first exhibition of the group had been held only seven years before, in 1874), fashionable painting was beginning to grow lighter in tone. 'They shoot us, but they pick our pockets,' remarked Degas sarcastically. This 'corrected and ameliorated Impressionism'* was affecting the work of Princeteau; it was a boon to Lautrec.

Princeteau was delighted with his pupil. As a result of his understanding kindness, as well as his astonished admiration for the 'increasing progress,' the 'miraculous progress,' the boy was making, he gave him the freedom of his studio. Lautrec went to the Rue du Faubourg-Saint-Honoré every morning to work with him.

At this time Princeteau was collaborating with Théophile Poilpot on a vast canvas that was intended to commemorate a famous episode in the war of 1870: the charge of Cuirassiers at Reichshoffen. He was to paint the horses, and Lautrec copied a number of his sketches—in particular, a Cuirassier—'so remarkably well . . . that it took my breath away,' said Princeteau. Lautrec often mingled his own drawings with those of his master in the latter's sketchbooks, and Princeteau sometimes had difficulty in determining which were which.

There was a constant coming and going between the various studios in the little colony of artists which Princeteau inhabited. The painters and sculptors who lived in it moved very much in the same world. They were mostly men who belonged to clubs, went to the races and fashionable parties. Among them were Petitjean, Butin, Lindon and the Viscount du Passage, whom Lautrec undertook to paint on horseback. But there were two in particular who attracted the boy. One was John Lewis Brown, a Bordelais of Irish origins. He was a hard worker and had now, at the age of fifty-two, acquired an enviable reputation as a painter of horses, both army and sporting. Napoleon III had bought two of his pictures in the past. Lautrec, who received a certain amount of advice from him, marvelled at his

* Émile Zola: *Le Naturalisme au Salon*, in *Le Voltaire*, June 21, 1880.

virtuosity and at the profound, almost incredible knowledge of horses he revealed in his painting.

The other was Jean-Louis Forain. This slender, pale young man, with sharp eyes and a bitter line about his mouth, was still more or less unknown. A friend of Degas, he exhibited with the Impressionists, where his water-colours had attracted attention, but for the moment, art did not provide him with much of a living. He was more often than not in financial difficulties and every now and then had the bailiffs in. But in anticipation of their visits he always took the precaution of putting his belongings in a place of safety—sometimes with Count Alphonse, who was a great friend of his and much admired his talent. Forain had an inexhaustible vein of mockery and, with roars of laughter, was always making devastating remarks that delighted the loungers who frequented his studio. He put his powers of observation to good use and started sending drawings to the newspapers (signing them with the impertinent pseudonym *Zut*), in which he gave free rein to his corrosive wit.

Lautrec was never tired of listening to him. He enjoyed his caustic humour that was generally turned against the conventional, the pretentious, the vulgar and the stupid. Nor did he ever tire of looking at his work: those sketches of Parisian life, those typical scenes, caught as it were on the wing, in cafés-concerts, backstage in the theatre, in the music-hall or on the promenade of the Folies-Bergère. Brilliantly incisive and superbly drawn, Forain's sketches rendered not only the outward appearance but the psychological truth of a character. There was never a line too many in them. They were direct, simplified, and beautifully observed.

Lautrec was never bored in the Rue du Faubourg-Saint-Honoré. He felt he was being reborn there. He could learn there, better than anywhere else, how to mock at fate. Princeteau's infirmity did not prevent his enjoying the spectacle of the world. He refused even to admit that he was a deaf-mute and was contemptuous of others similarly afflicted who had not the will to live a normal life in spite of it.

Princeteau often took his pupil to the circus or the theatre in the evenings. The circus was then very fashionable. Princeteau and Lautrec

nearly always went to the wood-built Fernando Circus at 63 Boulevard
de Rochechouart, which had some of the best turns at that time and
was very popular.*

The horses in particular were superb, and the men and women who
performed the *haute école* supremely talented. Lautrec was also delighted
by the acrobats, jugglers, tight-rope walkers, performing animals,
and by the perilous flights of the trapeze-artists. He had a taste, indeed
a cult, for perfection. Everything that was first-rate, particularly if
it was physical, excited his enthusiasm. These performers, so strong
and so supple, who had trained their bodies to such precise obedience
that difficulties seemed not even to exist, fascinated him.

'That's wonderful!' he would cry enthusiastically, the saliva trickling
from his swollen lips. The clowns reminded him of his own misfortune. They laughed at themselves, at their own clumsiness and
absurdity. And he, too, laughed at himself. Under the spell-binding
lights of the circus, the flour-white faces of the clowns were at once a
protest against human misery and its caricature.

Light and shadow were what Princeteau and Lautrec were in
search of when they went to the theatre. They were completely
indifferent to the text of the play. They did not even listen to it. All
they cared about was the décor, the play of colour created by the
actors' clothes as they moved amid the scenery. The gas footlights
threw up a curiously pale, yellow light that moulded the actors'
faces with a strangely violent chiaroscuro, it banished them from
everyday normality and threw each gesture into unusual relief. This
stage-lighting was a mask too; and masks were infinitely important to
Lautrec.

He was paying less and less attention to his lessons. They no longer
held any attraction for him. All he now cared about was painting.

There was, perhaps, some caprice mingled with this desire; caprice
and disappointment. But there was, too, a more serious ambition:
one day through his painting he intended to prove to the world, and
incidentally to himself, 'that he was not a failure after all.' What
importance could Latin prose and French composition have for him

* It was rebuilt and renamed, in 1898, the Medrano Circus, after its new
proprietor, Boum-Boum, the clown.

beside that? In July, he failed in the *baccalauréat* in French composition.

He concealed his disappointment with a joke, ordering visiting cards inscribed: 'Henri de Toulouse-Lautrec, failed B.A.'

*   *   *

Almost immediately after this rebuff, mother and son left for the south. Once again, Lautrec was to take a cure, this year at Lamalou in the Hérault, 'a ferruginous and arsenical (though only *slightly*, the doctor says) spa.'

Lautrec did not care for the countryside. 'A horrible hole in red earth,' he wrote to Devismes. 'It's much duller than Barèges, *quod non est paululum dicere.*' Though busy 'soaking himself inside and out,' he was very bored. But Devismes was to give him something to do and great pleasure at the same time: he had just finished a novel, *Cocotte*, and he asked Lautrec to illustrate it. Delighted that his friend had 'cast an eye over his rudimentary inspirations,' Lautrec quickly accepted the suggestion.

Cocotte is a story of very little originality which has for heroine an old mare that goes into quiet retirement with a kind country priest after having served in the army. One day, the mare's old regiment goes past. Excited by the trumpets, she sets off at a gallop and carries the priest into the middle of the ranks.

This rather thin anecdote at least had the merit of exciting Lautrec's enthusiasm and he made twenty-three pen and ink drawings, which were both amusing and alive.

As soon as he had finished the work, Lautrec sent it to Devismes. It seemed that he was aware now of what he was looking for in art, and could already foresee what he would accomplish. 'I have tried to draw realistically and not ideally,' he wrote. 'It may be a defect, for I have no mercy on warts, and I like adorning them with wanton hairs, rounding them off and giving them a bright surface.'

He signed the letter: 'A painter in embryo.' But he was anxious for Devismes' opinion and begged him not to delay in replying: 'Write me a line soon. I am feverish with anxiety.' He wanted so much to succeed in producing something good. Life had given him so many rebuffs that he now doubted everything, even his own gifts.

When he received Devismes' letter of praise, he could not restrain his joy. 'I thought I must be slightly mad when I read your charmingly kind letter,' he said gratefully. 'I could never have believed that such kindness existed: to receive my wretched drawings and then thank me into the bargain. And you need not be so scrupulous about my drawings. Just use those you like . . . But,' he concluded, 'I am madly, crazily happy at the thought that your prose, like so many fireworks, will frame my daubs, that you should have offered me a helping hand on the arduous road towards getting known, and finally that I have been able to do something in a small way to acknowledge our friendship which grows closer as it grows older.'*

Though at his mother's insistence obliged to go on working for his *baccalauréat*, Lautrec spent a great deal of his time painting. At Céleyràn and at Le Bosc, to which he returned after his cure, he worked at portraits, making his family sit for him.

He did not spare his patient models. If, out of affection and respect, his portraits of his mother are filial in feeling, it was not so with other members of his family. He painted one of his young cousins, full length and staring at a turkey, who does not appear to be very appreciative. As for his father, he painted him ironically in one of his favourite disguises: a Circassian costume, with a turban on his head, a hawk on his left wrist, and mounted on a horse adorned with the saddlery that had once belonged to the celebrated Imam of the Caucasus, Schamil-Effendi. But he treated animals more tenderly. He painted a portrait—a true portrait— of a white horse, called Gazelle, which is infinitely moving in its understanding.

The vigour and sureness of his touch lent considerable authority to most of these works. His mastery was growing. In his portrait of a priest, Lautrec succeeded in expressing all the man's humanity; the priest is shown sitting, red-faced against a red background, his head bent, sunk in reverie. The brush strokes are light and rapid. 'When my pencil starts moving,' he had written a little while before to

---

* Contrary to Lautrec's hopes, Devismes' 'pearl of prose' was of no use to him from the point of view of publicity. His friend's novel was not published at that time. It has since been published (Éditions du Chêne, Paris, 1953), but solely on account of Lautrec's drawings.

Devismes, 'it must be allowed its head or—bang!—nothing more happens.' And it was the same with his brush.*

In November, Lautrec sat for his *baccalauréat* again, this time at Toulouse, and succeeded. On the 22nd, writing from Albi, he happily announced the news to Devismes: 'Caught up in the whirlwind of the *baccalauréat*, I have been neglecting my friends, painting and every-thing else on earth that deserves attention for dictionaries and lesson books. Anyway, the Toulouse examiners have declared me passed in spite of the stupidity I displayed in answering their questions . . . I made non-existent quotations from Lucan, and the professor, wishing to show how erudite he was, received me with open arms.' The new *bachelier* drew a mocking portrait of the professor with a few strokes of his pen: great self-satisfaction, bald head and huge spectacles. 'Anyway, it's over and done with,' Lautrec concluded.†

It was over and done with. In no circumstances was he prepared to work for the second part of the *baccalauréat*. It was no use talking to him now of anything but painting. He was certainly not going to suffer the boredom of working for further examinations which, in any case, could lead to nothing.

His mother had not the heart to oppose him. She desired nothing but his happiness, that happiness already so compromised by his deformity. Painting as an occupation was compatible with the family dignity. Besides, it might perhaps help the unhappy boy to forget the things he would never have. His Uncle Charles encouraged him, and Princeteau declared that his 'foster child' had 'extraordinary talent' and that he might well have a 'brilliant future.' As for Count Alphonse, there was no opposition to be feared from him. Whether his son was good at Latin prose, whether he chose to spend his days in an armchair or whether he preferred amusing himself by 'daubing,' was of no importance to him, not even worth an expression of opinion, since

---

* There are some forty paintings attributed to this year, 1881.

† This letter is the last we possess of those written to Devismes. It would seem that the friendship between Lautrec and his friend from Barèges cooled rapidly from now on. Devismes was very pious. Thirty years later, in 1910, after his mother's death, he became a monk. Before retiring from the world, he had the touching thought of sending Countess Adèle the eight letters he had once received from Lautrec.

the descendant of the Counts of Toulouse was incapable of the only things in this world that really mattered: riding and hunting.

Though delighted at the idea of being 'made free of art,' as Princeteau put it, Lautrec was far from taking the matter lightly. He wanted to succeed, take his revenge in the one domain to which he was attracted.

Until now, he had worked rather at random, relying on his natural facility. But now the serious part of the business was to begin. Lautrec intended to enter the École des Beaux-Arts, and in the meantime to prepare himself for it in a well-known studio. 'To think that if my legs had been a little longer, I would never have taken up painting!' He would work hard to become a good artist. Oh, not a Forain, of course! 'If he could only paint as well as his great friend Princeteau, or as John Lewis Brown!'* He had learned a lot from Princeteau's teaching. But his instruction was limited. He must now go beyond it, submit to a necessary and more rigorous discipline. Princeteau himself advised this, suggesting that Lautrec should come to Paris and attend the classes of Léon Bonnat.

Bonnat had recently been elected to the Academy at the age of forty. He was a celebrated artist and a well-known portrait painter, the 'painter of millionaires.' No one could be more fitted than he to guide a Toulouse-Lautrec along the difficult path of art. His lessons— he was always called 'Monsieur Bonnat' as, in the past, the master of Montauban had been called 'Monsieur Ingres'—preserved with the utmost loyalty the great traditions of French painting, on which the Impressionists—'those humbugs and revolutionaries'—were trying to bring discredit. With Monsieur Bonnat no surprises were possible. Under his austere tuition, young Lautrec had a great prospect of achieving the splendid career Princeteau hoped for him, of becoming one of those high class painters who triumphed in the Salon and in fashionable circles, and of which a few—the cleverest—ended up in the Institut.

It also happened, that an Albi goldsmith, Ferréol, a friend of the Toulouse-Lautrecs, knew a banker in the town, whose young brother, Henri Rachou, was working in Bonnat's studio. Rachou promised to give Lautrec a letter of introduction to him.

* Thadée Natanson.

Lautrec arrived in Paris in March 1882. Princeteau introduced him to Bonnat, and by the end of the month he had entered that master's studio in the Impasse Hélène.

Countess Adèle was delighted with the arrangement and the future it seemed to offer her son. Lautrec was equally delighted. He was eighteen years old.

Lautrec and his father (*c*. 1875)
a sketch by René Princeteau

'*Au Chalet*'. Lautrec and friends (*c.* 1881)

The Atelier Cormon (1885)

...ec in the foreground; Émile Bernard standing back row, right; Cormon seated at easel

(left) *Lautrec, aged eighteen.* From a painting by Henri Rachou (1855-1944)

Émile Bernard

Lautrec by Émile Bernard. A previously unpublished sketch

left) Lautrec and Anquetin at *Le Mirliton*, Aristide Bruant's cabaret-bar (*c.* 1886)

Lautrec and Lucien Métivet in Lautrec's studio

Marie-Clémentine (Suzanne) Valadon (c. 1885)   Carmen Gaudin (c. 1885)

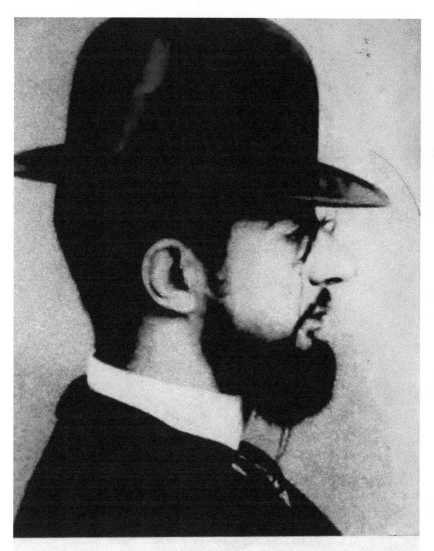

Toulouse-Lautrec (c. 1889)

CHAPTER TWO

The Sacred Grove

'Various Parisian celebrities passed vying with each other before
his eyes. Where are they going? Prometheus wondered.'
GIDE: *Le Prométhée mal enchaîné.*

LAUTREC's cab stopped every morning in front of Bonnat's studio.

With the assistance of his crooked stick, which he referred to
jokingly as his 'buttonhook,' Lautrec struggled to his feet with some
difficulty. He got out, tottered, regained his balance, and then waddled
as quickly as he could into the studio, where he hurried to his usual
corner. When he reached his 'donkey,' he put his huge hands on it, took
a flying leap and landed on it with his feet dangling.

The first day, the other pupils may have laughed at sight of the dwarf,
at his body balanced on two tiny legs covered in black and white
check trousers, at his disproportionately large head, his thick nose on
which rested steel-rimmed pince-nez, his swollen dribbling lips, and
his retreating chin on which a few black hairs, stiff as horsehair, were
beginning to appear. There is little tact in studios. On the other hand,
warned by Rachou, it is possible that the other pupils refrained from
rude remarks. Rachou introduced Lautrec. He shook hands all round,
and bore apparently impassively the stares of so many eyes. He was
always embarrassed on first entering a circle where he was not known.
Indeed, it was more than embarrassment, it was shame. But he rose
above it. He faced the glances of the curious; and held his head high—
which merely increased his waddle.

He knew all about the insults to which he was exposing himself
by his desire to lead a normal life. He had weighed the risks in advance.
But it had to be this; or nothing. And nothing meant a cripple's room;
compassion, but self-contempt; peace, but disgust.

His name and wealth were nothing now but rusty keys that could
open no doors. The great world was closed to him. If he wanted to

win a place in it, he must acquire and deserve other titles of nobility. He was like those younger sons of great families who, deprived of the advantages of their elders, go overseas to find fortune in virgin lands. For a while, he thought of becoming a doctor or a surgeon. To handle a scalpel and dissect bodies would have pleased him. But with his physique such an ambition was unthinkable, and so through art he would achieve the right he longed for: to live among men who were not monsters.

At first, he found some difficulty in adapting himself to the life of the studio. It was all so very different to the circles in which he had been born. He felt a certain nostalgia for the past; but with a determination worthy of his distant ancestors in the Albigensian war, he threw himself into his work.

He threw himself into life, too, and very quickly made a conquest of his companions. No doubt he paid the traditional entrance fee handsomely: punch, white wine, oysters, bags of fried potatoes, cigarettes and cigars. The banquet would have been lacking in nothing. But it was his personal qualities that made the real conquest of his companions. As a descendant of crusaders he might have been vain, but he was simplicity itself. As a young man on whom fate had played the most appalling of tricks, he might have been bitter and difficult, but he was all charm. Far from wanting to avenge himself on others, he accused no one and nothing. He touched people by his kindness and his power of sympathy. Nothing seemed to surprise or shock him. He was interested in everything. After knowing him for a while, they no longer noticed his disabilities; he was such good company. Used to living in a wide family circle, he had no difficulty in becoming one of a group. Besides, he needed friendship. He feared solitude and sought protection from it. This was obvious. And people responded to it. Had he whined, they would have turned from him. But he was the first to laugh at his misfortune. 'I'm a half-bottle,' he would lisp. He would grimace and caricature himself, amuse the gallery with an image of himself that was far from being a burlesque, for it became, indeed, by its very excess a form of concealment: the laughter was with him rather than at him.

Lautrec captivated people by his loyalty, his independence, his enthusiasm, his antics and his wit. People forgave him everything: his spoilt child caprices, his impatience, the way he had of turning even on his best friends when some stupidity irritated him; Rachou, for instance, with whom he soon made close friends, or Adolphe Albert, a young man of twenty-six, who had fallen under his sway. Besides, he always recovered his good humour very quickly. A joke could make him laugh; and if someone started singing, he always joined in.

But Lautrec's opinions were his own. He was not only clear-sighted about himself, but about others too, and perhaps with all the greater clarity since he felt himself to be standing outside things. He soon discovered which of the young men who surrounded him would never get anywhere, those who lacked determination, the talkers, the pretentious who believed that all you had to do to become an artist was to acquire the superficial and exterior attributes.* Pretentiousness and idle dreaming horrified him. He only liked people who rang true.

Lautrec worked extremely hard. In the mornings, he studied at Bonnat's; in the afternoons, he painted or drew with Princeteau or Rachou. He had already acquired a certain technique before coming to work under Bonnat. But he behaved exactly as if he had had no previous experience at all and started again from scratch. He listened submissively and attentively to the celebrated painter's advice, and did his best to put it into practice. He drew endlessly in charcoal.

Bonnat's first criticisms were not, it must be admitted, very encouraging. 'The master told him,' wrote Princeteau to his family, 'that his painting was peculiar in colouring. He also told him that he drew like a child.' It was a 'slap in the face.' But Lautrec responded energetically to his master's criticisms. Bonnat 'put ginger' into his veins. Rubbing out what he had done—'forward with the bread!'—Lautrec redoubled his efforts. How should he not take Monsieur Bonnat's opinions seriously, when that artist had 'a majesty,' as he remarked in a letter to his Uncle Charles, 'that forbids me to doubt him?'

As a fashionable portrait-painter, Bonnat frequented embassies, ministries and drawing-rooms. He was normally attired in an elegant frock-coat on which he changed the decorations according to where

---

* 'He was never wrong in his appreciation of our companions,' Rachou said later. 'He was an incredibly good psychologist.'

he was going. You could not get your portrait painted by him on a
mere whim. It was, indeed, a sort of consecration, and a very expensive
one. You had to prepare for it as if you were to be dubbed knight, 'by
fasting, prayer, and every sort of austerity,' a journalist wrote ironically.
'Then, when you have fully understood the importance of the act you
wish to accomplish, you must order a Bonnat portrait-dress; there
are special models. You must get yourself recommended by a General,
a Minister or an Ambassador, and then, but only then, Monsieur
Bonnat will consent to paint you standing upright, stiff as a post,
bright as crystal and lit from above.'

Concerned at his lack of stature, Bonnat increased it with a double
thickness of heel. His head held high, he trumpeted in a voice that still
had a Basque accent in spite of the twenty-five years he had lived in
Paris. His income was enormous; he spent most of it on a collection
to which he added continually with patience and love.* He held the
masters of the past in veneration and was humbly aware of the distance
that separated him from a Velasquez or a Michelangelo; when he
spoke of the Sistine chapel, his voice trembled.

Bonnat 'is not at all easy on his pupils,' wrote Countess Adèle.
'This seems to prove that he takes a real interest in them.' His severity
and his intransigent faith in principles he held to be incontestable
impressed Lautrec, who saw in him the prototype of the great artist
as his family conceived it. If he wished to succeed and 'not to be a
failure in everything,' he must endeavour to satisfy his master.

He submitted to all Bonnat's demands. In the past he had relied
on impulse, but now he exercised self-control, copying plaster casts
or pegging away conscientiously, and very academically, at working
from the life. He loved bright colours. Under Bonnat's teaching his
palette grew darker, and his studies became as cold and impersonal
as the portrait painter wished.

As well as going to the races and to horse-shows, Lautrec visited
numbers of exhibitions. But he did not stray from his own world,
frequenting the more fashionable galleries, the water-colourists' Salon—
'an exquisite exhibition splendidly housed,' he commented to his
uncle Charles, still under the influence of the excitement caused him by

* He eventually gave it to the Museum of Bayonne, his native town.

Béarnaise by Jacquet and *Scènes tunisiennes* by Detaille. He was equally enthusiastic about the Salon. 'There's so much to see!' he exclaimed. 'I might mention the *Portrait de Puvis de Chavannes* by Bonnat, *La Fête du 14 juillet* by Roll, *Les Derniers Moments de Maximilien* by J. P. Laurens.' His enthusiasms were conventional and reassuring. Uncle Charles' nephew was on the right path.

Sometimes, however, he felt a slight doubt. When Bonnat told him that his drawing was 'quite appalling,' he accepted it on trust, 'took his courage in both hands and began again,' trying to subdue the innate originality of a born draughtsman and become more conventional. But other sayings of Bonnat astonished him. 'When you draw the model's feet, look at her head,' the idealistic painter told him. Wasn't that strange?

And wasn't it strange, too, that this man, on whom so many honours had been showered and whose name was uttered with such respect in the fashionable circles in which he moved, should have derisive songs sung about him by students?

> *Bonnat,*
> *Tu peins très bien la redingote,*
> *Chacun sait ça,*
> *Chacun sait ça.*
> *Tu la*
> *Détaches couleur de botte,*
> *Sur fond caca,*
> *Sur fond caca.*

What could be the reason for these impertinences? In March, just when Lautrec arrived in Paris, the seventh exhibition of the Impressionists was being opened at 251 Rue Saint-Honoré, not far from the Cité du Retiro. Had Lautrec been to see the works of these notorious Impressionists, these Monets, Renoirs, Pissarros, Sisleys, Berthe Morisots and others, whose painting was the absolute negation of everything Bonnat and his circle said or did? It would at least be remarkable if Lautrec had not heard speak of them. The pupils often discussed things in the studio, and their tastes did not always coincide with those of the portrait painter. Some, indeed, would admit in a whisper that they were interested in Manet and the Impressionists. (Had Lautrec during his visit to the Salon, where he seemed to have noticed nothing but the Bonnats and Rolls, not stopped at least for a moment before Manet's great picture: *Le Bar aux Folies-Bergère*?) Imbued with the artistic prejudices of his own circle, Lautrec may well have been disconcerted by these opinions; but they must nevertheless have opened new and unsuspected horizons to him, have shown him that the domain of painting in the France of 1882 was not entirely and exclusively limited to the work of the official artists who shared among themselves the seats in the Institut and the commissions of the fashionable.

However, Bonnat's teaching was far from useless to him. Under his direction, he learnt the laws of composition. He also learnt from him that without discipline no fruitful work was possible, and that if he wanted to realise his ambitions he must pursue ever more vigorously and doggedly the education of his talent.

*   *   *

At the beginning of summer, Lautrec returned to the south and stood against the 'wailing wall' for the last time. He was barely five feet and would grow no more. He compared himself wryly to the Apostle Simon, who stood 'mocking a little, his head lowered, and above all very short' in a niche in the cathedral of Albi.

During these holidays he did a few landscapes and studies of horses, but mainly a number of portraits. The members of his family had to sit for him in turn: his mother, his grandmothers, Uncle Charles, Uncle Amédée, and his boy and girl cousins. Constantly in search of models, he also roped in peasants and servants (he paid them 75 centimes a sitting). It was continuous and profitable labour. His work was becoming surer and more individual. And now that he was away from Bonnat's studio, his palette was beginning to grow lighter again. His best portraits were bathed in light, particularly those of various farm labourers from Céleyran and that of young Routy among others. Was it the influence of Impressionism? Or was it the influence of the Salon painters who had gone rustic—cottages were fashionable at the moment—the Bastien-Lepages and the Jules Bretons? Lautrec's work was, however, still very unequal.* He was feeling his way; sometimes the delicate vitality of his work was such that it must certainly have gained a Sisley's approval, while at others it was muddy and dark.

At Le Bosc, among his other models, he persuaded an addict of the cafés, Père Mathias, to sit for him. He painted him collapsed over a table, his head resting heavily on his arms, a half-filled glass beside him. It is a startlingly realistic portrait. Père Mathias, with a deeply wrinkled face, is staring at the painter with dull, drunken eyes which are clearly revelatory of the sot. In its very simplicity, the painting is a document, a clinical note.

In Paris Lautrec often went to cafés with companions from the studio. He had plenty of money and liked only the best. They naturally enjoyed going with him and he was easily persuaded. His greed— 'I'm as greedy as a bishop's cat,' he admitted—led him on to drink and taste everything that 'was like a peacock's tail in the mouth.' He discovered that alcohol could irradiate dull days with a sudden gaiety of colour. Not that Lautrec wanted merely to get drunk. He drank for pleasure. But alcohol also gave him 'that excitement which seems like strength and that frenzy which simulates joy.'† Everything seemed so much simpler and so much easier.

On September 5, the new chapel in the Château du Bosc was to be consecrated. Mgr Bourret, the Bishop of Rodez, came to perform the ceremony. During the course of it, he addressed Lautrec in a fatherly way from the altar: 'My dear son,' he said, 'you have chosen the finest of professions, but also the most dangerous.'

* * *

On Lautrec's return to Paris, he found that Bonnat was giving up his studio. His pupils, somewhat disconcerted at first, took the initiative of going to ask another celebrated painter, Fernand Cormon, to take charge of them. And with his friends Rachou and Adolphe Albert, Lautrec began going to the studio the famous painter of *Cain* had opened at 10 Rue Constance, in Montmartre.

---

* There are some forty paintings attributed to the year 1882.
† Thadée Natanson.

Cain, which had been inspired by Hugo's *La Légende des Siècles*, had two years before been one of the triumphant successes of the Salon of 1880. The State had promptly bought it to enrich the national collections and had thus set the official seal on the talents, which were internationally recognised, of an artist who was not afraid of tackling great historical subjects. The son of a vaudeville writer, the author of *Deux Orphelines*, Cormon had been the pupil of Cabanel and of Fromentin. After painting *La Mort de Mahomet* and *Les Noces des Nibelungen* (which, in 1870, had earned him his first medal at the age of twenty-five), he had proceeded to the illustration of episodes from Hindu mythology, and then to *Cain*, whose success had encouraged him to search backwards in pre-history for scenes worthy of his brush. He had now reached the Stone Age. He dressed the pretty girls who were his models in skins, and transformed the boys of the Butte into bear-hunters and lake-dwellers. Because of his aesthetic tastes, and also no doubt due to the fact that he was remarkably thin—he was short, angular and emaciated, had a sparse beard and globulus eyes with heavy eyelids, while his body was incredibly bony—he had been nicknamed Père la Rotule.* Despite the irreverence, everyone admired him. Lautrec, for his part, thought he had 'an austere and powerful talent.'

Cormon was much beloved by his pupils. His success had not impaired his simplicity and cordiality. He was now thirty-seven and still a happy Bohemian, whom neither titles nor honours could make stiff and pompous. He was as ready for a lark as ever. On being decorated with the Legion of Honour, he had taken part in a students' masquerade. He had led a fantastic procession, armed with a happily innocuous sword and followed by a student holding an open umbrella over his head.

All the same, Lautrec regretted his old master. Cormon seemed to him too easy-going a teacher. He was not so strict as Bonnat had been, and was too often content, according to Lautrec, with the 'more or less.' He had to force himself to adhere to a more rigid discipline than his master imposed. This discontented and 'irritated him.'

Cormon came round the studio twice a week. He hopped bird-like

* Father Patella. (*Translator's note.*)

from easel to easel, correcting his pupils' paintings and drawings, suggesting alterations, telling some they should work more 'by planes' and others that they would do well to copy Veronese.

When the master was gone, the studio was left to its own devices. The thirty pupils often made a good deal of noise. They sang improper songs and told funny or, more generally, dirty stories. Though he seemed to his companions happy enough, Lautrec was not altogether so. 'A whole heap of sentimental considerations,' he said, were holding him back, which 'I must forget entirely if I'm ever going to get anywhere.'

But where this was he did not know. His work seemed to him to be bogged down in mediocrity. 'I am in no way to regenerate French art,' he wrote, 'and I am struggling with a miserable piece of drawing-paper, which has done me no harm, and to which, believe me, I am doing no good.' There was no likelihood of his provoking jealousy by giving himself airs. He thought little of his own work, while he was always ready to praise the work of his companions, such for instance as that of Louis Anquetin, the son of an Étrépagny butcher, for whom Cormon prophesied a brilliant career, and some of whose paintings—as a supreme reward—hung on the walls of the studio.

'Papa, of course, would look on me as an outsider,' said Lautrec. In his concern for the family honour, Count Alphonse had required his son to adopt a pseudonym. Lautrec had resisted and then, 'for the sake of peace,' had reluctantly resigned himself to it. He either signed his works with an anagram of his name: Tréclau—or did not sign them at all.

Was nothing to be left to him?

When he went home in the evenings to the Cité du Retiro, his mother was waiting for him with open arms. She was a loving refuge. Though she was self-effacing, Countess Adèle watched over her son and knew what he suffered. There was no need for bravado in her presence. Cormon's pupil, who laughed and joked and joined loudly in the choruses of bawdy songs in the studio, could stop playing a part. To his mother he could admit the pitiful truth. He could yield to the love and consolation he needed so much.

But love itself was a sword in his heart. Tomorrow, he would set out for Montmartre again and, playing the clown, would shout between two jokes: 'Oh, how I should like to find a woman who has a lover uglier than I am!' The studio would receive the jest with roars of laughter. Perhaps someone would remark that Père la Rotule was not exactly a handsome man, yet it did not prevent his keeping three mistresses at the same time—which was not the least of his merits.

'Pray for him, dear Mama,' wrote Countess Adèle; 'life in the studio, though excellent from the point of view of his profession, is a considerable ordeal for a young man.'

* . * *

The Montmartre of 1882 was still very much the same as that described by Gérard de Nerval in his *Nuits d'Octobre*: 'There are windmills, cafés and arbours, rustic elysiums and silent paths lined with cottages, barns and over-grown gardens, green fields bordering on precipices where the springs filter into the earth, gradually creating certain islands of verdure where goats gambol and feed on the acanthus clinging to the rocks; little girls, proud of eye and with the legs of mountaineers, guard them and play together.'

Gardens. Arbours. Green fields. Montmartre which had become part of Paris only twenty years before, in 1860, was still a village. Its peace, its wonderful views, the quality of its light and also the fact that life was cheap there had attracted many artists. There were studios more or less everywhere. Nevertheless, Montmartre was developing.

The building of the church of the Sacré-Coeur, which had been going on since the defeat, was continuing slowly on the summit of the Butte, and in lower Montmartre cabarets such as the La Grande Pinte, Le Plus Grand Bock and L'Auberge du Clou were beginning to appear. A certain Rodolphe Salis had begun organising meetings of poets, singers and painters in an establishment called Le Chat Noir on the Boulevard de Rochechouart; and there was dancing. There was also dancing at the Moulin de la Galette, the rustic dance-hall which preserved the two last of the thirty windmills whose sails had once turned on the hill. There was dancing, too, in the old Second Empire dance-halls, the Reine Blanche and the Boule Noire, whose last lights were shining out on the Boulevard de Clichy, while, on the Boulevard de Rochecouart, the Élysée-Montmartre dance-hall was attracting a crowd of customers with its wild music. Montmartre was becoming more and more gay.

The Rue Constance, containing Cormon's studio, gave on to the Rue Lepic, which curved round the flank of the Butte.

After work, Lautrec arm-in-arm with one of his companions, would hobble through the streets of Montmartre, in company with Rachou, Anquetin, René Grenier, a young man from Toulouse who was taking the studio course as an amateur, and with others, such as Charles-Édouard Lucas or Tampier, who went to all the exhibitions, talked endlessly about painting but would never touch a brush himself. Rachou, who had just painted his portrait (Lautrec, by way of thanks, had jokingly presented him with a '*sénateur*': a monkey that, according to him, looked exactly like the minister Méline), lived in the Rue Ganneron. Anquetin had a studio in the Avenue de Clichy.

Lautrec always left his companions with regret. By himself, he felt menaced, at the mercy of the first lout he encountered. Escorted by friends, he feared nothing. 'My dear big man,' he would call Anquetin affectionately as he looked up—Anquetin was some ten inches taller—at his friend's rough-hewn features. Anquetin was nearly four years older than he was and his crooked nose accentuated his resemblance to Michelangelo.

Lautrec admired Anquetin. Anquetin was everything he was not. He possessed iron health, great strength and a robust body, which he exercised daily in fencing and long rides. He was mad about horses; he possibly preferred them to painting, though he was convinced that he was going to be the great master of the future. Both his pride and ambition were limitless. When going in to the Louvre one day with other pupils from the studio, a guide offered his services, and Anquetin replied with contemptuous haughtiness: 'What for? We make the Louvre!' Extremely gifted, no difficulties existed for him as a draughtsman, and he intended to be—he said so himself—the Rubens of his century. He wanted to live as magnificently and already wore a velvet waistcoat and wide felt hat in emulation.

This very assurance dazzled Lautrec. What more could Anquetin possibly want? He lacked nothing—and women no more than the rest: sensual by nature, he had already lost count of his conquests. Women! As he sat in a café, Lautrec watched the women passing by while the others talked. Sometimes, when they noticed him sitting in a corner, looking still smaller and uglier and more of a caricature in contrast to his handsome friend, Anquetin, they would give a slight start and their eyes would open wide in astonishment, before they turned away and moved on. And Lautrec would drop his eyes, mortified by a glance that dared not even proclaim its disgust.

How he could have loved! But what had he to hope for? All his studio companions had mistresses, congratulated themselves on their good luck. But he had nothing. No woman would put her mouth to his drooling lips.

And then, raising his head, his eyes shining behind his spectacles, he would make a joke in his high-pitched voice, stuttering and lisping, with a sniff like a laugh at every three words, or some half melancholy comment in his own particular vein: 'Love'—sniff—'is when the desire to be desired'—sniff—'takes you so badly'—sniff—'that you feel you could die of it!' And then, with another sniff: 'Eh? What? Isn't that so my dear chap?'

All the emotion he could not expend in love, he expended in friendship. But his affection was despotic. Though, in his weakness, he sought out the reassuring presence of the strong, he made them yield to his slightest whim. Among his friends, he was like 'a general leading his troops.'*

His work also took the place of love in his life. It served as an outlet for his abounding and unused vitality. He drew desperately, covering the sheets of Ingres paper with firm, incisive lines. He was not of the sort who quietly elaborate their work. The lines seemed to spurt on to the paper in an effort to catch the model's salient characteristics.

But this was not precisely what Cormon wanted. Lautrec was 'floundering,' as he himself said, 'pitifully.' 'Oh, my dear Godmother,' he lamented, 'what a delusive profession! You would be wise never to hand yourself over, as I have, bound hand and foot to painting.

* Joyant.

It's much harder than Greek or Latin, if you want to do it seriously as I do.'

Fortunately—at least in Lautrec's eyes—Père la Rotule was being rather less easy-going than at first. 'For the last fortnight,' wrote Lautrec in February, 'he has been taking several pupils to task, of which I am one. I have begun working very enthusiastically again.'

Lautrec struggled to do his best with the subjects his master set him: allegories, a warrior fighting a vulture, Icarus, a Merovingian scene, the primitive village of a prehistoric tribe. But Lautrec was beginning to think these set subjects rather ridiculous. When Cormon asked him to paint a series of allegories of the Golden Age—*Le Printemps de la Vie*—in which he was to show youths and maidens frolicking with lions and leopards, he added ironically: '. . . and with bronze rattlesnakes.'

The aesthetic discussions that took place in the studio, which were in contradiction to Cormon's teaching since they lauded the experiments of such painters as Manet, the Impressionists and the other revolutionaries, gradually began to have their effect on him. He had just been visiting the fashionable exhibitions. Had their quality really deteriorated this year, or had Lautrec's eye changed? In any case, writing to Uncle Charles, he blasted them with a few adjectives: 'The Water-Colourists, pitiful; the Volney, mediocre; and the Mirlitons, tolerable.' He excused himself for criticising them 'perhaps rather summarily,' but, he added, 'they really don't deserve anything more.'

The energy with which Lautrec worked at his easel impressed his companions. The more clear-sighted among them had become aware of his unhappiness, and guessed the hurt that lay beneath the cripple's superficial nonchalance.

One day, Charles-Édouard Lucas, a jovial Norman, who loved all the good things of life,* had the charitable idea of freeing him from his obsession. He knew a great number of more or less 'loose' women. Of which one should he ask this curious favour? Was there one among them kind enough to overcome her repugnance? Lucas thought of a young model, Marie Charlet, to whom he had been useful on occasion. She was obviously cut out for the part. Boyishly slender, with huge

---

* Lacking all talent, he later went into industry.

eyes and a wide eager mouth, she was some sixteen or seventeen years old and anything but innocent. Born in the Rue Mouffetard, she had left home because her father, who was a drunkard, beat her, and had gone to live in a cheap room in the Rue de l'École-de-Médecine. Uninhibited, and something of a nymphomaniac, she would sleep with anyone and was always curious about the unknown.

Charles-Édouard Lucas threw her into Lautrec's arms.

*   *   *

Did Lautrec remember the evenings at Barèges when, four years ago now, he lay on his bed with his leg in plaster and hoped Jeanne d'Armagnac would come to see him? 'And I listen to her talk, without daring to look at her. She is so tall and beautiful! And I am neither tall nor beautiful.' The charm, the modesty, the moving quality of young girls . . . Lautrec emerged from his dream which, until now and in spite of everything, had not altogether faded. Marie Charlet revealed to him depravity, the shamelessness of an abnormal sensuality. Nothing remained of love but this obscene and perverse dance.

Charles-Édouard Lucas had made no mistake: Marie Charlet found piquancy in the adventure; Lautrec's monstrous constitution filled her with delight. She went about boasting happily of the dwarf's qualities as a lover and nicknamed him: 'Portmanteau.' This publicity attracted to Lautrec the attentions of the abnormal and of the nymphomaniacs.

With Marie Charlet he felt disgust and contempt. Was this love? Was this what women were like? Or, at least, the sort of love and the type of woman he was destined to have?

But he had no illusions. These vicious loves were but a new aspect of his wretched life. He was afraid of exciting pity; he inspired sadism. He could do nothing but acquiesce. 'One must know how to bear oneself,' he said sometimes. Besides, Marie Charlet had revealed to him the strength of his instincts which, once freed, now no longer knew restraint.

All was well, in spite of the disgust, the dreams and the melancholy he so quickly suppressed. Henri-Marie-Raymond de Toulouse-Lautrec Montfa was, after all, only Tréclau. Outside art, there was nothing left to him but pleasure. He threw himself into it with the same impetuosity that he applied to his work; and what did it matter if it was to destroy his life? Laughing and joking, Lautrec disappeared into the streets of Montmartre.

The Butte became increasingly the centre of his life. Day by day, he began to feel more at ease there than anywhere else. Paris seemed to wash up its scum there. Besides the prostitutes and roughs, there was every kind of eccentric, society's outcasts living no one knew how, the unemployed, failed poets, anarchists, art students with wide-brimmed hats, models waiting to be hired. Every Sunday round the fountain in the Place Pigalle there was a model market: down-at-heel Sicilians in bright rags prepared to sit as God, Neapolitans as ready to prostitute themselves as to pose for the Madonna, and many other 'phenomena,' to use Lautrec's word: over-pretty boys in too-tight trousers, and women alone, the disciples of Sappho. But this world of outcasts was a friendly one. It was a 'court of miracles.' Each had his idiosyncrasy, physical or moral. Once the first astonishment was over, peculiarities ceased to attract attention. The normal would have been much more likely to be considered strange. Lautrec could wander about without embarrassment. He was beginning to be known; people were becoming used to his appearance; they no longer turned when he passed. He fitted in to his surroundings and recovered his equanimity.

On the surface, there had been no change in his relations with the people of his own world, but little by little, he was growing away from his family. He went back every night to the Cité du Retiro; and the letters he wrote to Le Bosc and to Albi were as affectionate and intimate as ever. But a profound transformation was taking place within him. Princeteau, in spite of a great success at the Salon this year with his *Intérieur d'Étable*, which earned him a medal, left Paris; deprived of his friendship, Lautrec no longer went to the races.

He still dreamed about horses, but beauty existed everywhere, not only on the race-course. In his own staccato language, heavily sprinkled with 'Eh!' and 'What!,' he was continually spluttering with enthusiasm about something or other: 'Eh? What? Magnificent, isn't it?' But it was not the conventional beauty that appealed to Bonnat and Cormon which excited his admiration. Lacking as he was in imagination, Lautrec cared only for the real. The distinguishing characteristics that marked a man, that underlined his personality, these and these alone delighted his insatiable curiosity; and made him seize his brush. Even ugliness had its 'beautiful aspects'; you simply had to be able to see them.

In the spring, there was an extensive exhibition of Japanese art at the Georges Petit Gallery. Lautrec was fascinated by the clear and delicate colouring of the prints, by their flat, simple tones and their vigorous, eloquent line.

In his enthusiasm, Lautrec began making a collection of prints. He even intended to go to Japan one day, to that land of short men where dwarf trees grew. His mother at once offered to pay the fare. But he declined. To accept it, when he still had so much to learn, was quite impossible. He was still striving to satisfy Cormon. The unreal conventions Cormon imposed discouraged and disheartened him; nevertheless, he did his best. 'I can't do it, I can't do it,' he wrote in despair. 'I simply can't help turning a deaf ear to it and banging my head against the wall—yes—and all for an art that escapes me and will never know all the trouble I have taken on its behalf.' It was an exhausting and sterile struggle.

Unlike Anquetin, who spent long hours in the Louvre, magnifying-glass in hand, studying the paintings of the great masters and trying to pierce the secrets of their technique, Lautrec could raise no enthusiasm for masterpieces that were merely painting and too far removed from reality. Those historic personages congealed in conventional pomp! Those angels, sirens and satyrs . . . no doubt, those canvases were painted with dazzling technique, but what was the use of technique, except to state something, to enable painting to be primarily a means of giving expression to the truth about life?

In May, Countess Adèle bought the Château de Malromé in the Bordelais, a few miles north-east of Langon. It was a fine house whose towers and turrets were concealed amid extensive woodlands in some hundred acres of land. Countess Adèle was now a neighbour of her Pascal cousins, who lived nearby and whose company she liked. Abandoning the Languedoc and the Albigeois, she spent the summer there with her son.

Lautrec was delighted with Malromé. He enjoyed working in these agreeable surroundings. Though he painted a few rural scenes, in particular during the grape harvest, he spent most of his time on portraits.* Landscape and still-life were senseless exercises as far as he was concerned. Only man existed (animals belonged to the paradise of his childhood), not mankind idealised into archangels and nymphs, embellished, and disincarnate through intellectual abstractions, but simply as he was in everyday life. Lautrec painted his father and mother again. He painted his mother having breakfast, sitting in a chair, a cup in front of her, her eyes lowered, looking thoughtful and a little melancholy.

The young painter scrutinized his mother's features pitilessly, and he put on his canvas the face of a woman who gave no indication that she was the Countess of Toulouse-Lautrec, but whose disappointment, anxiety and the pained surprise life caused her are evident at first glance. Here is a little bourgeoise, whose life should have been cast in a mould of simple happiness but who, between the husband she had chosen and the son who had been born to her, was the victim of an extraordinary fate; a woman who had suffered humiliation but was resigned, who feared the worst but would submit to it with a sad docility since it was God's will.

Lautrec's passion for painting, though he was no doubt only obscurely aware of it as yet, was simply a passion for humanity. There were no other means of expression open to him. (He preferred to explain his meaning by a sketch rather than by words; and when he wrote a letter it was invariably crude, lacking both taste and style). The paintbrush was the instrument of his curiosity.

After the grape harvest, he left the woods and vineyards of Malromé and returned to Montmartre, that stew in which so many of the men and women were outcasts like himself.

*   *   *

Lautrec was working harder than ever. The weeks and months went by without any relaxation of effort. 'Henri is working like a black and gets very tired,' wrote Countess Adèle in 1884.

* There are some twenty paintings dating from 1883.

He even gained Cormon's approval. Indeed, Cormon went so far as to consider enlisting him (together with Rachou) as a collaborator with a few other artists in illustrating an edition of Victor Hugo's works. And this was not all: Bonnat—Monsieur Bonnat—had also complimented him. What more could he hope for?

Countess Adèle declared herself much gratified by these good reports which proved that her son was 'not the least in the studio from what one hears.' Her confidence in his future increased. 'He seems,' she said, 'to be more and more established in his path and vocation.'

But what precisely was his vocation in her view? For Countess Adèle, her son's aims of two years ago, when he had first entered Bonnat's studio, remained unchanged. They were the École des Beaux-Arts, fashionable exhibitions, the Salon, decorations and one day perhaps the Institut. She was quite unable to imagine a painter's career taking any other form. The irresistible urge which was sweeping Lautrec away altogether escaped her. She did not know that Montmartre had acquired a permanent hold over her son; she did not even suspect it. Montmartre was so very far from the world in which she moved.

But, for that matter, was Lautrec himself very clearly aware of the urge that was driving him on? He was stimulated by the praise of Bonnat and Cormon, which gave him real pleasure. 'I'm glad not to be completely ineffectual.' Yet can we be certain that he attached as much importance to their approval as he would have done two years ago? Both Bonnat and Cormon still inspired him with respect. However divergent their preoccupations and conception of painting, Lautrec had not lost his esteem for his two masters; while the uncertainty and sense of inferiority which the circumstances of his life had developed in him constantly inclined him to think others right and himself wrong.

He was, nevertheless, compelled to obey the impulsion of the forces that drove him on. When, in the spring of 1884, he visited the exhibitions, he made a note of his impressions. His spontaneous criticisms were irreverent and he gave free rein to a certain mischievous irony. Though he was prepared to admit the 'masterly flexibility' of a Carolus Duran or the 'precise and implacable drawing' of a Delaunay, he made no bones about the mediocrity of what he saw. 'But, Monsieur Delaunay,' he cried, 'why those green leaves which make so disagreeable a contrast with the reds of your general? Too many laurels, Monsieur Delaunay!' And of another exhibitor: 'Are you trying to sell, Monsieur Sergent?' he asked ironically. 'Certainly, the way you wipe your brush clean is marvellous, but international art will really not be regenerated by its enthusiastic contact.' Faithful to his friendship with Princeteau, he said impertinently: 'Monsieur Princeteau seems to me to estimate club exhibitions at their proper value. He sends along the first sketch that comes to hand, but this does not prevent his being in the front rank and with honour.'

It was not only at the pictures Lautrec looked with a mocking eye, but also at the people who came to see them, the fashionable society whose pretentions and affectations irritated him. 'The Mirlitons in the Place Vendôme, opposite the column! What a crush! A lot of people, a lot of women, and a lot of nonsense! It's a crush made up of gloved hands manipulating tortoiseshell or gold lorgnettes; but it's a crush all the same!' Lautrec much preferred his friends in Montmartre to this brilliant throng.

This year, at the Salon, where Cormon exhibited to the admiration of the crowd his *Retour d'une chasse à l'ours à l'âge de pierre* (which was immediately bought by the Nation), Puvis de Chavannes aroused great excitement with his painting, *Le Bois sacré cher aux Muses et aux Arts*, which was destined to decorate the museum at Lyons. This huge canvas, which, so one critic noted, 'transports us into a light, harmonious world of Elysian serenity,' was greeted with divided opinions by Cormon's pupils: some praised it warmly, others criticised it severely. Lautrec, for his part, found in it a pretext for a laugh. In this 'Elysian' canvas, representing half-naked Muses in draperies with carefully studied folds, he detected a 'sniveldrop quality' as he termed anything that seemed to him ridiculous. With the help of some of the other pupils in the studio, he spent two afternoons making a parody of it, introducing an army of art students into the Sacred Grove, watched over by a policeman; he put himself in the front row in a burlesque attitude, his back turned to the Muses.

If Countess Adèle ever saw this canvas she must have trembled at such disrespect for the glories of the hour. But she would have been even more concerned had she known where her son went to find his models. Desiring to paint a nude, Lautrec* asked a decayed prostitute, Grosse Maria, to sit for him.

He painted her blighted body, her ravaged and almost dolorous face, with a sympathy that must, had they seen it, have been seriously disquieting to his family. But had he not felt a profound fellowship with Grosse Maria's decadence, would he have been able to give the nude he painted of her such an emotional quality? Like himself, she had no illusions.

Lautrec was now twenty. Montmartre had slowly tightened its grip on him. It was there only, as he limped from street to street, delightedly sniffing their gamey odours, that he wanted to live. One day, he announced to his astonished mother that he intended to set up house there. His family protested and refused to allow him the money to lease a studio. But Lautrec was not deterred. He belonged by temperament to the breed of men in whom caprice is all-powerful, and independence a passion. Leaving the Cité du Retiro, he went to live with his friend Grenier who, with his wife, Lily, lived at 19 *bis*, Rue Fontaine.

* Only five or six paintings survive from the year 1884.

CHAPTER THREE

Montmartre

'What is Montmartre? Nothing. What should it be?
Everything !'

RODOLPHE SALIS

RENÉ GRENIER was a few years older than Lautrec and had served in the
cavalry as a non-commissioned officer. At the end of his period of
enlistment, his colonel had sent for him. 'Why the devil do you want
to go on being a soldier when you've got a private income?' the
colonel asked, and strongly advised him to take up some other
profession, painting perhaps.

Grenier followed this advice. His family were very well off (they
owned part of the Ternes district), and he had an annual income of
some 12,000 gold francs.

Though he was not without talent, he went to his easel only at spare
moments. But he liked living among artists and the bohemian
atmosphere suited his temperament. He probably looked on himself
merely as an amateur, and certainly considered Lautrec as one. Nor
did he care for his friend's work.

This charming man, whose good humour everyone remarked
on, had married a plump girl very much to the taste of the period.
With a body that might have been modelled by a sculptor, a milky
skin covered with tiny freckles and bright red hair, Lily could have sat
for Rubens. She had in fact been a model for Degas, who painted her
bathing. Since the days when as a little peasant girl from Brie-Comte-
Robert she had sat for the first time to Princess Mathilde, she had
appeared in all her resplendent nudity before some twenty artists.
She had many devoted admirers. But though perfectly aware of her
attractions, she never abused her power. Lautrec nicknamed her
'Lily-la-Rosse.'

He was amused by her vitality, by her delight in having made so good a marriage with such little trouble (she was just twenty), and in having money to throw about. She was like a healthy young animal, intoxicated by the scents of spring. He was amused too by the social blunders she made, by her off-hand manner and the superb and peremptory airs she assumed.

She amused him, and he was wise enough to conceal the fact that she attracted him. He was not going to make himself ridiculous by entering into rivalry with such handsome men as the actors Silvain and the younger Coquelin. Lily, he knew, had 'no taste for half-dwarfs'. Nevertheless, the domineering young woman showed him an almost maternal tenderness. She would sometimes take his hand to lead him across the street as if he were a child. She was the best and kindest of friends to him in all sorts of ways. On several occasions she consoled him in moments of distress. Perhaps she understood him better than anyone else, knew his regrets for all he could not have and which she could not give him. Lautrec enjoyed the warmth of her presence. He liked walking with her too. He was proud to be seen with her in public places.

The Greniers went out a great deal and had many friends. Lautrec shared all their amusements. From time to time, Lily, with the help of professional actors, organised entertainments in fancy dress. Lautrec would dress up as a woman, a Japanese or a Spanish dancer, flirting with fan and eye. He was the life and soul of the party, and people said how splendid it was of him to overcome his deformity in this way and show no bitterness But this dressing-up was like the jokes with which he made the studio laugh (and with which he salted his parts in these masquerades): it was a deliberate pose by which he endeavoured to substitute, even if only for an instant, another personality for his own. There had always been good reasons for dwarfs turning themselves into court jesters.

In the evenings, Lautrec, the Greniers, Anquetin and other friends from Cormon's would go to the various pleasure haunts on the Butte, whose numbers were continually increasing. 'What is Montmartre? Nothing. What should it be? Everything!' proclaimed the 'gentleman tavern-keeper', Rodolphe Salis, whose Le Chat Noir Lautrec and his friends frequented. Salis was a great showman, who was never at a loss for new and amusing ideas; and he was putting all his verve into launching the Butte.

Tall, red-haired and restless, the son of a Chatellerault distiller, he had tried and failed in a dozen professions before his thirtieth year. Having first studied mathematics, he had been in turn a caricaturist, an engraver of medals, an archaeologist, and a painter. He had even painted decorations for a building in Calcutta. But success had always eluded him. Then, one day in 1881, he had had the idea of turning the studio he had fitted up in a disused Post Office, at 84, Boulevard de Rochechouart, into an artists' cabaret. It was not a new idea. Writers and artists were already meeting at La Grande Pinte, which had been started three years before in the Avenue Trudaine, and where the more fashionable customers came to listen to literary discussions and hear poets, singers and musicians give impromptu performances. Salis decided to organise systematically the attractions which had contributed to the brief vogue of La Grande Pinte.

He had a gift for detecting talent and he succeeded in persuading a group of young poets and painters, the Hydropathes, to desert the café in the Rue Cujas on the Left Bank, where they had had their headquarters, and come to Montmartre. He also managed to persuade them—for he was as avaricious as he was able—that he was doing them a great honour by suggesting they should come regularly to his tavern and drink there as copiously as possible at their own expense.*

It was thus that the Chat Noir was born. And soon all Paris was to come and drink Salis' beer, which was baptised 'hydromel', among the real or false Louis XIII furniture, the tapestries, pictures, Church windows, stuffed stags' heads, armour, rusty swords and worm-eaten wooden statuettes, to all of which had recently been added a huge canvas by Willette, the *Parce Domine*. It showed a crowd of pierrots, art students, singers and young women with the sardonic face of death appearing from behind the clouds, for which the artist had been paid the princely sum of 250 francs.

---

* Among the frequent customers of the Chat Noir may be mentioned Alphonse Allais, Émile Goudeau, Verlaine, Jean Richepin, Maurice Rollinat, Charles Cros, Jean Moréas, Édmond Haraucourt, Jean Lorrain, Jules Jouy, MacNab and Maurice Donnay.

Behind the big room was a smaller one, pompously called the Institut, and reserved for artists and heavy drinkers—the waiters were all dressed in the uniform of Academicians—and Salis, with pointed beard and wearing a tightly-buttoned grey frock-coat, would harangue his customers, shouting in his harsh voice: 'Montmartre, the town of liberty! Montmartre, the sacred hill! Montmartre, the salt of the earth, the mind and navel of the world, the granite breast from which the generations athirst for the ideal come to refresh themselves!' Montmartre owed a great deal of its prosperity, which was now beginning, to Salis.

There was, however, a certain disingenuousness about Salis with which Lautrec was not in sympathy. He did not care for his swash-buckling effrontery, his exhibitionism and his publicity-seeking. Salis had once announced his death and put a notice on the door saying: 'Open because of death', and then presided over his own funeral in a golden robe.

Shown in by a scarlet-clothed Swiss, halberd in hand, the customers were welcomed by the master of ceremonies: 'This way, my Lord!— Will you take a seat, Monseigneur?— What will you have to drink, your Highness?' This bumptious obsequiousness, this bowing and scraping of a lemonade-seller over-proud of his success ('I spit in the beer of the cads who order it contemptuously'), this mercenary charlatanism of Rodolphe Malice—for so Willette called him—whose grandiloquence was a mask for his petty meannesses (Salis had the reputation of never returning forgotten umbrellas), profoundly irritated Lautrec. Besides, Lautrec cared too little for poetry, literature and the discussions of writers to see in the main attractions of the Chat Noir anything but snobbery and affectation, which were all the more irritating for being organised.

He could find the noise, the movement and the turbulent rowdiness, which were for him the only charms of the Chat Noir, in many other places on the Butte. Accompanied as always by his protectors, he went to the dance-halls, to the Élysée-Montmartre at No. 80, close to the Chat Noir and on the same side of the street, which had revived the old *chahut* under the name of the naturalistic quadrille. Or he would climb to the top of the Rue Lepic, to the Moulin-de-la-Galette, to drink its speciality—mulled wine, spiced with cinnamon and cloves. But it was a long way for his crippled legs.

Besides, he was not particularly attracted to the Moulin-de-la-Galette. On Sundays, the glass-walled shed that was the tavern's main room was filled with counter-jumpers, errand girls, laundresses, small shopkeepers, poor artisans, Batignolles work-girls chaperoned by their mothers, hoydens who had escaped from their homes, wearing kiss curls fixed with salad oil, to meet 'their young man at the corner of the Impasse Girardon',* waistcoat-makers, artificial flower-makers and pale-faced clerks all dancing waltzes, polkas or family quadrilles with a happy propriety to the band in which the brass was dominant, while the cashier shouted: 'Pay your money!'

You paid two sous for waltzes, four for quadrilles. The entwined couples jerked about the floor for the sole pleasure of dancing; there was all the lack of ceremony of the popular dance hall. On Monday nights, on the other hand, the Moulin was full of roughs, apaches and pimps, who quarrelled over their prostitutes and went out to fight with knives or pistols in the dark little alleys of the neighbourhood: the vicinity of the Moulin had a bad reputation.

None of this held any enchantment for Lautrec, the Sunday routine no more than that of Monday. The Élysée-Montmartre, with its high-kicking professional dancers, was a very different matter.

Beneath the gas lamps, to the rhythm of the stentorian music marking with shattering chords the figures of the quadrilles, among a whirlwind of frills, a rectangle of flesh would be revealed from time to time. And Lautrec discovered an ineffable pleasure in the feverish, breathless, overheated atmosphere.

Sitting at a table with a drink in front of him, he watched, scribbling in a sketch-book or on an odd piece of paper the outline of a body or a head with the burnt end of a match. He drank and drew interminably, always watching the crowd that jostled in the dance-hall, the provocative gestures of the women, the congested faces of the men, surprising a wink here, a bargain being made there.

It was himself and his own damaged life he saw in the stigmata of lechery imprinted on the faces of these men and women. Decadence

* Montorgueil.

and sophistication cast their spell over him. He returned continually to the spectacle, could not tear himself away from it. All that accorded with his inmost, secret suffering was here in this temple of movement, where he played with such intensity the only part to which he could pretend: that of an observer. His painter's eye discerned with an ineffable sensuality, a delight which would have been morbid had he possessed any illusions about himself, a pale face with bistre lines about the hollows of the eyes, the blue shadow softening the hollow of an arm, the feverish brilliance of eyes too large and too made-up, the greenish tone of a cheek.

He noted pitilessly what he saw, with neither tenderness nor cruelty, but with the cold, precise irony of someone who had nothing to lose and was calmly drawing up the balance sheet of his own insolvency.

Nothing escaped him. Everything held his attention: the dancers high-kicking amid a froth of underclothes, sometimes removing a spectator's hat with a quick, light kick before sinking to the ground in the glissade of the splits; the band leader, Louis Dufour, once a musician in the Guard, fat, jovial, apoplectic, who panted and sweated and waved his baton frenziedly, stimulating with gesture and eye his forty musicians and the dancers; the Commissaire of the Moral Police, Coutelat du Roché, called Père La Pudeur, whose duty it was . to see that the girls did not overstep certain limits of decency and who walked up and down in his black uniform with a steel chain across his chest, his hands clasped behind his back, his complexion stained by thirty-five years' exposure to the fetid atmosphere of dance-halls, and who kept a melancholy, slightly weary eye on the swaying skirts, persuaded for a long time past of the uselessness of his functions; the girls who, as soon as Père La Pudeur's back was turned, took the opportunity of showing an extra length of black open-work stocking, and garters of delicate hues; the young girls from the suburbs come to sniff the odour of debauchery ('Mama, we worked terribly late at the shop'); pimps scenting their quarry; and, finally, Valentin le Désossé, the dance master, who during the day was a wine merchant in the Rue Coquillière and at night transformed himself into the leader of the quadrilles. Valentin le Désossé who, with his overlong but wonderfully supple arms and legs, had triumphed in all the dance halls of the Second Empire, from the Hermitage to the Tour-Solferino, who had been the anointed king of waltzers and had been carried in triumph by three thousand people to the Tivoli-Vauxhall, and who led his partners indefatigably into the rhythm of his irreproachable timing, dancing with his eyes half shut, his top-hat tilted forward a little on to his forehead, his bony, mournful face completely imperturbable, 'his head stiff and motionless on his long, emaciated neck in which only the Adam's apple seemed to show any emotion.'

Lautrec watched and drew, and drank!

*   *   *

Lautrec was still going to Cormon's studio, but he was something of a rebel now. He had adopted a casual attitude towards the sage precepts of the painter and devoted himself to individual and highly characteristic work, which would no doubt have annoyed Cormon, if done by anyone else.

But Cormon, who was not nearly so narrow in his views and opinions as certain of his official colleagues, showed infinite patience with Lautrec. The dwarf's vitality, good humour and buffoonery, all disposed Cormon to tolerance.

There were continual discussions in the studio. The artistic world was in a state of considerable ferment. Manet, who had died two years earlier,* was becoming increasingly important; the fame, that had for so long eluded him, was now accruing posthumously. The Impressionists were still struggling, but their group was dispersed; yet their theories were already having an effect on younger painters. The year before, in 1884, the first Salon of the Société des Artistes Indépendants —a salon without a hanging committee—was held in the hall of the Ville de Paris in the Champs-Élysées. And, also in 1884, an *avant-garde* club, the Société des XX had been founded in Brussels. The theories of the various schools, which must ultimately determine the evolution of art, scarcely interested Lautrec. He cared little for aesthetic doctrines, took no more account of conformity than he did of rebellion, merely assimilated what he needed from wherever he happened to find it and

* April 30, 1883.

looked no further. All he wanted to be able to do was to express what moved him in a model, to have a technique available that was sufficiently proved and effective to enable him to say what he wanted to say. He was not at all intransigent; sometimes, to please Cormon, he tried hard to be 'pretty, pretty'—though, it must be admitted, without much success.

Nevertheless, his own tastes were becoming more precise. He liked Renoir (whose colour delighted him), Pissarro and Raffaelli. His liking for Forain's work had grown no less: he spoke of a drawing Forain had done of Count Alphonse as 'a marvel'. But his greatest enthusiasm of all was for Degas.

While most of the Impressionists were open-air, landscape painters, Degas had dealt with a number of subjects which obsessed Lautrec, scenes in cafés-concerts, paintings of night-life, dancers and musicians. By an odd chance, Degas occupied a studio in the same building as the Greniers, at the farther end of the courtyard. But Lautrec certainly dared not accost him. He knew too well Degas' reputation as an old bear even though he looked on him as a master among masters.

His assiduous attendance at cabarets, dance-halls and at the brothel at No. 2, Rue de Steinkerque, a few yards from the Élysée-Montmartre, had in no way impaired Lautrec's fever for work. Contrary to what one might expect he now had remarkable physical stamina. His compact body had become vigorously muscular and he could swim, row and do dumb-bell exercises without fatigue. No excesses could impair his vitality. Had his companions always joined in his excesses of work as in his excesses of pleasure, he would soon have exhausted them. He hardly slept, went to bed very late, and got up at dawn.

An elderly photographer, Père Forest, had given him permission to paint in his garden, which lay at the bottom of the Rue Caulaincourt, next door to a big yard belonging to a timber merchant.* The garden was only partly cultivated; the rest was allowed to run wild, and was covered with long grass, shrubs and thickets of brambles. There were a few limes, sycamores and planes and many lilacs. Père Forest was a great amateur of archery, and would come two or three times a week

* The site is occupied today by the Gaumont Cinema. The Rue Forest perpetuates the memory of these gardens and their proprietor.

to shoot with his friends. Except for this, the gardens were solitary and ideally peaceful. Lautrec could work there in complete tranquillity. A little summer-house sheltered his apparatus, as well as an assortment of bottles. 'One should drink little, of course,' he remarked; 'but often!'

He was constantly in search of models. To perfect his technique, he painted portraits which were to him what practising scales are to a musician. 'My homework,' he called them.

Although he chose to sit his models in the open air, it was for reasons quite other than those which tormented the Impressionists. He took no particular account of the gardens. He was not interested in the subtle analysis of light, the play of shadow, the diversity of colour according to the time of day and the season. On the contrary, he was hoping to obtain, under a more direct light than that of the studio, a pristine clarity, free of ephemeral elements, that would not hinder him in his quest for the mystery of a human being as such. He wanted to paint faces that had been utterly stripped of the fortuitous.

He had recently got to know a painter called Zandomeneghi, a Venetian who had come to Paris in search of fame, and was now bitterly unhappy at having to vegetate in an obscurity for which he blamed the French: they had disappointed the hopes he had placed in them. Zandomeneghi had recommended a young model to Lautrec, a girl of twenty, called Marie-Clémentine Valadon, who lived in the same house as he did.

The daughter of an unknown father and a seamstress from Bessines-sur-Gartempe, in Limousin, she had been brought to Paris before she was five years old. Her mother made her living as best she could by going out charring. After attending a school run by nuns for a short while, the little girl had found employment at the age of eleven as a seamstress. Since then she had been a nursemaid at the Tuileries, a waitress in a cheap restaurant, and had sold vegetables in the Batignolles market. Attracted to the circus, she had joined Molier's amateur circus at the age of fifteen and had become a trapeze-artist. A few months later, she had had a fall which had put an end to her career as an acrobat. That had been five years ago.

She was physically attractive, though her beauty had a slightly acid quality; but she was fond of drawing. She had drawn all her life on anything that came to hand, including walls and pavements, using a bit of coal or a piece of chalk. Somewhat reluctantly helping her mother, who had set up as a laundress in the Impasse de Guelma, she delivered linen to artists, among others to Puvis de Chavannes in the Place Pigalle, and she became his model. She sat for Puvis in the studio at Neuilly. The Muses and the ephebi in the *Bois Sacré*, which Lautrec had parodied, were no other than Marie-Clémentine, painted in a variety of attitudes.

She also sat for Zandomeneghi and for Renoir, inspiring his *Danse à la Campagne* and his *Danse à la Ville*, two panels which date from 1883. At the end of this same year, December 1883, she gave birth to a child, Maurice, whose father did not think it proper to publish his identity. She then went to live at 7, Rue Tourlaque, at the corner of the Rue Caulaincourt, in a flat on the first floor, on the same landing as Zandomeneghi, with her mother and her son.*

Valadon suited Lautrec as a model. And she was all the more to his taste because of her wildness. Maria—for so she was called in the studios —was extremely independent and lived a turbulent love life. The inhabitants of the Butte would have found it difficult to name Maurice's father, to decide whether it was Boissy, the singer, a Bohemian alcoholic who performed in the cabarets or the distinguished Miguel Utrillo, a Spaniard, who so delighted in the charms of Montmartre that he lived in the Moulin-de-la-Galette; or even Puvis de Chavannes, whose wife, born Princess Cantacuzène, kept a discreet eye on the models her famous husband employed. Maria enjoyed making love and Lautrec's peculiar constitution and his ardent nature were far from frightening her. Nor was she repulsed by his deformity. The painter very soon made her his mistress.

They seemed born to understand each other. The working-class girl had no more prejudices than had the descendant of the Counts of Toulouse. She had seized every opportunity of learning the secrets of their trade from the artists she knew, and she was immediately

---

* Eight years later, Maurice was recognised by a Spaniard, Miguel Utrillo y Molins. As for Marie-Clémentine, she later changed her Christian name to Suzanne.

appreciative of Lautrec's talent, his lucidity, his inability to be 'pretty, pretty', and of the often aggressive precision of his brush.

Lautrec painted two portraits of her in Père Forest's garden. He did not flatter her. Renoir, who was still summoning this attractive girl to sit for him, was in process of painting a half-length portrait of her in *La Natte*, in which he painted her big blue eyes, her large sensual mouth, her abundant brown hair and her full, round bosom with a voluptuous delicacy. Lautrec gave her features a more angular, harsher aspect, depriving her of the wild beauty of her twenty years only to return it to her in a less transitory reality.

Suspicious, jealous of her private life and inclined to put off the curious with lies, Maria had never told anyone that she drew. Lautrec, therefore, did not know that in 1883 she had drawn a self-portrait in pastel in which she had been no more indulgent towards herself than he had.* It would not have occurred to her to reproach him with a lack of gallantry; she undoubtedly admired the precision of his draughtsmanship.

* * *

On Wednesday, June 10, 1885, at midnight, an extraordinary procession set off from the Chat Noir.

Preceded by two little pageboys in short coats, a big banner which flapped in the wind, the Swiss making his halberd ring, and the major-domo dressed as a sous-préfet, Rodolphe Salis, who for the occasion had donned the uniform of a préfet of the first class, led seven or eight musicians, beating drums and blowing bugles as loud as they could. Four waiter-academicians, torch bearers, a whole company brandishing halberds, arquebuses and swords were followed by a crowd of customers and friends, whose numbers were increased at every step by the idle and the curious.

Rodolphe Salis was moving house. He was leaving the Boulevard de Rochechouart to set up his cabaret on new premises five or six hundred yards farther on.

Things had not been going well for him in the district these last

---

* 'I paint people so as to get to know them,' said Suzanne Valadon later . . . 'Never bring me a woman to paint who is in search of the polite or the pretty, I shall most certainly disappoint her.'

months. Since he prided himself on the high social standing of his customers, the roughs who hung about the Élysée-Montmartre had picked a quarrel with him. One night, one of these '*dos verts*', his cap over his ear and a cigarette dangling from the corner of his mouth, had tried to force his way in. Salis had thrown him out, with a good deal of dramatic posturing and considerable shouting. A little later, the roughs came back in force, and there was a battle which cost Salis two slashes. But this was not the most serious part of the business. Whirling a stool round his head, Salis had the bad luck to hit one of his waiters, who died that same night. Ever since this incident, Salis had been extremely nervous. Disgusted with the neighbourhood of the Élysée-Montmartre, he had given up his lease at the end of April and taken No. 12, Rue de Laval,* the house which had previously been occupied by the Belgian painter Alfred Stevens.

Salis was afraid that someone might take the opportunity of re-placing him on the Boulevard and was far from reassured when he heard two or three days later that a new cabaret, the Mirliton, had been started in his old premises. It was founded by a man whom he had helped, an unknown song-writer whom he had allowed to sell his work at the Chat Noir: Aristide Bruant, the singer of blackguardly songs. There was no danger of his being attacked by the roughs from the Élysée. However, no one would go to the Mirliton.

But soon, alas, everyone was going there. They crowded in. But what was going on? Incredible though it seemed, people went to Bruant's to be insulted!

From almost the very first day, Lautrec had been a regular customer of the Mirliton. Bruant delighted him. Tall, clean-shaven, with a sneering, bitter mouth, an impudent manner, a face like a Roman emperor's, and a loud voice, 'a voice for riots and barricades, a voice to dominate the roar of the streets on the day of revolution',† Lautrec felt that enthusiasm which was always aroused in him by people endowed with overwhelming vitality.

Emptied of Salis' furniture, the cabaret had now only a few tables, chairs and benches. The singer walked up and down, one hand grasping

---

* Today, Rue Victor-Massé.
† Jules Lemaitre.

Lautrec with Zidler, director of the Moulin Rouge (*c.* 1891)

Lautrec. A double portrait by Maurice Guibert (c. 1890)

(right) Lautrec working on the painting *La Danse au Moulin Rouge*, in his studio at 27 rue Caulaincourt (1890)

'La Goulue' (right) and 'Grille d'Égout'

'La Goulue' (seated) and her sister

Lautrec. Self-portrait with his cousin Gabriel Tapié de Céleyran. Detail of the painting *A[t the] Moulin Rouge* (1892)

(*Right*) Lautrec (*c*. 1892

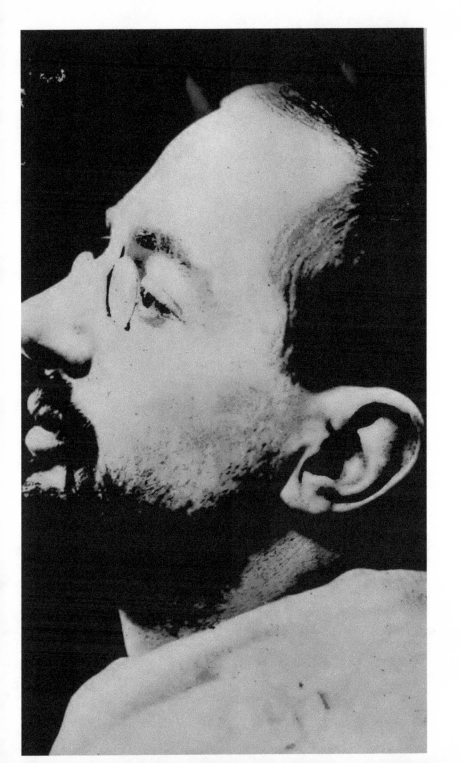

a cudgel, the other on his hip, dressed in a red flannel shirt, black corduroy coat and trousers, and sewer-man's boots. Lautrec's curiosity had no doubt been aroused by the flamboyant effect of this costume which was completed by a wide, 'go to Jericho'* felt hat, a black cape, and a scarlet scarf. But Bruant's forceful personality was even more striking.

Lautrec delighted to hear him receiving his customers. Salis' 'gentle ladies' and 'my lords' were over and done with. 'Here's something fancy coming,' the singer would cry as new customers arrived. 'No dregs this time. Something choice, three star tarts. And the gentlemen following behind are undoubtedly pimps or ambassadors! This way, ladies, this way! Sit beside the little fat fellow here! It's all right, you're only fifteen on that bench! For Christ's sake move up a bit at the end there! And you, moon face, sit down there with your two girl-friends!'

Unconventional himself, Lautrec was delighted at Bruant's welcome to the fashionable customers in tail coats and smart dresses, who were in search of a taste of low life.

The fashionable customers liked it too. They asked for more. One night, a general shook Bruant warmly by the hand and said: 'I've enjoyed my evening very much. Thank you! It's the first time I've ever been called an old so and so, at least to my face!'

Bruant discovered the peculiar attraction of his establishment by mistake. On the day the Mirliton opened, only two or three loungers came in. He had risked in the business not only all his own savings, but quite a considerable sum of money he had borrowed. Faced with an almost empty room in which, in Salis' time, he had so often seen a jostling crowd, Bruant turned morose at the prospect of his enterprise failing and lost his temper with a customer who was demanding another song. 'What? What's that? Who's that c—— complaining?' The day after, the same man came back to the Mirliton with a number of friends. Bruant sang. But his customers seemed dissatisfied. 'What? No bouquets today?' the man cried. Bruant realised immediately the implications of this somewhat unexpected remark. The gentlemen wanted to be insulted. Very well, they should have their money's

* Courteline.

Lautrec painting Berthe 'La Sourde' in the garden of Père Forest (1890)

worth. From that moment his public grew day by day. He was soon
able to put up a sign:

AT THE MIRLITON
CUSTOMERS WHO LIKE BEING BLACKGUARDED

The cabaret was full from ten o'clock at night till two in the morning. 'I'm going to sing you "*A Saint-Lazare*," ' Bruant would
announce, exaggerating his vulgar accent. 'And the rest of you, you
bastards, try to bawl the chorus in time . . . Monsieur Marius, give me
the chord of F sharp . . .'

But Bruant did not have to try very hard to play his part. Lautrec,
who very soon became his close friend, knew very well that Bruant
had nothing but contempt for the people who came up to Montmartre
to seek out low life in his establishment. 'They're a lot of idiots,' said
Aristide, 'they don't even understand what I sing to them, they can't
understand, because they don't know what it is to starve. I take
my revenge by treating them worse than dogs. They laugh till
the tears run down their cheeks; they think I'm joking. But it's the
thought of the past, and the horrors I've seen, that make me speak as
I do.'

Bruant had suffered thirty-four years of poverty. Born in the
Gâtinais, he had lived in Paris with a drunken father and an ill-tempered
mother in a series of sordid lodgings which they had left one after the
other because his father drank away the little money they had. Remarkably enough, he had preserved the soul of a young countryman;
wherever he might be, he had only to look up at the stars to be reborn
and forget. Healthily ambitious, he had worked in a lawyer's office,
with a jeweller, and with the Compagnie du Nord Railway, before
branching out to try his luck in the cafés-concerts. There was a latent
poet in him. At first, he had sung songs in the contemporary fashion,
light, comic numbers and marching songs; then, when he went to
Salis, he had changed his repertoire and made himself the troubadour of
the down-and-outs.

Like Lautrec, but with a more humanitarian indignation and a
deeper anger, he sympathised with the world of the outcasts. In a
direct, robust and highly coloured slang, he sang of the dregs, the dens,

the brothels and the prisons, the waste-lands, where slept the down-and-outs and the roughs of the district fought their battles. He sang of the women who walked the streets on melancholy winter evenings:

> *A sont des tas*
> *Qu'a plus d'appas*
> *Et qui n'a pas*
> *D'sous dans leurs bas,*
>
> *Pierreuses,*
> *Trotteuses,*
> *A marchent l'soir*
> *Quand il fait noir,*
> *Sur le trottoir,*
> *Sur le trottoir.*
>
> *A n'ont plus de pain,*
> *A n'ont plus d'feu,*
> *A prient l'bon Dieu,*
> *Qu'est un bon fieu,*
> *D'chauffer leur pieu.*

Lautrec did not share Bruant's compassion. He was a complete stranger to the pity that flavoured his friend's songs. The romanticism with which Bruant endued his vagrants and prostitutes touched him not at all. As an aristocrat, he felt nothing but repulsion for the dismal sordidness of poverty, for what he called 'the poor side of life'. Mediocrity caused him as much impatience as the rabble did repulsion. 'Let's go,' he said one day to his companions at the Moulin-de-la-Galette, when it was invaded by the Sunday crowd; 'all this luxury of the poor is even more nauseating than their misery.' It was not that he liked splendour and wealth for their own sakes. He saw no difference between the marquises of the aristocratic Faubourg and the prostitutes of Pigalle, except in standing, and this was of no importance. Socially, he no longer belonged to any particular circle. It was humanity alone that interested him—and that passionately. What so delighted him about Bruant were precisely those gifts of observation the singer used so surely, and his frank, direct language.

La dernièr'fois que je l'ai vu,
Il avait l'torse à moitié nu
Et le cou pris dans la lunette,
A la Roquette.

Bruant was a tender-hearted man behind his roughness. Lautrec recognised something of himself in him. Beneath the irony and cynicism he concealed a bruised sensibility. Like Lautrec, the one thing he hated most was emotional dishonesty.

Lautrec went almost every evening to the Mirliton, and took his friends with him, the Greniers, Anquetin and others.

Oh! là là! C'tte gueul', c'tte binette!
Oh! là, là! C'tte guel' qu'il a!

shouted the regular customers as soon as anyone entered the establishment.

Beneath the huge reed-pipe that hung from the ceiling, Bruant went to and fro among the tables, from time to time jumping on to one to sing a song, stamping his boots to mark the beat. If the toffs would only continue to make his fortune while he insulted them, he would be able to retire to the Gâtinais in ten years.

'All together!' he would cry; and at a wave of his cudgel the whole room would take up the chorus:

Tous les clients sont des cochons,
La faridondon, la faridondaine,
Et surtout les ceuss' qui s'en vont,
La faridondain', la faridondon!

Trees, grass and the murmuring of water under the willows, these were what Bruant wanted; and to make his fortune as quickly as possible and bow himself out into a purer air!

Oh! là, là! C'tte gueul' . . .

With a gesture, Bruant would stop the chorus. He could see the little figure of Lautrec coming in. 'Silence, Messieurs,' he would order. 'Here's the great painter Toulouse-Lautrec with a friend and a bastard I don't know.'

Lautrec hobbled through the crowd, his head held high. He knew now that his true nobility was to be a painter. His work was his rehabilitation. How could he fail to agree with Bruant's contempt for the incompetent, the idle? He could listen, mocking and unmoved, to the popular singer, who stood there with his hands in his pockets lashing the ineffectual rich, without feeling that it was directed at himself:

> *Tas d'inach'vés, tas d'avortons*
> *Fabriqués avec des viandes veules,*
> *Vos mèr's avaient donc pas d'tétons*
> *Qu'a's ont pas pu vous fair' des gueules?*
> *Vous êt's tous des fils de michés*
> *Qu'on envoy' têter en nourrice.*
> *C'est pour ça qu'vous êt's mal torchés . . .*
> *Allez donc dir' qu'on vous finisse!*

*　　*　　*

During the summer of 1885, Lautrec went to stay for a while in a charming village in Brie, Villiers-sur-Morin, where the Greniers had a pied-à-terre.

To travel the forty kilometres between Paris and Villiers was at that time something of an expedition. You had to take the train as far as Esbly, and then go by diligence to the valley of the Grand Morin, which took at least an hour.

It was a pleasant solitary place where many artists went to paint. Lautrec spent his holiday in the company of several friends from Cormon's studio, in particular Anquetin. These were all staying at Père Ancelin's inn on the church square, not far from the Greniers. The beautiful Lily was the queen of the colony. To the scandal of the natives, she rode about the countryside, her hair blowing in the wind and—height of immodesty—riding astride. Oh, these artists!

The parties they held by the waterside, in a place called the Pré-Salé, horrified the natives even more. Lautrec was happy. He fished and felt like a countryman. He would have liked, so he wrote, 'to be a faun and walk about the woods naked'.*

* Quoted by Francis Jourdain.

And yet, his break with nature was complete. Unlike his friends the landscape painters, it never occurred to him to take up his brush to paint the beauties of that countryside. Only when it rained did Lautrec seize the opportunity of working, and then in his own fashion. He painted four decorations on the walls and doors of the Ancelin inn, but instead of being scenes of rustic life they were of the theatre. One was of the call-boy summoning the company on to the stage; another of a dancer in her dressing-room; a third of a ballet; and a fourth of the audience in the gallery. He painted himself among the audience dressed as an apache, a peaked cap on his head and a red scarf round his neck.

It was not long before he was back in Montmartre and he plunged into the iridescent night life of the Butte with more delight than ever.

Montmartre was becoming more popular week by week. The Élysée, the Chat Noir and the Mirliton were full every night. Artists, authors and journalists, the fashionable world and the demi-monde, the wealthy and the impoverished all came to applaud the quadrilles of Valentin le Déssossé and his two favourite partners, Grille d'Égout and La Goulue, to listen to the poems and songs at Salis' establishment or suffer the ratings at Bruant's.

'An aristocrat waggles her behind when she runs!' sang Bruant, but his head was not turned by success. As a good son of the soil, he liked the ring of sound money, and he made the most of his opportunities. He served his customers the worst beer he could lay his hands on. 'What's the matter?' he would say if someone complained. 'It's not my drink you pay for, it's the right to see me and hear me bawl. The rest's just thrown in.' And, more than this, he reduced his *bocks* to the size of glasses of Madeira, sold them for eight sous and called them 'galopins'. On the slightest excuse, because a party seemed to be about to make a complaint, or, above all, because he guessed them to be well off, Bruant would order himself a drink at his customers' expense. 'Maxime, bring me a *galopin* to the table of those bastards over there!' All this delighted Lautrec.

Under Bruant's influence, he began larding his talk with slang. He knew all his friend's songs by heart and was continually singing them. The friendship between painter and singer soon became a collabor-

ation. For Bruant was decorating the Mirliton little by little. He bought anything that took his fancy at the curio-dealers: statuettes of saints, shaving dishes, string-less guitars, warming pans. There was even a chamber-pot which, in the middle of 'an asymmetrical trophy of boarding axes and Tunisian chibouks,' looked like 'a fantastic sun'.*
Bruant was a great admirer of Steinlen and hung his pictures on the walls of the Mirliton. He asked Lautrec for a work, and the latter drew the heroine of one of his songs, *A Saint-Lazare:* a prostitute writing from the famous women's prison to her man:

> *C'est de la prison que je t'écris,*
> *Mon pauv'Polyte.*
> *Hier, je n'sais pas c'qui m'a pris*
> *A la visite;*
> *C'est des maladi's qui s'voient pas*
> *Quand ça s'déclare,*
> *N'empêch' qu'aujourd'hui, j'suis dans l'tas*
> *A Saint-Lazare!*

Thanks to Bruant, Lautrec now had free entry to the Élysée-Montmartre. If he could acquire sufficient mastery of technique, he would soon be painting the scenes of the Mirliton and the Élysée. Above all, he wanted to paint the quadrilles, the whirling frenzy of the dance.

The naturalistic quadrille had recently acquired an artist of the first order, La Goulue, who suddenly threw the other stars of Montmartre, Nana la Sauterelle, Georgette la Vadrouille, La Torpille and Demi-Siphon, into the shade. The sixteen year old Alsatian girl—whose real name was Louise Weber—had been given this peculiar nickname because of her remarkable appetite. She was so greedy that, on occasion, she would even empty the dregs in the glasses on the tables. La Goulue was a foul-mouthed guttersnipe, whose conversation was a stream of obscenities; but as soon as she started to dance, to perform one of those improvisations that were her secret, she was transfigured. She was not merely a dancer; she was the dance itself. At first glance, Valentin had discerned her talent. He had protected, guided and taught

* Courteline.

her. They had become an incomparable couple. They danced to enthusiastic applause at the Moulin-de-la-Galette and the Élysée-Montmartre.

Lautrec never tired of watching them. She had a small mouth and blue eyes and was pink and chubby, yet her profile was aquiline. She had a harsh, cruel, almost metallic glitter about her, carrying her head, helmeted with a high chignon of fair hair, like an empress. As she kicked her legs towards the ceiling, her petticoats boiled like foam; she was a bacchante, possessed by rhythm, whirling disdainfully, indifferently, among a circle of infatuated men. While he, tall and supple, beating time with his coarse hands, his large feet never misplaced for an instant, followed every movement she made, every figure she evolved, his body taut, slanting slightly backwards, his greasy top-hat pulled low over his angular, morose and ravaged face.

Self-assured, haughty and insolent, La Goulue would disappear from the floor, followed by a hundred pairs of eyes. She did not bother to acknowledge the audience's ecstatic applause.

As if they were the slender, quivering legs of a thoroughbred, Lautrec seized his pencil to record what he himself could never enjoy: the exquisitely turned legs of La Goulue and the long, supple legs of Valentin unwearingly beating out the measures of the quadrilles.

He sat and drank and soaked himself in the atmosphere. Intoxicated by the odour of sweat, dust and tobacco, he was totally unable to drag himself away from the spell of these dance-halls. 'Let's go and see the darlings dance. They're so sweet, so Fontanges . . . No, I assure you, there's really no danger to me in drinking . . . I'm so close to the ground, eh?' And he would give a sniff.

*   *   *

In the autumn, Lautrec left the Greniers and went to live with Rachou, at 22, Rue Ganneron, behind the Montmartre Cemetery.

He continued his series of portraits, either in the studio, or in a little garden belonging to Rachou. One day, as he was leaving the Restaurant Boivin with his friend, he noticed a girl in the Avenue de Clichy. She looked rather unhealthy but had a splendid aureole of red hair.

'How beautiful she is!' remarked the painter. 'What a jade she looks! If I could only have her for a model.' Rachou spoke to the girl, and after some hesitation she finally agreed to sit for Lautrec.

The red-headed girl, whose name was Carmen Gaudin, was not at all 'the redoubtable bitch' the painter had imagined, but a decent working-girl. She had all the qualities of a good model and was soon making a career for herself with the painters. Cormon, and then Stevens, were soon employing her. For Lautrec, she had the great merit of flaming hair which was for him the most important attribute of a beautiful woman. 'When a woman has red hair! But really red!' he said (and the adjective seemed to clutter his mouth). 'Red!—The love of the Venetians!' All the women who attracted him, whether Lily or La Goulue, had either fair or red hair. Valadon was the only exception.

Lautrec painted at least four portraits of Carmen.* Did he tell her of the feelings she aroused in him? Probably. But he was not in the habit of admitting to his amorous temptations—nor to the rebuffs they brought him. 'The best way of possessing a woman,' said Ingres in his old age, 'is to paint her.' Nevertheless, Lautrec preferred less platonic loves. His contemptuous and sarcastic remarks did not deceive his friends. When they heard him lisp with a shrug of the shoulder as a pretty girl went by: 'I could have that one whenever I liked for fifty francs,' they knew that it was not 'the height of cynicism, but despair.'†
But Lautrec was not the man to give himself away. Impassivity was his supreme quality.

> *Quand on cherche une femme à Paris,*
> *Maint'nant, même en y mettant l'prix,*
> *On n'rencontre plus que des débris,*
>   *Ou de la charogne* . .

In the studio, where the classes had begun again, Lautrec sang Bruant's songs at the top of his voice. The dissension between Cormon and his pupils was increasing. A certain number of the pupils, among whom were Anquetin, and above all a slender young man of seventeen

* There are fifteen of Lautrec's paintings attributed to the year 1885.
† Thadée Natanson.

with a thatch of hair from Lille, whose name was Émile Bernard, and who had joined the studio only during the last year, openly criticised Père la Rotule's 'little method of academic construction'. Bernard exhorted everyone who would listen to him to rebellion. 'What we're being taught is based on nothing,' he said categorically. Cormon? He was a bad master and an appalling Philistine. 'He sits down beside each pupil,' said Bernard, 'retouching an arm here, a head or a chest there, with no more reason or logic than that he *sees it like that* and that you must see it like that too. He has only one piece of advice to give the more advanced: darken, blend and soften with the brush, that's to say *cheat* . . . After a year, you know less than you did before you came to him.'

> *Mais pour trouver c'qu'on a d'besoin*
> *Il existe encore un bon coin . . .*

From the moment of Bernard's arrival, Lautrec, Anquetin and Tampier had made friends with him. They had taken him to the Louvre to see the paintings of Velasquez, the drawings of Michelangelo and Luca Signorelli; they had taken him to Durand-Ruel, in the Rue Laffitte, to see the paintings of the Impressionists. With his characteristic impetuosity, Bernard had at once joined the rebel camp. With his three friends he had been able to examine the works of a certain Cézanne which a poor colour merchant, the Père Tanguy, kept in his little shop in the Rue Clauzel, in lower Montmartre. From then on he proclaimed that Cézanne was the great master of the period.

> *C'est au bout d'Paris, pas ben loin;*
> *Au bois de Boulogne! . . .*

If Bernard had received the first impulse from his friends and principally from the argumentative Tampier, he very soon asserted himself among them. He had read much, had great facility and a quick and lively intelligence. He was perfectly at home with theories, and would develop them, link them, and ceaselessly re-concoct them. Convinced that his opinions were soundly based, he was always prepared to argue. He looked on art as a sacred vocation. Genius and fame were his favourite words. To become an artist, which incidentally he was doing against his parents' wishes, seemed to him like a call to the priesthood. Though he had to come on foot from Asnières where he lived, he was nevertheless always first in the studio in the mornings. Religious by nature, and with a leaning towards mysticism, he hated the climate of Cormon's studio, its lewdness and frivolity. 'The whole spirit of the place,' he said, 'is an insult.' And when Anquetin persuaded him to go to the Mirliton one night, he came back 'appalled', nauseated, he said, by the 'unhealthy folly' of the place.

Lautrec listened rather absent-mindedly to Bernard's arguments. It was his friend's face that interested him. He asked him to sit for him. In twenty sittings, he made an excellent portrait of him, capturing with great subtlety his sitter's serious, censorious attitude towards life, and the resolute gaze of his small, rather narrow-lidded eyes.

At the beginning of 1886, the situation at Cormon's grew worse. Bernard had no hesitation in frankly adopting the clear colours of the Impressionists. Cormon was furious at such effrontery, sent for the young painter's father and told him he could no longer keep so undisciplined a pupil in his studio, for he was as insolent as he was gifted. The father returned to Asnières in dismay. He threw his son's brushes into the fire, while the latter shut himself up in his room and refused to come out.

Though less overt, Lautrec's behaviour was just as rebellious. But Lautrec avoided conflicts. Though in Père la Rotule's eyes he was 'taboo,'* he would not have risked showing him some of his canvases, particularly the two on which he was working at the moment: *Le Refrain de la chaise Louis XIII chez Bruant* and *Le Quadrille de la chaise Louis XIII à l'Élysée-Montmartre*.

Rodolphe Salis had forgotten this Louis XIII chair when he moved house. He kept on worrying Bruant to give it back to him, but the singer would not allow the chair to leave his establishment for anything in the world. However, since it did not belong to him and he was afraid of its being damaged, he hung it up near the door of the cabaret and he composed a song about it which he made his customers sing in chorus from time to time.

* Gauzi.

Ah! Mesdames, qu'on est à l'aise
Lorsqu'on est assis sur la chaise Louis XIII.
Elle est à Salis, et cependant,
Pour s'asseoir dessus, faut aller chez Bruant.

In both these pictures, Lautrec introduced some of the familiar figures of the Mirliton and the Élysée: Bruant, his waiter Maxime, the bandleader Dufour, Père la Pudeur, Anquetin and another pupil at the studio, François Gauzi from Toulouse, who often accompanied Lautrec on his evening excursions. In the picture *Quadrille*, La Goulue and Grille d'Égout are dancing together, both doing a high kick.

Between work on these two canvases, Lautrec amused himself by exhibiting at the Salon des Arts Incohérents. He exhibited 'soda-water colours', some 'sculptures in crumb of bread' and an 'oil painting on emery paper': *Les Batignolles, trois ans et demi avant Jésus-Christ*, under the name of Tolau-Segroeg, who was described as 'a Hungarian of Montmartre, who has visited Cairo and lives with a friend, has talent and proves it.'

During the spring, while Lautrec was busy with these jokes, and Bernard, having put an end to his voluntary seclusion, was setting off on foot to Brittany, a strange new pupil arrived at Cormon's.

He was a good deal older than most of the others and was a native of Holland. The young men in the studio were surprised by this man with the ravaged face. They knew nothing of him except his Christian name—Vincent. Vincent covered his canvas with enormous speed, making the easel shake under the vigour of his brush. The impetuosity with which he painted and his concentrated vehemence, which was so much at variance with the light-hearted atmosphere in which they lived, made them uneasy. No one dared to play the customary practical jokes on the newcomer. But how would the master react to his work which, like its author, had a quality of violence?

Cormon absolutely refused to allow any change whatever in his pupils' reproduction of the model, but Vincent altered everything. He turned the stool on which the nude woman was sitting into a divan; he put a blue cloth over the divan; and transformed the dirty curtain that served for background into sumptuous hangings. The malicious were delighted. They could already hear Père la Rotule's outraged remarks, for his disputes with Bernard had not made him any the more inclined to make concessions. Cormon felt his prestige with his pupils was diminishing, and it vexed him.

When Cormon arrived, he was greeted by a deep silence. It became deeper still as he went from easel to easel, drawing gradually nearer the Dutchman. There was no sound but the scrape of charcoal. Cormon reached Vincent's easel, glanced at the canvas and stopped. Standing perfectly still, he gazed at it for several minutes without a word. Then he made a few rapid remarks about the drawing of this surprising composition and went on to the next pupil.

Little by little, Lautrec got to know the Dutchman. He was attracted to him. They very soon made friends. Though there were basic differences, they had much in common.

Vincent was the brother of Théo Van Gogh, the manager of the Boussod et Valadon Gallery in the Boulevard Montmartre. He was at this time thirty-three and had suffered every kind of unhappiness and disaster. He had been drawing for only six years, and painting for only four. He had wandered over the plains of the north with an empty stomach and a passionate heart. Like Lautrec, he had been driven into his destiny as a painter. He would have liked to lead what he referred to sadly as a 'real life'. But it was impossible. Like Lautrec, he was an outcast. He was not the man to laugh at the cripple's legs. He knew too much about the harshness of fate. Everything he had ever attempted had failed. But his heart was full of an immense love that no one wanted.

Lautrec could no more associate himself with the love and compassion which filled Van Gogh at the sight of suffering, than he could adhere to Bruant's humanitarianism. Lautrec was not moved to pity by anyone, even himself. He looked on others as implacably as he looked on himself. He neither condemned nor approved: he observed. He did not judge: he analysed. He was as alien to sentiment as he was naturally indifferent to morals. He wanted simply to surprise life in all its nakedness; and nothing more. Van Gogh was all charity; Lautrec all lucidity. Their temperaments seemed to be at opposite poles. Nevertheless, the ardour which consumed them was the same.

In the meantime, new incidents had occurred at Cormon's. A pupil had called Père la Rotule an 'old academician'. Anquetin, whose current mistress liked the Impressionists (she owned some Caillebottes), forgot Michelangelo and Rubens and became an 'intransigent.' For his part, Van Gogh, in his harsh French, raged against Cormon. Lautrec himself rebelled: 'I'm here to learn my trade,' he said, 'not to let myself be absorbed.'

Cormon closed the studio in a fury.

*   *   *

When Lautrec finished the two canvases on which he had been working, Bruant hung them on the walls of his cabaret.*

Lautrec was sailing before the wind. In imitation of Salis, who published a little newspaper, Bruant had been producing *Le Mirliton* since the previous October. Though he preferred Steinlen's art to Lautrec's, he promised the latter to reproduce his *Quadrille de la chaise Louis XIII,*† and asked him also for some cover designs. Furthermore, the publicity agent for the Pastilles Géraudel, Jules Roques, had founded a magazine two years earlier which was entirely devoted to the pleasures of Montmartre, *Le Courrier français*. Much to Lautrec's delight, for he wanted to get his talent known, Roques also invited him to supply drawings. Lautrec sent him six.‡

This summer he went to his family in the south. Countess Adèle—'my poor saintly mother', as the painter called her—was much alarmed by the life he was leading. Her principles, religious faith and respect for convention were all traduced by her son's life in Montmartre. She was greatly distressed.

But her reproaches died on her lips at the sight of her son. When she saw him waddling along in his little boy's suit, leaning on his 'button-hook', when she heard him roar with laughter, it was not the frequenter of the Élysée-Montmartre and of No. 2, Rue de Steinkerque she saw, but the child whose distress she understood better than anyone,

---

* Lautrec painted five or six other canvases in 1886, *Danseuses, La Femme au noeud rose, Chez la Blanchisseuse*, etc.

† It appeared in December on a double page.

‡ In fact, only one was published: a scene in a bar, *Gin-cocktail* (No. 39 of *Le Courrier français*, September 26, 1886).

the 'moral suicide', as Lautrec once called himself. She knew he could use and abuse her love, and that she would accord it to the end.

Lautrec was happy. 'Life is good!' he exclaimed. The sun was shining on the vines. His father, as a protection against the heat, was happily indulging in a régime which he had acquired, so he said, from Armenia: it consisted in bathing his feet in a basin of milk while applying slices of lemon to his head. Lautrec drew scenes of the family waging battle against phylloxera. They were humorous sketches, their legends full of puns and rebuses, in which the name of his cousin, Gabriel Tapié de Céleyran, a tall young man of seventeen, who had become fond of him and whom Lautrec tyrannised, appeared in twenty different and ludicrous forms: 'Tapiedeussellerang,' '7 l'air rend,' 'M. Tap. hier 2 c'est l'airan', 'M. Tapise et deux selles erang' . . . Childish jokes that were very much in keeping with the student's jests he had exhibited at the Salon des Arts Incohérents.

Countess Adèle asked an archbishop to luncheon so that he might point out with the utmost kindness the duty her son owed, in spite of everything, to the name he bore. Sitting on the prelate's right, Lautrec waited humbly for the sermon, and 'questioned him in the most Christian spirit, while seeing to it that he was served with the choicest dishes, about the state of the souls in his diocese'.* A prince of the Church was clearly not going to refer to the prostitutes of Pigalle in Bruant's direct terms. The sermon, which began with the pudding, consisted of many obscure allusions; the argument was developed at length; it meandered on and threatened never to come to an end.

But the summer ended in triumph: his family at last agreed to allow him sufficient money to lease a studio. There happened to be one vacant on the fourth floor of the house in which Valadon lived in the Rue Tourlaque. Lautrec took it at once. At the same time, he made arrangements with his friend Bourges, a medical student, who was now walking the wards of a hospital, to share a flat at 19, Rue Fontaine, close to the Greniers' house.

* J. E. S. Jeanès.

Indomitable

PART TWO
[1886—1893]

CHAPTER ONE

Rosa la Rouge

All'a l'poil roux, eun têt' de chien.
Quand a passe, on dit: V'là la Rouge,
A Montrouge.

ARISTIDE BRUANT

HAVING weeded out some of his pupils, Cormon re-opened his studio.
Lautrec was not among the banished. Nevertheless, he took little
advantage of this favour: from now on, his life as a painter developed
elsewhere.

During this winter of 1886 to 1887, the friendly group he had
formed with Anquetin, Bernard and Van Gogh was, artistically
speaking, in full development.

On his return from Vétheuil, where his meeting with Monet had
proved very disappointing, Anquetin had definitely decided to take
up the *divisionnisme* of Seurat, who had again exhibited his *Grande
Jatte* in August and September at the second Salon des Indépendants.
On his return from Britanny, Bernard had also declared himself for
divisionnisme and had painted views of Asnières in Seurat's technique.
But then came an abrupt change.

Having shown his canvases in a small exhibition at Asnières, Bernard
had received a visit from Signac, the indefatigable apostle of *divisionnisme*. Signac had taken him to his studio near the Place de Clichy.
What happened during the interview? No one knew. The fact
remained that Bernard immediately adopted a precisely opposite
theory.

What we must seek, he said, is a 'personal and highly coloured
simplism,' a technique of flat, synthetic, circumscribed tints.
The Japanese paintings on silk, many of which Van Gogh had
bought on the quays of Anvers immediately before coming
to France, indicated the path to follow. Anquetin approved; he
was by now jeering at *divisionnisme*. 'When you've got oil paints

115

and glosses,' he declared, 'it's idiotic to paint with maggots and confetti.'

Experimenting with their new conception of painting, Bernard painted his *Chiffonnières au Pont de Clichy* and Anquetin his *Bâteau sous des branches*. Upon which Anquetin set about synthesising even more audaciously. Having discovered that by looking at a landscape through differently coloured glass, you obtained specifically varied impressions, green producing an effect of dawn, yellow of sunlight, red of dusk, and blue of night, he painted his *Faucheur* in yellow tones, and his *Avenue de Clichy, le soir* in blue.

What an artist! Everyone marvelled at his mastery. Bernard judged him to be 'very good.' 'He's a painter!' said Lautrec, who considered that no one since Manet had been endowed with 'such high qualities.' 'I'd like to be able to paint like him,' he admitted. Van Gogh, for his part, was wildly enthusiastic, particularly over the *Faucheur*. 'Excellent! Excellent!' he kept repeating excitedly.*

Van Gogh, who was irritated by the official opposition to the innovators, conceived the project of a huge exhibition which would include Anquetin, Bernard, Lautrec, himself and two or three other painters, his 'pal' Gauguin and a fellow-countryman, the Dutchman Koning. Only in this way could their group assert its existence before the public. But how could he find a gallery? Since Vincent ate from time to time in a popular restaurant in the Avenue de Clichy, near the Fourche, it occurred to him that the hall of the restaurant, which was huge and perfectly lit, would lend itself remarkably well to their project, and all the more so, the humanitarian Vincent thought, since it would be no bad thing to try to touch the generous heart of the man in

---

* Later, at Arles, Van Gogh was inspired by Anquetin's canvas to paint a *Faucheur* in his own manner. And Anquetin would undoubtedly have been dumbfounded if anyone had predicted that the future would show complete indifference to his work. In 1897, Signac wrote the following appreciation of him: 'A man who knows his profession well, he is able, even too able, and seemingly powerful if one does not know the originals of which he makes a pastiche. His work is a mixture of Daumier, Manet, Michelangelo, Renoir, and Degas, all very well done. The tenth part of his talent, in the hands of an original creator, would have sufficed to produce marvels.' (Extract from *Journal de Signac*, published in the *Gazette des Beaux-Arts*, April 1952).

the street directly. Van Gogh approached the management and obtained permission to hang as many paintings on the walls as he liked.

The 'Petit Boulevard group' (as Vincent called it to distinguish it from the Impressionist group, which he called the 'Grand Boulevard group,' that is to say of the Boulevard Montmartre) therefore exhibited its work to the customers of the restaurant in the spring.

The customers, as they drank their soup and ate their fried potatoes, were somewhat startled and inclined to make ironical remarks about this manifestation of avant-garde painting. A few artists and amateurs, however, went to look at the pictures. Bernard and Anquetin each had the luck to sell a canvas. But the exhibition came to an abrupt end. Irritated by the ungracious remarks of the customers, Van Gogh was soon quarrelling with the management. In a fury, the Dutchman hurried off to find a handcart to remove the pictures. The 'Petit Boulevard' had had its day.

Lautrec did not attach very much importance to all this commotion. *Divisionnisme* and *synthétisme* both left him cold. He felt an instinctive dislike for all schools. He was going his own way.

In this, he was much closer to Van Gogh than to Anquetin or Bernard. Van Gogh never took radical dislikes and was always able to discover, even in work that was profoundly foreign to him, something to admire or to learn. Enthusiasm was the climate in which he lived.* He assimilated with lightning speed the most diverse and contradictory influences. Lautrec was also ready to learn from outside. He was as widely receptive; but, unlike Van Gogh, whose every action was informed by a warmth of overflowing sympathy, Lautrec's receptivity was due to a fundamental simplicity and a complete absence of pride. Sectarianism suited him no more than it did Van Gogh.

Lautrec followed Vincent's development with profound attention. His passionate tenacity and the ardour of his convictions moved and impressed Lautrec, who understood impetuous characters better than most people. Van Gogh might appear eccentric and fanatical to the

* A quarter of a century later, Émile Bernard honestly admitted: 'Nothing could have been more different from my blind absolutism than Vincent's eclecticism. Today, I know he was right . . .' (Preface to the *Lettres de Vincent Van Gogh*, Paris, Ambroise Vollard, 1911.)

art students of the Butte; but the ferment in which he lived and which
surprised and baffled others seemed quite normal to Lautrec. After
all, Van Gogh was no more extravagant in his behaviour than Count
Alphonse. In fact much less so: Count Alphonse's life, since he was
quite incapable of setting himself a goal worthy of his ambitions, was
null and void; while Van Gogh's had the hall-mark of the absolute.
In the Dutchman's company Lautrec could not help realising that
painting had offered him a justification for existence.

Lautrec was now twenty-two. His art was beginning to bear fruit.
He studied more closely the Japanese prints on the walls of Van Gogh's
room at 54 Rue Lepic. In the same house lived Portier, a small picture
dealer and connoisseur of the art of Hokusai, Hiroshighe, Outamaro,
Toyokouni and Haru-Nobu, and Lautrec often bought prints from
him. Or, when he could persuade the dealer, bartered his own paintings
for them.

He was more than ever under the influence of Bruant. And this
influence, together with that of Van Gogh, who was always talking to
him of the time when he used to spread the word of God among the
miners of Borinage, and of the artistic community he wanted to
create, caused Lautrec to turn to subjects of more or less social
significance.

In three consecutive numbers, January, February and March 1886,
the *Mirliton* published on its cover drawings of his in which he represented street scenes: workmen, a little errand-girl being accosted
by an old rip in a top hat and white beard: 'How old are you, my dear?'
'Fifteen, monsieur . . .' 'Hum! Already rather old . . .'

The same spirit was often present in the pictures Lautrec was then
painting of the Moulin-de-la-Galette and of the Élysée-Montmartre.
In these works, which were more difficult to compose than portraits,
the painter's ambition was still clearly greater than his technique. He
knew he must work like Van Gogh, with the same humility and the
same energy. 'I have the right only to a little indulgence and encouragement,' he wrote to his Uncle Charles on May 15.

He visited all the exhibitions. Though he found the highly polished
floors tiring, he went everywhere, often trying to persuade a friend
to accompany him in wheel-chairs through the rooms. 'They'll push

us, it'll be so amusing!' he would insist, laughing. 'You don't want to?' No matter, it was simply a good opportunity for a laugh lost.

And so Lautrec braved the crowds. They watched him as he clung to the guard-rails that were too high for him, moving from one picture to the next, stopping, moving on again, sometimes halting for a long time in front of a canvas. Was it as good as all that? His face contorted with pain, Lautrec was merely resting before going farther. But nothing daunted him. He went to the Salon, where Cormon this year was showing his *Vainqueurs de Salamine* ('les Vainqueurs de Salaminette,' said Lautrec), he visited the Millet Exhibition and the International Exhibition in the Georges Petit Gallery, where was hanging Renoir's *Baigneuses* for which Valadon had sat ...

'A woman's body, a splendid woman's body, you see,' lisped Lautrec, 'is not for making love ... It's too beautiful, eh? For making love anything goes ... anything ... anything at all, eh?'

'Quite by chance,' he had seen some of Valadon's drawings. The cunning girl would, of course, never have dared to show them to him! Lautrec declared that no one could fail to attribute them, in their virile energy, to a master and delightedly hung some on the walls of his studio. Bartholomé, the sculptor, saw them and insisted that Valadon submit her drawings to Degas. 'You're one of us,' Degas told her; a rare compliment from such a misogynist.

The 'terrible Maria,' as Degas called her, had now formed a close connection with Lautrec. It was difficult to say if she had any precise intentions towards him. She was all guile and evasion. She would go off and then come back, and sit to him only when it suited her. Nevertheless, each week, when Lautrec gave a little party to painters in his studio, she was always there.

Lautrec's studio—a huge room connected by a staircase to a little room on the floor below—was remarkable for its disorder. It was like a junk shop. Sofa, stools, chairs and a coffee table were mingled with easels, a model's throne, a high step-ladder, half-finished canvases, stretchers, frames and a quantity of indescribable litter among which could be distinguished such an unlikely mixture as pink dancing shoes, reproductions of Uccello and Carpaccio, old newspapers, pieces of Persian pottery, books with broken backs, a clown's hat, a boot with a high heel, a pair of dumb-bells, kakemonos, netsukes, a cup and ball, a Japanese wig and empty bottles. On the wall opposite the big window hung the parody of the *Bois Sacré*.

Lautrec was constantly pulling out of the dusty lumber some object —a Samurai's lacquered helmet or an ordinary hamper in which his mother had sent him provisions—for the admiration of his guests. 'Eh, what? Beautiful, isn't it? Magnificent!' Every object precisely adapted to its function was to him a work of art. The logic and efficiency that determined its shape delighted him. Showing them a knife, he would delicately run his finger down the blade and say delightedly: 'The technique of assassination.' He would emphasise the word 'technique,' which constantly appeared in his conversation.

'Let's drink!' With a felt hat pulled down over his eyes, which sparkled behind his spectacles, Lautrec busied himself in shirt sleeves behind a low bar covered with zinc and laden with a variety of bottles and all the utensils required by an expert barman. He set to work paring lemon peel, crushing ice and playing with ten bottles at once as he made cocktails for his guests.

At Lautrec's, if you were to retain his esteem, you had to drink whether you liked it or not. Nor were the drinks of a simple kind. One of the first Frenchmen to practise the art of the cocktail, he passionately enjoyed trying out new and fancy combinations, which were sometimes delicious and sometimes appalling. Delighted when · one of his guests approved an original composition, he exulted no less when he dismayed another with some strange and terrible concoction. He would give a diabolical laugh and drink the appalling stuff as if it were water. No one could stand up to him; no one could equal his capacity to drink the most murderous mixtures.

While Lautrec was making both himself and his visitors drunk, Van Gogh would be sitting in a corner of the studio in front of one of his own pictures, which he had brought with him. Placing the canvas as best he could in a good light, he waited for someone to catch sight of it and deign to speak to him about it. He would hopefully watch people's eyes. But no one ever paid the slightest attention to his work. And, at last, weary of waiting, he would pick up his canvas and go away.

Valadon had noticed this performance, which was repeated every week. Though silent in the past, she was now beginning to express her opinions. 'Painters are brutes!' she said, as she saw Vincent leave.

What was she looking for from Lautrec? Life was war to the knife. You needed every weapon you could lay your hands on. From her experience as a model, she knew that 'Forain threw the money he owed the poor girls on the floor, while a certain member of the Institut paid them in bad coin . . .'* 'The technique of the jungle,' Lautrec might have said.

Her lover's drunken parties left Valadon completely unmoved. So did his more fantastic jokes. From time to time, Lautrec would take her to a meal in the flat he shared with Bourges in the Rue Fontaine. A servant called Léontine, who was an excellent cook, looked after the flat; but she was very respectable and Lautrec delighted in teasing her.

One night, when Valadon was dining with him, Lautrec suddenly said: 'Take off your clothes, and we'll see how Léontine reacts.' Valadon did so and then sat down again, assuming an expression of the utmost dignity; she had retained only her shoes and stockings. Léontine gave a start when she came into the room; but she said nothing and continued imperturbably to serve dinner.

Nevertheless, Léontine complained to Bourges the next day that 'Monsieur Henri had insulted her.' The medical student, who was a short, fat, peaceful character, a hard-working, serious man, who always wore a bowler hat, lectured Lautrec. But what could be done with anyone so undisciplined? 'After all, Léontine must know very well what a woman's body looks like. I was dressed. I'd taken nothing off but my hat,' Lautrec protested. And, when it came to the point, Léontine had to admit that 'Monsieur Henri' was very generous with his tips. And, what was more, he never bothered to look into the housekeeping accounts!

Bourges, who was saddened and disquieted by his friend's behaviour which, in his opinion, was linked to his deformity, was sparing neither with admonition nor advice. He considered Lautrec's way of life with its continual drinking and late nights utterly pernicious. He hoped

* Robert Beachboard: *La Trinité maudite.*

to persuade him to a healthier régime and entreated him to moderation. Lautrec, of course, paid no attention whatever to 'Bi's' advice. He would put an end to his homilies with a joke and, seizing his little stick ('Monsieur! Monsieur, you've forgotten your stick!' someone shouted one night, wickedly handing him a pencil), he would go off to the Élysée-Montmartre or the Mirliton, singing Bruant's latest song.

*   *   *

Having spent part of the summer at Malromé, Lautrec returned to the Butte.

While in the Bordelais he had painted several portraits: his mother, his cousin Pascal, who was now working in an insurance business, and Mme Pascal. They were simple exercises in a manner that was very close to that of the Impressionists.

On his return to Montmartre, he made a portrait in pastel of Van Gogh in a spontaneous, rather wilful pose. The peculiar thing about this work is that it is executed in Vincent's own technique of nervous hatching.

This technique suited Lautrec so well that he started another canvas, in which were mingled the aesthetic influence of Van Gogh and the moral influence of Bruant. *Gueule de Bois ou la Buveuse* was a naturalistic scene for which Valadon sat once again. Sitting exhausted at a table, the girl dreams, her eyes vaguely staring and her mouth a bitter line, a bottle and a glass in front of her. Vincent took a great interest in the painting of this picture, which so clearly bears his imprint.

With the approach of winter, Van Gogh became depressed. A second attempt at a popular, and this time permanent, exhibition in the Tambourin, a restaurant-cabaret in the Boulevard de Clichy, with Lautrec, Bernard and Anquetin as his fellow exhibitors, had come to an equally abrupt end. Vincent had exhausted the lessons of Paris and its school of painting. He was impatient to be off. He wanted more light and more sun. His mind turned to sunnier lands, to what he called his Japan, to the South, to Africa. Ah, when would that colony of artists be founded, where the 'poor cab-horses' of painting could find a warm refuge and be protected from the harshness of life? Lautrec was rich. Why shouldn't Lautrec help to create a communal studio? When Van Gogh had a plan in mind, it was impossible to make him forget it. Lautrec, who was temperamentally averse from any form of philanthropic system, became annoyed by Vincent's insistence. He found it very difficult to evade so overwhelming a friend. Particularly since he would not have hurt the Dutchman for anything in the world. But when he realised that Van Gogh wanted to leave Paris, he did his best to hasten his departure.

Van Gogh was hesitating between Africa and Provence, and then between Marseilles and Aix. He discussed it endlessly; there appeared to be drawbacks everywhere. Why not Arles, Lautrec suggested? It was a nice little town, in an aesthetically virgin country, where Vincent could 'measure his brush against the sun.' Besides, he could probably live there very cheaply. Van Gogh got excited about it. Arles would be his Japan. And who could tell, perhaps later on, when he had cleared the ground, friends might come and join him and establish there a 'Studio of the Midi?' Suddenly, he made up his mind. 'I'm leaving tomorrow,' he said one evening in February.

Before leaving Paris, Van Gogh persuaded his brother, Théo, to acquire some of Lautrec's canvases for the Boussod et Valadon Gallery. During the course of the winter, Lautrec had also received a visit from Théodore Van Rysselberghe, who had been sent to him by Octave Maus, the founder of the Group 'XX' of Brussels. 'The little dwarf's not at all bad,' said Van Rysselberghe. 'He's got talent! He's just right for the XX!' Lautrec was invited to send pictures to their exhibition of 1888. He was delighted. The exhibition in Brussels, to which he sent eleven pictures and one drawing, took place at the very moment Van Gogh reached Provence.

The 'Vingtistes' were one of the more vital groups of the period. They had no fear of scandal, indeed they felt more inclined to arouse and provoke it. Every year, their exhibition was greeted with explosions of anger from the Belgian press. 'What is Maus going to show us this time: green rabbits, pink blackbirds?' The paintings in this exhibition of February 1888 ran true to form and included Signacs, Ensors, Whistlers and Forains. Lautrec, however, disarmed most of the critics. Though he was reproached for 'sometimes having a very hard line' and for 'orgies of dirty, clashing colours,' his gift for analysis was praised as well as the way he 'expressed the intimacies of heart and mind,' his 'rather coarse vitality' and his 'well-observed figures.'

Encouraged by these promising beginnings, Lautrec was not idle. On March 10, the weekly magazine of the Boussod et Valadon Gallery, *Paris illustré*, published a drawing of his, the *Bal masqué*, in which he showed La Goulue in a tutu and some of his friends, such as kind Adolphe Albert who, like Bourges, vainly exhorted him to a more moderate way of life. Lautrec was also preparing for *Paris illustré* a series of four drawings to accompany an article on *L'Été à Paris.** Inspired by a song of Bruant—who was as sensitive to the misery of animals as of humans—Lautrec chose for his subject one of the extra trace-horses that were put to the omnibuses on steep streets. On the other hand, his satirical spirit led him to draw a scene of mocking realism, *Un jour de première communion*, in which he showed a husband and wife dressed in their best and walking with their crowd of brats.

These drawings were in no sense secondary matters to Lautrec, and he worked at them with the same scrupulous care that he devoted to his paintings, making repeated studies until he was absolutely satisfied. This was a basic part of his nature. He was incapable of working otherwise than seriously and conscientiously. And he judged men as he judged things: he appreciated and respected only those who fulfilled their role faithfully, honestly and unpretentiously. 'Say what you've got to say,' he often remarked. He could no more bear slackness than he could fatuity or superfluous ornament.

For the husband in *Un jour de première communion*, Lautrec asked François Gauzi to sit for him. Their friendship had become closer since Gauzi had come to the Rue Tourlaque and taken the studio opposite Lautrec's. Gauzi's cheerful and impulsive character delighted Lautrec, who twice painted his portrait. They met practically every day. They went together to the dance-halls, to the Mirliton, and to the Fernando Circus in the Boulevard de Rochechouart, beloved by Degas, Seurat and Renoir.

Constantly in search of new and unusual aspects of humanity, Lautrec was always pestering Bourges, who was now a house-surgeon at the Bicêtre Asylum, to let him visit that establishment. Bourges

* They appeared in the number published on July 7, 1888.

eventually agreed to take Lautrec, Gauzi and Grenier to visit a patient, a man of letters suffering from persecution mania.

Bourges met them and led them across a courtyard where a nurse was in charge of a group of abnormal children. Seeing Lautrec the children rushed towards him with wild gestures, and 'hoarse, inarticulate cries, a sort of incomprehensible barking.'* These deformed, crippled and idiot children, thinking a new companion had arrived, shouted their delight. At that moment, Lautrec felt no desire to laugh. He hobbled off as quickly as he could, protected by his friends, who were much embarrassed by the unfortunate incident. Bourges and his guests succeeded in escaping the crowd of half-witted children only when they reached the garden where the writer was awaiting them.

Lautrec did not pay much attention to the sufferer from persecution mania. How could he help thinking of the children who had taken him for one of themselves and through whom he would have to pass a second time on the way out? After this, Lautrec was no doubt not so keen to visit lunatic asylums.

* * *

Valadon continued to play her disconcerting game. She would absent herself, then reappear with the most unlikely excuses, which annoyed Lautrec. 'She suffers from no lack of imagination, and lies cost her nothing,' he said bitterly.

One afternoon, when Gauzi was painting, there was a violent ring at his studio bell. Before he had time to put his palette down, the bell rang again, even more imperatively. Gauzi hurried to the door. Outside was the anxious, breathless figure of Lautrec. 'Come at once. Maria is going to kill herself.' 'What nonsense is this?' 'No, it's very serious; come quickly, follow me.' And Lautrec started hopping hurriedly down the stairs.

They reached the first floor and found the door of Valadon's flat ajar. The two young men pushed it open but were stopped in their tracks. They could hear sounds of quarrelling coming from the near-by kitchen. Valadon and her mother were having an argument. 'You've

* Gauzi.

made a fine job of it! You've frightened him off and he won't come back. A lot of good you've done yourself!' the model's mother screamed at her. Lautrec listened, pale as death.

They heard Valadon say sourly: 'He wouldn't play. I did all I could.' 'You ought to have had a little more patience!' replied her mother.

Followed by Gauzi, Lautrec went into the kitchen. The two women were so startled by his appearance that they fell silent.

'This is a pretty story!' exclaimed Gauzi. 'What's all the fuss about?' He turned to Lautrec: 'My poor friend, you see they've been making a fool of you!'

Lautrec and the two women looked at each other. None of them said a word. Suddenly the painter turned on his heel and went out. He never saw the 'terrible Maria' again.

*   *   *

'Here, you, fatty, place your fat carcass next to Madame. And you, you long sausage, put your skeleton between these fools who're laughing like a couple of idiots at God knows what!'

Bruant was on the way to making a fortune. Year in, year out, his business was bringing in fifty thousand gold francs.* At the special request of the fashionable world, he had made Fridays smart days, when 'galopin' cost five francs instead of eight sous. And on these days, Bruant surpassed himself in insults. He ordered himself drinks at every table, swallowing two or three hundred francs worth of beer at his customers' expense during the course of the evening. 'God, how disgusting it is!' he thundered. Fortunately, the 'galopins' were not very large.

Bruant had not changed. As a place of rest from his trade, he had leased a mud-walled cottage at the top of the Butte, at the corner of the Rue Cortot and the Rue des Saules; it stood in the middle of a large, open space, where there were trees, grass, shrubs and a few square yards of vines. There, in the silence, far from the customers he assailed with his insults, he was happy. Wearing clogs and an old cap, he idled in the sun in company with his chickens and his dogs.

* About £9,000 in terms of modern money.

All the dogs in Montmartre knew that there was food for them at Bruant's house.

At two o'clock in the morning, when he had counted his takings and locked up the money, Bruant could climb the deserted alleys of the Butte to his 'domain' without fear of being attacked. The roughs would not meddle with him. They knew his songs and respected him; besides, they would not have dared. Their admiring women called him 'the general of the boys.' They were nearly all secretly in love with him. One of them even had his name tattooed on her buttock.

> *Quand j'vois des filles de dix-sept ans,*
> *Ça m'fait penser qu'y a ben longtemps,*
> *Moi aussi, j'l'ai été, pucelle,*
> *A Grenelle.*

On nights of police raids, when the police were rounding up the prostitutes on the boulevard, the women hurried to his cabaret. Bruant found room for them among his customers, mingling them without further ado with the aristocratic ladies. Interrupting his usual invective, he would talk to them almost tenderly.

Bruant gave the titles of some of his songs, *A Grenelle, A Batignolles* and *A la Bastille*, to pictures by Lautrec, which came one after another to complete the Mirliton collection. They were portraits of prostitutes and, in their own way, good illustrations of the singer's works.

And all this time Lautrec never stopped painting, or drinking; like a defiant young cock, he paraded his dissoluteness and responded with cynical unconcern to Bourges, Albert and everyone who was distressed by his conduct.

He would laugh: 'One must learn how to bear oneself.'

He painted Bruant's prostitutes, the so-called *filles de joie*, but there was a new sadness about the figures, and sometimes he would say, though one could not tell to whom he was referring: 'Those who say they don't care a damn do care a damn, because those who don't care a damn, don't say they don't care a damn.'

For some time, Lautrec's attention had been attracted to a prostitute who haunted the promenade of the Élysée-Montmartre. Her red hair fell in long straight locks about her narrow, surly face.

C'est Rosa, j'sais pas d'òu qu'a vient,
All'a l'poil roux, eun têt' de chien . . .

Lautrec soon made this girl one of his favourite models. He painted several studies of her. In his picture *A Montrouge*, which Bruant hung in the Mirliton, he placed her in front of the window in a dark room, half turned towards the light, one lock of hair hanging over her eye. Her profile and her shock of hair were silhouetted against the light. It is a haunting and dramatic work.

Someone charitably warned Lautrec against being too intimate with Rosa la Rouge: 'Be careful, my dear chap, she might give you an unwelcome present you'd never be able to get rid of!'

But Lautrec laughed at the warning, for Rosa la Rouge had already infected him.

          *   *   *

Lautrec's production increased.* In the autumn, he painted a big picture, one metre by two, of the Fernando Circus, in which a circus-rider is performing under the eye of M. Loyal, who has a whip in his hand. It is a masterly picture—the painter was now twenty-four—in the audacity and decision of its construction. Lautrec seemed to have discovered his formula, and brought 'his trade of a builder's labourer' towards perfection.

Breaking away from naturalistic representation and the conventional laws of perspective, as well as from the researches of Impressionism, Lautrec profited by the lessons he had learned from the Japanese. He invented a new means of rendering movement by the rhythm of his line which, like his colour values, was reduced to essentials.

The Fernando circus-rider was a young woman, a member of a rich family who, having fallen in love with her riding-master, had divorced and gone in for *haute école* and mounted gymnastics. Lautrec asked her to sit for him in the Rue Tourlaque. He combined in these works the technique of Van Gogh and a process of Raffaelli. This process consisted in applying to the cardboard paint that was very

---

* There are still in existence thirty pictures attributed to this year, 1888. In 1887, Lautrec had painted fifteen.

[OPPOSITE] 1890. Lautrec aged twenty-six

Lautrec as a Muezzin, Taussat (1889)

'Carmen' Lautrec on the arm of René Grenier. In the background, Lily Grenier (c. 1892)

Lautrec dressed as a choirboy for the *Bal des Quat'z-Arts*, at the Moulin Rouge. With René and Lily Grenier (Spring 1894)

Lautrec as a Japanese (c. 1892)

More dressing up . . .

diluted in spirit and, on being absorbed, took on the matt appearance of pastel. Boldly applying hatching to this base, he drew as he painted, giving his line a vigour and an emphasis which could not be achieved in work that was more delicately modelled in accordance with traditional methods. Lautrec had found his technique.

Was his disease partly responsible for this rapid progress and for his intellectual ferment?

In obedience to Bourges, who looked after him, the painter submitted himself to energetic measures. There could be no doubt that the life he led was most unsuited to his condition. Bourges constantly warned him. 'More than anyone, the syphilitic requires a sufficient number of hours' sleep . . . he cannot overwork his intelligence and abuse his mental activity with impunity . . .'*

Taking advantage of a moment when Lautrec was temporarily depressed, Bourges succeeded in persuading him to go to the country to recuperate. He went to Villiers-sur-Morin with the Greniers, and spent three winter months there: three eventless months, during which he fished and painted, notably portraits of Grenier and Lily.

In the evenings, after dinner, both to give himself something to do and amuse his hosts, he drew interminably. From an apparently inexhaustible imagination, he pencilled endless scenes, nearly always ridiculous and frequently erotic.

Lautrec returned to Paris during the first weeks of 1889. 'I need a change,' he said as he left Villiers.

Restored by his stay in Brie, he plunged impatiently back into his old way of life. His thirst both for work and pleasure was intense. He finished some drawings for Roques' *Le Courrier français*,† but above all he painted. He painted Rosa la Rouge; he painted women in Père Forest's garden; he painted the hall of the Moulin-de-la-Galette, a big canvas full of life and extremely original in construction; and he also painted a work inspired by the theatre, the first of real importance he had made in this particular field, an ironic portrait of the actor

---

* Bourges, who became interested in the question, possibly because of Lautrec, published in 1897 a work entitled *L'Hygiène du Syphilitique*. The treatment at that time was far from being as effective as it is today. The specific cause of syphilis, Spirochaeta pallida, was discovered only in 1905.

† Four appeared in the spring (April 21, May 12 and 19, June 2).

[OPPOSITE] 'Mademoiselle' Lautrec

Henry Samary playing in Jules Sandeau's *Mademoiselle de la Seiglière* at the Comédie-Française. It was more the portrait of a costume than of a man, who was himself, indeed, nothing but the costume.

Lautrec exhibited this year at the Artistic and Literary Club in the Rue Volney, which in the past had been so dear to Princeteau; he also exhibited—for the second time—at the Salon des Arts Incohérents under the pseudonym, which he had already used, of Tolau-Segroeg—address 'Rue Yblas, under the third gas lamp on the left, pupil of Pubis de Cheval,* specialist in family portraits with a yellow pastel background'—he submitted the *Portraits d'une malheureuse famille atteinte de la petite grêlure.*

Lautrec also wanted to exhibit in company with Bernard and Anquetin at the exhibition of the Impressionniste et Synthétiste Group which Gauguin was organising at Volpini's, the manager of the Café des Arts at the Universal Exhibition; but Gauguin refused to invite him.

At the beginning of the year, Gauguin, who had gone to join Van Gogh at Arles two months previously, had suddenly returned to Paris. The Studio of the Midi had suffered an even more lamentable fate than the popular exhibitions poor Vincent had tried to organise: at Christmas, Vincent, while suffering from a nervous breakdown, had cut off a part of his ear, and had been confined in a lunatic asylum.

What did Lautrec think of his friend's fate? Did it make him consider his own circumstances? The disease from which he suffered had sometimes, after years of quiescence, the most ghastly effects. One day, when he was looking at a reproduction of André Gill's painting, *Le Fou*, which showed a man, his mad eyes dilated with horror, struggling in hopeless terror in a strait-jacket—it was the last work Gill painted before his mind entirely gave way (he had died in the Charenton Asylum four years earlier, in 1885)—Lautrec said calmly to Gauzi: 'That's what's in store for us!'

But, in the meantime, life continued to be gay. Lautrec went everywhere. At the Universal Exhibition, which was being held on the Champ-de-Mars and at whose entrance rose the Eiffel Tower, he drew Arab women, whirling Dervishes, Javanese stomach-dancers

* A reference to Puvis de Chavannes.

and Annamites weaving. Though it was intended to commemorate the centenary of the French Revolution, the Exhibition extolled the future more than it recalled the past. People thought it marked the dawn of a golden age. Confident in the genius of industry, everyone believed in a future of unlimited wealth and happiness. Lautrec visited it all. He went to the corridas which were held in a newly built bull-ring in the Rue Pergolèse.* He went to the uproarious fancy-dress ball which the *Courrier français* gave each year to its supporters. He went to the theatre with the Greniers. Their evenings sometimes ended up in the police station. Whether Lautrec and his friends were really displeased with the play, one does not know. But they were inclined to take their shoes off and throw them on to the stage. Lautrec sang:

> *C'est des maladi's qui s'voient pas*
> *Quand ça s'declare,*
> *N'empêch qu'aujourd'hui, j'suis dans l'tas . . .*

Amid all these dissipations, there was a really great joy in store for him in the summer. Having published in the *Courrier français* a drawing of his *Gueule de Bois ou la Buveuse*,† he made a present of it to some friends of his family, called Dihau, who lived at 6 Rue Frochot. The Dihau family—Désiré and Henri, and a sister, Marie—were musicians. Marie gave piano and singing lessons. Désiré, who was over sixty, played the bassoon in the orchestra at the Opéra; he composed tunes and wrote the music for songs produced at the Chat Noir. Lautrec often visited them in their third-storey flat, attracted not so much by their talents as by their pictures. They owned a number of paintings by Degas, who was a close friend. Among them *Musiciens à l'orchestre*, in which the artist had depicted Désiré, and two portraits of Marie,

---

* The corridas in the Gran Plaza de Toros in the Bois de Boulogne were forbidden three years later, in 1892, and the bull-ring demolished. According to Théodore Duret, Lautrec drew and painted many episodes of the corridas, portraits of toreros, etc. None apparently survive. But it is possible that Lautrec gave most of them to their models and that they either lost them or destroyed them. Ferran Canyameres records that one of the toreros, El Agujetas, exclaimed when he saw Lautrec's portrait of him: 'If my mother saw me looking like that, she'd have a fit!'

† In the number published on April 21, 1889.

with whom Degas had been rather in love some twenty years earlier. 'My cruel friend,' he called her in a letter of 1872.* The Dihau family, kind, simple, quiet people, regarded 'Monsieur Degas' with the utmost respect. Lautrec shared their admiration.

It so happened that Degas saw Lautrec's drawing at the Dihaus' flat, examined it and exclaimed, not without a certain melancholy: 'To think a young man has done this, when we have worked so hard all our lives!'

The remark was repeated to Lautrec and filled him with pleasure and pride. He had wanted to meet Degas for a long time now and Marie Dihau set about arranging it. A few days later Lautrec was admitted to Degas' studio.

The compliments he received from Degas gave him the liveliest satisfaction. But there was no further meeting then. Degas never wanted to make new friends.

*   *   *

Lautrec spent several weeks of this summer of 1889 at Malromé, in the Bordelais, and on the Bassin d'Arcachon, on board a little yacht, the *Cocorico*.

He had lost none of his passion for the sea. He swam, fished, sailed his yacht, followed the regattas and baked himself on the beaches of Arcachon and Taussat at hours when they were not too frequented. Or he wandered about the hills, among the pines and gorse. This country of sea, sand and pines delighted him. Sitting in the bows of his boat, he tried to paint seascapes, but above all, as he himself said, he 'soaked and restored his carcass.'

At Malromé, Lautrec found his father and his cousin, Gabriel Tapié de Céleyran, who had begun his medical studies at the Catholic Faculty of Lille.

Tapié was now twenty. He was a tall, spotty young man, with a slight stoop; his cheeks were covered with whiskers in the Austrian fashion; his hair, which was black and glossy with grease, was divided by a central parting that ran down the back of his neck and was combed forward over the temples. He wore huge rings on his long,

* *Les Musiciens à l'orchestre* and the portrait of *Mademoiselle Dihau au piano* are today in the Louvre.

slender fingers; a heavy watch chain ran across his stomach; gold-rimmed spectacles reposed on his pimply nose; and he nonchalantly extracted his cigarettes from an enormous silver case engraved with a coat of arms. He also wore a stone in his tie-pin. If asked what sort it was, he would reply slowly in a soft, grave voice, that it was neither a chrysoprase nor an agate, but the 'extreme end of a sea-shell seven yards long,'* for which he would obligingly furnish the Latin name.

Lautrec made Cousin Gabriel his slave. He caricatured him frequently, subjected him despotically to his whims, and never allowed him any initiative of his own. As soon as the 'Doctor' looked as if he might be about to express an opinion, a curt 'that's no business of yours, Charlotte!' immediately brought him to heel.

*　　　*　　　*

On September 3, the fifth Salon des Indépendants opened in the hall of the Horticultural Society in the Rue de Grenelle. Introduced by Adolphe Albert, Lautrec exhibited three works: his recent canvas, *Bal du Moulin de la Galette*, a study of a woman, and the portrait of one of his friends, M. Fourcade.

The Salon des Indépendants closed on October 4. On the following day, Saturday 5, there was great excitement in Montmartre. Joseph Oller, the prince of Parisian pleasures, the founder of the Pari Mutuel, the Théâtre des Nouveautés, the Grande Piscine Rochechouart, the Nouveau Cirque, and the Montagnes Russes, summoned all Paris to the opening night of his new dance-hall: the Moulin Rouge.

Oller, a Catalan of some fifty years of age, had never had a failure yet.† This time, however, everyone predicted a fiasco. Disregarding the geography of Montmartre night-life, Oller had not established his dance-hall on the Place Pigalle or the Boulevard de Rochechouart, where Bruant and the Élysée-Montmartre were being so successful: the scarlet sails of his Moulin were turning near the Place Blanche at 90 Boulevard de Clichy, on the site of the old Reine Blanche, which had been pulled down four years before. It was clearly madness!

---

* Recorded by Paul Leclercq.
† He was a distant relation of the painter Francisco Oller y Cestero, who had been a friend of Cézanne and Pissaro.

It may have been madness, but that night all Paris came to applaud the stars of the dance, La Goulue and Valentin le Désossé, Grille d'Égout and Rayon d'Or, Marie Casse-Nez and La Môme Fromage, whom Charles Zidler, Oller's partner, had attracted away from the Élysée-Montmartre. The aristocracy, the arts and literature were represented; Prince de Sagan, Aurélien Scholl, Élie de Talleyrand, Stevens, Gervex, Prince Troubetskoi and Count de La Rochefoucauld were all there in the huge high room. As light as day with its gas footlights, globes and chandeliers, the Moulin was hung with flags and looked even bigger than it was since one wall was entirely covered with mirrors.

From the opening night onwards, Lautrec was always there. He and the Moulin Rouge were to be inseparable from now on. He had his own table kept for him every night. Zidler, a friend of Portier, foreseeing this, had invited Lautrec and hung his canvas, *L'Ecuyère du cirque Fernando*, in the Moulin's purple hall.

And, indeed, there was no other spectacle in the world so likely to attract Lautrec as that of the Moulin Rouge. The pleasure, interest and material he had derived from the Élysée and the Moulin-de-la-Galette were here enormously increased. Here again were the quadrilles, and here also, more insolent and striking than ever, La Goulue who, in her sky blue satin blouse and her black skirt five yards wide, displayed with such agility her sixty yards of lace. 'Higher, La Goulue! Higher!' cried her excited admirers.

With his bowler hat either pulled down over his eyes or balanced on the back of his head, Lautrec drew, soaking himself in the noisy, vibrant atmosphere of the dance-hall which was, indeed, more than a dance-hall, a market, a fair of love. The public did not dance. They came to see the quadrilles. Between the dances, the over-excited men fell an easy prey to the women seeking 'customers.' Blue, red, green, white and yellow dresses moved to and fro, mingling with top-hats, felt hats and bowlers. There were even caps to be seen. 'Darling, will you buy me a drink?' The glittering, multi-coloured parade had all the luxury of a fashionable brothel. Champagne corks popped. Décolletée to the navel, a black watered-silk ribbon round her neck, a bunch of flowers in her hair, La Goulue would pass arrogantly by, queen of the dance and of the vendors of love. A little while before by way of salutation she would have displayed her drawers with a jerk of the hips and revealed a heart embroidered on her bottom.

*   *   *

Invited once again to exhibit in the XX Exhibition, Lautrec this time went to Belgium himself. He was accompanied by one of his friends from the Moulin Rouge, Maurice Guibert, an agent for Moet-et-Chandon champagne.

If Lautrec had his good geniuses, friends like Bourges and Adolphe Albert, who took him to task for his dissolute life, he had his bad angels too, and Maurice Guibert was one of them. An assiduous frequenter of bars and brothels, he was, so it was said, 'of the whole capital the man who knew the prostitutes best.'* Lautrec was fond of him but never stopped teasing him, demanding ten times a day, for instance, that he should twist his features into a hideous grimace; with which Guibert, good chap that he was, docilely complied. What a tyrant the little dwarf was! Like all weak people, he had to provide himself with the illusion of power. He sometimes carried it to cruel lengths, but his friends took it all in good part. His natural candour, his wild spirit, his inexhaustible vitality and constant enthusiasm gave him 'an ascendancy over them which was like a spell.'†

Lautrec had sent five canvases to this Exhibition of the XX of January 1890: studies of women and his picture *Bal du Moulin de la Galette*, to which he seemed peculiarly attached since he had already shown it at the Indépendants. In the 'Vingtistes' Exhibition he was not only hanging side by side with Renoir, Signac, Odilon Redon, Sisley and even Cézanne, who had sent three canvases from his solitude in Aix, but with his friend Van Gogh, who had also been invited to contribute.

Van Gogh, who was now a voluntary patient in the asylum of Saint-Paul-de-Mausole, near Saint-Rémy-de-Provence, was fighting a tragic battle against his disease. He was constantly on the watch for the successive attacks, and spent the intervals hard at work, 'labouring like a man possessed.' Van Gogh's six pictures were like a triumphant

* *Fin de Siècle*, July 7, 1895.
† Thadée Natanson.

fanfare on the walls of the Royal Museum of Modern Art, where the XX Exhibition was being held. Lautrec gazed in admiration at the two canvases of *Tournesols*, at the *Lierre*, the *Vigne Rouge*, the *Champ de blé au soleil levant* and at the *Verger en fleurs*. Had one to be mad to attain to these heights? Had achievement such as this always to be paid for in suffering and derangement?

There was, however, no unanimity about the merit of Van Gogh's work. On January 18, the day of the opening, there was a great dinner held for the 'Vingtistes' and their guests, Lautrec and Signac among them. Forty-eight hours earlier, one of the 'Vingtistes,' the Belgian painter Henry de Groux—a puny little man, barely taller than Lautrec himself, whose weakly body was usually covered in the folds of a huge green cloak (he had been nicknamed The Bell owing to his appearance)—had threatened to withdraw his own works unless the 'execrable' daubs of Van Gogh were removed. During the dinner, de Groux repeated the offence, shouting that Van Gogh was an 'ignoramus' and a 'charlatan.' Lautrec, who normally hated scenes, clambered to his feet and, indignantly waving his little arms, cried that it was 'a disgrace to insult such an artist.'

But de Groux refused to be silenced. The quarrel reached such proportions that he and Lautrec were heard through the general hubbub challenging each other to a duel. But Signac's voice was suddenly heard above the din saying coldly that, if Lautrec were killed, 'he would issue a challenge himself.'*

The banquet had taken a tragic turn and Octave Maus was much concerned. He was well aware how pathetically grotesque a duel between the two dwarfs, The Bell and Lautrec, would be and next day hurried off to try and extract an apology from de Groux. With some difficulty, he succeeded in doing so. De Groux resigned from the 'Vingtistes.' If he ever heard of it, Lautrec would have been delighted to learn that shortly after this incident someone had bought one of Van Gogh's canvases, *La Vigne Rouge*: it was the only picture his friend had ever sold—the only one he ever was to sell.

While the Belgian press was fulminating as usual against the painters of the 'XX'—though, as on the first occasion, it was on the whole

* Octave Maus: *La Lanterne magique*, a lecture given in Lausanne in 1918.

fairly indulgent towards Lautrec's 'spicy modernism'*—the painter was looking round Brussels with Maurice Guibert. The women on whom he cast his eye did not please him: 'Rubens in flesh and blood.' With a grimace, he decided they were 'shapeless.' However, the wine cellar of the barrister, Edmond Picard, whose portrait he drew, obtained his whole-hearted approval.

On his return to Paris, Lautrec took the risk of painting Désiré and Marie Dihau. The risk, he felt, was whether his portraits 'would stand up beside those of Monsieur Degas' or whether they would look 'ridiculous.'

He painted Désiré reading a newspaper in Père Forest's garden, and Marie at her piano. In the latter work, he concentrated attention on the musician's hands. He wanted to make a 'portrait of those hands' which were often more eloquent for him than faces. 'People who botch hands are no good . . . I can't stand it!'

Lautrec exhibited one of the portraits at the club in the Rue Volney, and the other, in March, at the sixth Salon des Indépendants, where he must certainly have examined at length a picture by Seurat, who had recorded in his own particular technique a moment at the Élysée-Montmartre.

Lautrec was now busy painting scenes of the Moulin Rouge. Bruant's influence had lapsed. If Lautrec had been attracted for a time by 'naturalism,' he was escaping from it. Now, in this dance-hall, he was obeying nothing but his own instinct.

He had started work on a big canvas, 60 in. by 56 in., *La Danse au Moulin Rouge*, which was the third of his big compositions (after *L'Écuyère du cirque Fernando* and *Le Bal du Moulin de la Galette*) in which he arranged the audience at the Moulin to include his friends Guibert, Gauzi, and the photographer Sescau.

But this was only the beginning. The Moulin Rouge had much to teach Lautrec and he had yet much to learn about life.

One night he heard two women arguing at the Moulin Rouge. 'You mean to tell me that's a pedigree dog!' one of them cried, pointing to the animal. 'Just look at its dull coat and crooked paws. What a miserable brute.' 'Not at all,' replied the other; 'look at its

* Edgar Baes, in *La Revue belge*, February 15, 1890.

lovely black face. Of course it's a pedigree dog with markings like that! You don't know what you're talking about!' And, turning to Lautrec, she said: 'Am I not correct, Monsieur, in saying that the dog may be ugly and yet have a good pedigree?' Lautrec rose to his feet, gave her a military salute, and said: 'You're talking to the right man!'

At this time, caricature was what pleased him most. And during this period there was an element of it in his portraits of street-walkers, drawn with so rapid a line that one might think Lautrec was in a hurry to rid himself of some anxiety. At the sight of these canvases, in themselves so revealing, one recalls Lautrec's angry remark: 'In the first place, you don't know and never will know; you know and only ever will know what one is prepared to show you!' But his works speak for him.

At the end of May, Van Gogh returned from Provence, and went to live at Auvers in the valley of the Oise. On Sunday, July 6, Lautrec had luncheon with him at Théo's in the Cité Pigalle. The climate of the little flat was peculiarly oppressive. Lautrec knew that Théo's business was not prospering and Vincent himself seemed highly nervous. He did his best to cheer up his hosts and after luncheon, took Van Gogh to his studio to show him his latest works, in particular his portrait of Mademoiselle Dihau, which Vincent thought 'really surprising.'* Then the two friends parted.

They were never to meet again. Exactly three weeks later, Van Gogh, in despair, climbed the hill at Auvers and shot himself in the chest. 'Sorrow will last all one's life!' he said as he was dying. He was thirty-seven.

Lautrec went on painting. He painted the life of pleasure and gaiety, searching constantly 'not for the inhuman but, on the contrary, for what was appallingly human.'† Like Van Gogh, he had to go on to the end of the road.

---

* Vincent had himself just painted a rather similar portrait: *Mademoiselle Gachet au piano*.

† Francis Jourdain. There are some twenty paintings for each of the years 1889 and 1890.

CHAPTER TWO

The Surgeon

'Asile, asile, ô Tourbillon!'
VALÉRY

THE fame of the Moulin Rouge had soon crossed the frontiers of France. Its name was known all over the world. From now on Paris was Montmartre, and Montmartre the Moulin Rouge.

'God created the world, Napoleon founded the Legion of Honour and I have made Montmartre!' announced Salis at the Chat Noir, while Zidler, the grumbling old man with a red face and white whiskers, who reigned over the dancers—'Louise, you're losing your drawers,' 'Paulette, don't make eyes at the gallery'—grew nostalgic when he talked of the success he had made of his life. 'At ten years old,' he would say, 'I used to stand in the stinking water of the Bièvre,* tanning cow-hides. I was fourteen when I learned to read and write, and I'm not very good at it yet. But my intelligence has taken the place of education . . . I had a flair for organising pleasure . . .'

Lautrec's picture, *La Danse au Moulin Rouge*, was hardly dry when it was bought by Oller. Zidler hung it in the hall, on the right, above the bar, as a companion piece to *L'Écuyère du cirque Fernando*.

Lautrec and his friends were there every evening. When a new customer entered the Moulin and saw the funny little man lisping witticisms, drinking hard and surrounded by a crowd, he was inclined to think he was one of the attractions of the establishment, like the 'pétomane' who, every evening between eight and nine, aroused the audience's hilarity by producing musical sounds from his behind, imitating bass, baritone or soprano on demand.

Lautrec's life took on a wilder rhythm. He would go from the

---

* This Parisian tributary of the Seine, the 'river of the Gobelins', as it was called, was completely covered in at the beginning of the twentieth century. In course of time, the tanners had transformed it into a drain.

Mirliton to the Chat Noir to the Moulin Rouge, from a brothel to a circus or a café, dragging with him anyone he happened to meet clinging to them, forcing them to accompany him. Had it been possible he would never have gone home to the solitude he feared.

His circle of friends was increasing. Some he admitted because they amused him or because he was attracted to them by some eccentricity —a curiously shaped head or the most splendid waistcoats in Paris— others because they were never reluctant to accompany him on his interminable rounds of pleasure. There were others again in whose company he felt safe.

There was 'Guibert's band,' consisting of Numa Baragnon, whose ogreish appetite was not daunted even by a whole leg of mutton; Sescau, who used his photographer's studio mainly for the purpose of seduction, and was so terrifyingly thin that Lautrec promised to 'pad his end'; and Henry Somm, a fat, fair, childish-looking man who was a caricaturist and etcher, a painter of 'little ladies' and author of the famous song of the Chat Noir:

> *Un escalier qui n'aurait pas de marches*
> *Ne serait pas tout à fait un escalier . . .*

Then there was Maxime Dethomas, so immensely tall that Lautrec called him 'the big tree'; a peaceful giant with a weak heart who was so shy and anxious to efface himself, that 'even the black of his coat looks darker than that of other people'.* To Lautrec's stupefaction, he remained impassive even in the most exciting haunts, had a horror of saying 'I,' laughed silently, and never did more than make the faintest of gestures even when Lautrec was bickering with some stranger and threatening in his 'golden voice': 'Just wait till he knocks you down!'

There was Charles Maurin, who drank rum by the litre, was a taciturn anarchist with a taste for violence, and hated dogs as much as he did policemen; he was a painter—'who knows how to paint hands!' exclaimed Lautrec—very absorbed in all the problems of technique, and always on the lookout for innovation. He was an anti-senti-mentalist, infatuated with scientific exactitude, and prone to repeat in a

* Thadée Natanson.

flat, dragging voice and provincial accent details of the observations he was making at the zoo upon the amorous habits of monkeys.

There were also the English who frequented the Moulin Rouge, the poet Arthur Symons and the painter Charles Conder, who had recently arrived from Melbourne, seemed always half asleep from drink and worked like a somnambulist. Lautrec liked the reserve and dignity with which the English took their pleasures. Besides, Anglomania was now all the rage in society. People had their clothes made by Poole, the Prince of Wales's tailor. It was even said that 'certain districts of Paris had become so English that you saw London beggars in them.'* British tourists invaded the Moulin Rouge in knicker-bockers and golfing caps, where they moved among a 'very select demi-monde.'†

Finally there was Maurice Joyant, his old friend from the Lycée Fontanes.

*   *   *

Joyant was a young man of good family, great tact and beautiful manners. In October 1890, he was sent for by the owner of the Boussod et Valadon Gallery at 19 Boulevard Montmartre. 'Our manager, Théo Van Gogh, has gone mad like his brother the painter and is in an asylum,'‡ said M. Boussod. 'Go and replace him, and run it as you please.'

'Théo Van Gogh,' M. Boussod told Joyant, 'has accumulated the most appalling stuff by modern painters; they're a dishonour to the firm. There were a few Corots, Rousseaus and Daubignys, but we've removed this stock as it will be of no use to you. You'll find too a certain number of canvases by a landscape painter, Claude Monet, who's beginning to sell a little in America, but he does too many of them. We have a contract with him to buy his whole production, but he's overwhelming us with them, and they're always of the same subjects. As for the rest, they're horrors. Just do the best

* Articles in *La Vie Parisienne* of July 30, 1892 and June 9, 1894, quoted by J. Adhémar, in *Lautrec peintre-graveur*.

† *Fin de Siècle*, September 23, 1891.

‡ Two and a half months after Vincent's suicide, Théo had suddenly shown signs of serious mental illness and was confined in an asylum at Utrecht. He died there a few weeks later, in January 1891.

you can and don't bother us, or we'll be obliged to close the branch down!'

Somewhat disconcerted by all this, Joyant made an inventory of the paintings with which his unfortunate predecessor had filled the two little rooms of the entresol. Among the 'horrors' signed by Gauguin, Degas, Pissarro, Raffaëlli, Guillaumin, Daumier, Jongkind and Odilon Redon, he discovered the Lautrecs Vincent had made his brother buy.

Once or twice, during the preceding years, Joyant had met his old school-friend by chance. As the painters who had pictures in the gallery came one by one to ask about them, Joyant thought Lautrec would probably appear one day too. He did and found his old school-friend depressed. There were no customers and no money; and the few people who did come in shook their heads and were pessimistic.

Lautrec, cheerful as usual, offered encouragement. Before long the gallery became a little centre for the new school of painting. Gauguin, who was about to leave for Tahiti, Émile Bernard, Sérusier, Schuffenecker and Charles Morice used to meet there, and Lautrec went every day.

*   *   *

The Moulin Rouge closed 'officially' shortly after midnight. By then only the real habitués were in the hall, and the dancers would perform for their own pleasure and for these regular customers, inventing the most acrobatic steps, their whirlings reflected in the mirrors on the walls which multiplied their wild improvisations.

This always excited Lautrec. Sketchbook in hand he would quickly capture the frenzied feet of Nana la Sauterelle; the arabesque of La Macarona, an audacious plump girl who was continually tossing up her 'packet of linen' to reveal black diamanté drawers; and the ethereal dancing of Grille d'Égout, the delicate, childish virtuosa, whose restraint ('women who show their flesh disgust me') contrasted with the sensuality of La Goulue.

Lautrec drew La Goulue's or La Môme Fromage's variations with the phlegmatic Valentin le Désossé or those of Vif Argent or Pomme d'Amour or Rayon d'Or, serpentine of movement and honey-coloured of hair, who beat out the time with her satin slipper. He watched Nini Patte en l'Air, a former shopkeeper, wife and mother, who had been seized by the demon of the dance and who now, her body bent over backwards, was whirling round her partner, high kicking at every step, her pale, sickly face with its huge dark eyes illumined by a sort of ecstasy; 'death dancing,' as someone said.

Or he would watch the solo performances of the strangely aristocratic Jane Avril, the intellectual friend of writers such as Arsène Houssaye and Barrès, who had nicknamed her 'Petite Secousse'; she was young and fragile-looking and had the beauty of 'a fallen angel';* she danced with a languid, ambiguous smile on her lips, 'dreaming of happy things.'

> A shadow smiling
> Back to a shadow in the night . . .

the poet Arthur Symons murmured to Lautrec.

When it was time to go home Lautrec would try to persuade one or other of his friends to accompany him round Montmartre looking for a bar that was still open.

Leaning on his little stick, he would take two or three steps, stop, gaze up at his companion's nostrils (he paid as much attention to nostrils, which he knew better than anyone, as he did to the hands in his portraits†), look about him, make some witty and often biting remark, then move on, his body bent, towards the nearest light—that haven in the night.

'The technique of ascension,' he would mutter, heaving himself up on to the high stool of a bar.

He was always thirsty. He preferred the best, and always carried a nutmeg in his pocket to spice his port. But he was content to drink whatever he could find, from the 'vinegar' in some little wine shop to the finest of old brandies. From being a pleasure, drink had become a necessity. He had hardly got out of bed in the morning before he started drinking. Vermouth, rum, white wine, armagnac, champagne, cocktails; he would drink at any hour of the day.

* * *

* Arthur Symons.
† Thadée Natanson.

Canvases were piling up in his studio in the Rue Tourlaque, but Lautrec's subjects did not alter much: women, portraits of friends, scenes in dance halls. The Dihaus, Bourges, Sescau and others sat for him. In Père Forest's garden, in February 1891, he painted *A la Mie*, in which Guibert and a model were sitting at a café table. The model was a pretty girl and Guibert a jolly fellow. But Lautrec painted this scene* so that their faces reflect nothing but vice and degradation.

It was a significant deformation. Lautrec's manner was acquiring greater vigour and precision every day. He was now twenty-six and his hypersensibility was finding expression in a violence that went straight to essentials and was devastating in its probing. His style, so intimately linked to what he had to say, had developed a terseness and refinement of expression. Every line, however simple, bore the stamp of his experience and could have belonged to no one else.

He was going more and more frequently to brothels with his friend Guibert, and he painted the women in all the intimacy of their lives. He was fascinated by the stealthy silence and drowsy atmosphere of these places, by the wan complexions of the women, by their mutual love affairs.

Himself deprived of love he watched their Lesbian loves with emotion. 'No one could be more loving,' he said. 'You've no doubt never seen them together. They're like two birds burying themselves in each other's feathers . . .'

Nevertheless, there were women in Lautrec's life. The Panthère, for instance, red-headed and green-eyed, with a strange, icy beauty, to whom Zidler introduced him one night at the Moulin Rouge. But to Lautrec these were fugitive loves, ardent in their sensuality but disappointing . . . 'Real life' lay elsewhere.

Was Lautrec thinking of what he might have been when, during these weeks, he several times painted a woman who in no way belonged to the world of his ordinary models, Mme Honorine P——? How delicately his brush brought to life the fresh, elegant, aristocratic face of the *Femme aux gants*.

One night, when visiting friends, Lautrec said to a girl: 'Wait a moment, I shall sit behind you . . . I can talk to you just as well from

* There is a photograph of it taken by Sescau.

there. I shall be just as close to you . . . I don't need to look at you, I know you by heart.'

And when hidden behind her, he added in a different tone: 'I'd also rather that you didn't have to look at me,' the girl, it is told, restrained her tears with difficulty.

* * *

In January, 1891, Lautrec exhibited at the Cercle Volney his *Bal du Moulin de la Galette* (which he was now showing to the public for the third time), portraits of Sescau and Henri Dihau, and a study of a prostitute. In March, he exhibited at the seventh Salon des Indépendants (and this year he was a member of the hanging committee together with Seurat and Signac); he showed several works, among them *A la Mie* and *En Meuble,* in which a prostitute stands by her bed, reading a letter.

At the Cercle Volney, a critic had reproached him for his choice of colour: a palette reduced to neutral tones. Octave Mirbeau said the same thing in March though he recognised the quality of his work: 'In spite of the black with which he unnecessarily darkens his faces,' the critic wrote in the *Écho de Paris,* 'M. de Toulouse-Lautrec shows a real spiritual and tragic force in his study of faces and understanding of character.'

Lautrec took these remarks to heart and turned to lighter, more varied colour-harmonies.

And now something occurred of major importance: Oller and Zidler asked him to do a poster for their establishment for the autumn season.

When the Moulin had first opened, Jules Chéret had designed the poster. In this field, which usually exploited the worst possible taste, Chéret was dominant. He excelled in drawing Pierrots and Columbines —the 'appetising Chérettes,' as they were called. 'Life is often sad enough,' he said, 'that's why it must be represented as happy and delightful. There are blue and pink chalks for the purpose.' His works occupied first place in all the collections of posters, which were astonishingly fashionable at the moment. People would stop at nothing to acquire the latest examples; they tore them from the walls, or bribed the bill-stickers.

And it was generally considered that Chéret had surpassed himself in his poster for the Moulin Rouge. Lautrec had therefore to meet severe competition in the public eye when he accepted the commission; nevertheless he was delighted.

Longing, as he did, to make his name, never missing an opportunity to appear in an exhibition, this was an unhoped-for opportunity. His contributions to magazines were still rare. He had also quarrelled with Roques, the editor of the *Courrier français*. Roques had not only failed to pay him for his drawings, but had had the impudence to sell the unpublished ones at the Hôtel Drouot auction rooms. Lautrec, very angry indeed, had served a writ on him. The dispute had been settled, but they were still at daggers drawn.*

The dissipated life Lautrec was leading prevented his working regularly for newspapers and in any case he had neither the time nor the taste for keeping up with topical events. Besides, most newspapers preferred amusing, mocking, 'Parisian' caricature and the semi-pornography that went with it. None of this appealed to Lautrec.

But now thanks to this poster, his work would be seen even by the crowds in the street. Was it minor, commercial art? Hardly. Daumier and Manet had not hesitated to design posters. Lautrec admired Chéret's work. He had also seen this year a poster by Bonnard, for *France-Champagne*: he had been so delighted with it that he had made friends with the young artist though Bonnard had one grave fault in his eyes: he politely but resolutely refused to drink.

Lautrec worked hard at his new task. To him the Moulin Rouge was La Goule and Valentin; they symbolised it entirely in his eyes, and in his poster he gave them a role which was not usually accorded to them at that period, when the actor and actress were more often looked on as mere mummers rather than stars.

It did not take Lautrec long to realise that the medium of the poster suited him, for he was continually aiming at achieving the maximum of effect with the minimum of clutter, and the poster encouraged him to apply what he had learned from the Japanese and from Degas.

* The sale at the Hôtel Drouot took place on June 1 and 20. Lautrec's drawings went for a few francs each.

He worked on with enthusiasm, making sketch after sketch in charcoal reinforced with colour.

The spontaneity of Lautrec's work is in a great measure due to the labour he devoted to it. It was his practice to sketch whenever he was still—even for a moment. At the counter of a tobacconist's, for instance, while one of his friends bought cigars, indicating in a few lines the curve of a neck or a forehead, the wave of a girl's hair or the contour of a chin. These incessant exercises taught him to have, as he said, 'his drawing in his hand,' and later to improvise from them, or from memory, with astonishing brilliance. But he was not easily satisfied. The improvisations themselves were rarely definitive. A line, which seems to have come from his pencil or brush with such ease and simplicity, was more often than not the result of long and patient effort.*

Modifying his first attempts by a series of studies, from which he eliminated all superfluous ornament, Lautrec gradually achieved the forceful poster design he wanted.

He treated the group of spectators as one large continuous black mass, outlined by an ingenious arabesque which silhouetted the men's top-hats and the feathered hats of the women. Against this mass he placed La Goulue, with her golden hair, pink corsage and white petticoat. He projected all the light upon her and made of her the very image of the dance. In the foreground, opposite Valentin, who is grey against the light and in his familiar attitude—eyes closed, body bent, arms in movement, large hands beating out the time—the yellow dress of an invisible dancer is caught in flight.

As soon as it appeared on the walls of Paris towards the end of September, Lautrec's poster created a sensation. Its vigour, its novelty of accent, its mastery and its undeniable power to arrest, all astonished. Enthusiasts followed the advertising vans parading it through the streets and tried to decipher the signature. Lautrec had abandoned his 'Tréclau' pseudonym for the last three years. But his name was difficult to read. Was it Hautrec or Lautrec? His fame was beginning, at least as a poster artist.

*   *   *

* 'Michel Georges-Michel has counted forty studies for the angle of a dancer's legs, and for the pacing of a circus horse,' records Michel Florisoone.

At about this time, Gabriel Tapié de Céleyran came to Paris to continue his medical studies.

From now on, Lautrec was always in the company of his cousin. The two young men met every evening. They formed a striking contrast, which no doubt delighted Lautrec, the lanky 'doctor' emphasising still further his own shortness and ugliness which he incessantly proclaimed and constantly caricatured. The sight of the tall, stooping medical student following the dwarfish painter was not one that could be forgotten.

Tapié felt real affection for Lautrec, and also a compassion which, though he took care not to show it, nevertheless made him as long-suffering and forebearing as a big dog under the teasing of a child. He was peaceable, kindly and good-natured, and always gave way to Lautrec. He also admired his talent.

Lautrec, whose one desire was to live the life of a normal man, would have refused to admit that people might have shown him less tolerance had it not been for the compassion he aroused. 'Of all the talents he had, the one he prided himself on most was getting his own way.'* A childish characteristic for a twenty-seven-year-old man. But there was something childish in Lautrec's nature, in his caprices, his impatience, his sudden angers, in the way he stamped with rage if his wishes were ignored, and also in his propensity to be amused at everything.

Tapié became his butt. He forbade him to talk politics, which were the 'doctor's' hobby but Lautrec's phobia. He forbade him to discuss art. 'Don't worry about that! It's none of your business!' He forbade him to shake hands with anyone who was not in his own good books, or to whose face he happened to take a dislike. He was continually rebuking him. 'In-com-pet-ent!' Lautrec would exclaim, emphasising each syllable. Tapié would fall silent, lower his spotty forehead, but never lose his temper. Indeed, one might have thought he derived a certain pleasure from being insulted.

As for Lautrec, he could no longer imagine life without the 'Tapir de Ceylan.' The 'doctor's' company had become indispensable to him.

* Thadée Natanson.

Cousin Gabriel was not living in Montmartre, but near the Madeleine in a flat with very low rooms—'a flat for a fried sole,' said Lautrec. He was working at the Saint-Louis Hospital, where he had been appointed assistant to a famous surgeon, Péan.

Lautrec was particularly attracted by surgery. The brush and the pencil were so often a scalpel in his hands that he felt a natural attraction towards the art of the bistoury. He was a dissector by nature. He did not rest till Tapié had obtained from Péan permission for him to attend operations.

There was very little difficulty, for the celebrated Péan, the glory of French surgery, enjoyed playing to the gallery. He operated before an audience consisting not only of a crowd of students and of doctors who had come from all over the world, but of laymen present out of mere curiosity.

Lautrec, who soon began going to the Saint-Louis Hospital every Saturday morning, became very enthusiastic about Péan, a huge man, who handled a scalpel with the mastery of a virtuoso, and, as had happened when he met Bruant, Lautrec attached himself to this powerful personality.

Péan was the son of a poor miller in the Beauce, had begun life at the plough, had studied on his own for the *baccalauréat*, and had then gone into medicine. Now, at sixty-one, he was at the height of his fame. He had invented the haemostatic forceps, and had performed the most daring operations with success, including the first excision of the spleen, the first resection of the pylorus and the first oophorectomy; he had opened up an immense new field to surgery.

On Saturdays Lautrec was at the door of the hospital even before Péan arrived, watching for the surgeon's carriage drawn by two chestnut horses, with a coachman and footman on the box, resplendent in gold-emboidered liveries. He followed him everywhere.

In the operating-theatre he would approach as near as he could and watch with close attention the incredible dexterity with which Péan operated. Lautrec was fascinated by the precision and dexterity of his hands. Everything about the surgeon attracted and delighted him: his overflowing vitality; his solemnity; his liking for ceremony which induced him to operate in a frock-coat with only a towel tied round his neck; his flow of small-talk, which never ceased, even when he was most urgently at grips with death, though he had no greater ease of elocution than had Lautrec himself; his self-satisfaction, which was no doubt amply justified, but was nevertheless a little ridiculous.

Quite insensible to the aspect of operations that others might consider unpleasant, Lautrec went to them as to the play. He drew every aspect of Péan, expatiating, mopping his forehead, composing his 'operating menu,' working on a patient, washing his hands . . . 'Magnificent! . . . Eh? What?' Cousin Tapié had provided Lautrec with the greatest possible pleasure.

Lautrec also made two paintings: *Une Opération de Péan* and *La Trachéotomie*. The painter's interest in operations was clinical. He treated these scenes with discretion, avoiding the more repugnant details. He did not hide the fact that he adored 'seeing people cut up.' But he enjoyed it in the same way that he enjoyed acrobatics at the circus. The cleanliness of the operating-theatres and the surgical instruments delighted him as much as the 'splendid work' of the surgeon —which, he remarked, was, of its kind, less clever than the way Charles, the head-waiter at Durand's, at the Madeleine, carved a duck.

There was nothing sentimental about Lautrec's approach to surgery. Just as there was nothing sentimental about his approach to life. He neither approved nor disapproved. He recorded. He was a spectator who stood outside morals. Bodies never yielded up their secrets so surely as in illness; and life was never better exposed than in corruption.

Dance-halls and brothels were Lautrec's operating-theatres.

* * *

At the end of 1891, a year which had been fruitful from every point of view, Lautrec had another opportunity to exhibit some of his works.

Paul Vogler, a painter of more pretention than talent, had succeeded in persuading an art dealer, Le Barc de Boutteville, in the Rue Le Peletier, to abandon the Dutch and Italian masters and devote himself to the young 'hopefuls' of French painting.

Le Barc was an elderly man and he was kind. He had made a certain amount of money and might well have retired from business to his property in Pierrefitte. But, after all, why should he not help young painters?

Putting such painters as he still possessed into store, he had his shop repainted and renamed 'Impressionnistes et Symbolistes', and he invited a few of the artists whom he thought most worthy of attention to exhibit in it.

In December Lautrec took part in the first exhibition together with Bernard, Anquetin and a few others such as Bonnard and Maurice Denis.

The exhibition attracted a certain amount of interest. The *Écho de Paris* even sent one of its reporters to interview the artists of the group. Anquetin declared superbly: 'No theories, no schools. There are only temperaments! What do I call myself? I call myself Anquetin, nothing more.' Bernard received the journalist in the little wooden studio he had built at Asnières, on whose walls he had inscribed his profession of faith: 'Art is the vision of the sublime,' beside a list of the artists he admired. Bernard talked at length of his aesthetic theories and fulminated against the official celebrities: 'Cabanel, Carolus Duran, Cormon, etc.,' he said, 'are all cretins, who have never understood anything about the masters they want to emulate . . . As for Meissonier, his early pictures are like well-made cakes, his later ones like gravy.'

Lautrec, though he was enjoying the beginnings of success, seemed overshadowed by his two loquacious friends. It did not occur to him to be proud of his success. 'I work in my own little corner,' he said modestly. The official painters? He had no opinion about them. Meissonier? 'He has worked very hard,' Lautrec said, 'and people who work hard should always be shown at least a little respect.' That was all.

Lautrec clearly did not wish to indulge in sensationalism. His growing reputation was nevertheless a fact; though in the eyes of his family it was far from being an enviable one. 'Who is your favourite painter?' someone asked Countess Adèle one day. 'Certainly not my son,' she replied.

That he should sign his works 'Lautrec' in spite of his being for-bidden to do so, naturally displeased Count Alphonse very much indeed. Why did his son not paint military scenes, like Neuville or

Detaille? How could he be persuaded to change both his subjects and his manner? 'For the honour of the name,' said one of his uncles, 'it would be better if he selected his models elsewhere than in Montmartre.'

For the honour of the name! Lautrec guffawed. From then on he always called this uncle 'L'Honneur-du-Nom' and announced that he proposed 'to have no further relations with him except those of burial.'*

* There are some thirty pictures attributed to the year 1891.

CHAPTER THREE

A Little Bunch of Violets

'You men can never talk of anything without deciding
immediately that it is stupid or sensible, right or wrong. And
why? Have you ever sought the motives of an action in all
their detail? Do you know the causes that produced it and
made it inevitable? If you knew them, you would not be so
quick to judge.'

GOETHE

LAUTREC was now exhibiting continuously: in January, 1892, he
exhibited with the 'XX'; immediately afterwards at the Cercle Volney,
and then with the Indépendants. His press was good, often excellent.
Yvan Rambosson wrote in *La Plume*, on March 15, that his contribution to the Volney had 'great value amid the surrounding banality.'
People were beginning to understand and admire Lautrec. Octave
Maus saw in his work: 'An art stripped of all convention and all
literature. It suggests grave matter for thought by its very crudity'; it
was an art 'of bitterness, fever and immodesty.'*

Lautrec seemed to be everywhere at once. In May, he went to
London.† A month earlier, he had gone to Toulouse, where he supervised the printing of a second poster, an arresting design in black and
white, which Arthur Huc, the editor of *La Dépêche*, had commissioned
from him to announce a new serial.

But even if Lautrec had remained constantly in Paris, his production
could not have been more abundant. He was making painting after
painting inspired by the Moulin Rouge; and in them La Goulue and
Jane Avril constantly appeared.

---

* Quoted by Dortu, Grillaert and Adhémar: *Toulouse-Lautrec en Belgique.*
† Possibly in company with Pissarro. Pissarro wrote to his son Lucien:
'Lautrec is also going to London, perhaps we shall take the same train.' (May 17,
1892.)

Jane Avril—who was also called La Mélinite—was very different from the other dancers at the Moulin and particularly interested Lautrec. She was the natural daughter of an Italian nobleman and a demi-mondaine of the Second Empire. In childhood, she had suffered much from the brutality of her mother, whose charming exterior had not succeeded in hiding, even from her lovers, her cruel, irascible, rather morbid and unbalanced nature. This woman had fallen on hard times and had found poverty intolerable. At times she became depressed and believed herself to be persecuted, at others she grew excited to the point of delirium with dreams of grandeur, and always she avenged herself on her daughter, whom she terrorised and threatened with drastic punishments should she cry out or complain to the neighbours. She also forced her to go out begging and to sing in the streets for money. Unable to bear this treatment any longer, the girl finally ran away and ended up as a patient of Charcot in the Salpêtrière, where she was treated for a nervous ailment. She was then sent back to her mother, who tried to turn her into a prostitute. At seventeen, she ran away again, this time for good, and for the rest of her life had a horror of violence and 'all that was low, vulgar and coarse.' She had protectors, but did not sell herself; she brought affection to her intrigues. Music and dancing were her refuge. After working as a circus-rider at the Hippodrome in the Avenue de l'Alma, then as a cashier at the Universal Exhibition of 1889, she went to the Moulin Rouge, where Zidler welcomed her with much kindness.

Lautrec also grew fond of this frail young woman who, with her pale face and turquoise-blue eyes, seemed astray among the other dancers, who called her: 'Jane-la-Folle.' She did not belong to their world; her delicacy, refinement and her touch of 'spirituality' set her apart from her companions at the Moulin and, as was only natural, they heartily disliked her.

The dance, for her, had none of that carnal frenzy which gave La Goulue her lubricious fame. For her it was a language. Lautrec was delighted by the subtle figures she created, by the colour-harmonies of her clothes (Jane Avril was the only dancer at the Moulin who did not wear white underclothes), in which black, green, lilac, blue or orange were exquisitely juxtaposed. He was fascinated by her unusual face, and painted her indefatigably. Her reserve made her all the more provocative, giving her a disquieting and perverse charm. As Arthur Symons described it: 'an air of depraved virginity.' Lautrec painted her dancing; he painted her coming out of the Moulin Rouge putting on her gloves or, wrapped in a voluminous coat, with her hands in her pockets, and always he lingered over her narrow, strangely melancholic face. Some people assumed she was a morphia addict, while others took her for 'the more or less crazy daughter of a good English family, whom her people had got rid of by paying her a remittance.' Her bedside book was Pascal.

Jane Avril fully returned Lautrec's friendship. She admired his talent, and was always ready to sit for him in his studio, where she sometimes acted as hostess. She often went to lunch or dine with him in the famous restaurant of Père Lathuile, in the Avenue de Clichy; and she frequently met him at Bruant's.

Would Lautrec have been so faithful to Jane Avril had he still been as attracted by the quadrilles? It seemed that these no longer aroused the same creative impulse in him. His paintings of the Moulin Rouge, although they were still numerous, represented only rarely the whirl-wind of the dance. If he still painted the quadrille, it was before the orchestra had played the opening bars, while the dancers were standing motionless, face to face in apparent defiance.

He certainly painted two women clasped in each other's arms in the waltz at this time, but he was more interested in their personalities and their sapphic love. 'Look at them dancing, gazing into each other's eyes, even when they're closed!' he said delightedly. And when he painted La Goulue, it was no longer to catch her in the snowy whirlwind of her lace, but on the arm of some young ass between waltzes, or again, in the company of her sister Jeanne, looking round the dance-hall with an insolent eye for 'a customer.'

Moreover, La Goulue was beginning to get fat and becoming more like her sister, a heavy, intolerably vulgar young woman, who fre-quented the Moulin only for the most obvious reasons. Jeanne Weber was not much liked. When Zidler bought a canvas in which Lautrec had painted her with La Goulue and hung it with the others that decorated the dance-hall, the dancers would gather in front of it to jeer: 'Goodness me, how ugly she is! What an elephant!—I think it flatters her!' These remarks became so frequent that Zidler had to take the picture down.

As if he wished to set the seal on his three years of research at the Moulin, Lautrec set to work on a big canvas, 55 in. by 47 in., in which he placed at a table in the foreground La Macarona, Guibert, Sescau and the critic, Édouard Dujardin, a tall man who wore an eyeglass and was 'shaggy, bearded and thick-lipped';* in the background Tapié, and Lautrec himself, are passing by, while La Goulue is pinning up her hair in front of a mirror.

It was clear that Lautrec's explorations into poster design had been of undeniable value to him, inducing him to strip away inessentials to achieve an extraordinary immediacy and authority.

*   *   *

From time to time, Lautrec disappeared for a few days and no one knew where. His friends could not find him at the Moulin Rouge, nor at Bruant's. He was not in Montmartre. The studio in the Rue Tourlaque was empty.

But the mystery was soon solved; it was discovered that Lautrec descended the Butte and went to stay in the brothels of the Rue Joubert or the Rue d'Amboise.

He painted, ate and slept in them.

Lautrec was not the man to make a scandal, though there was perhaps a certain ostentation in his contempt for public opinion: eccentricity, in the proper sense of the term, was, with him, only an affectation, a manifestation of his desire never to appear astonished.

'Bordel! What do you mean, bordel!' he would exclaim to the disapproving. 'They're the houses of the *bord de l'eau*. They need a lot of water, eh? Technique of ablution.'

If he shocked people—and particularly his own family, who looked on his continual back-sliding with bewilderment—it was to some extent in spite of himself. He had no choice and, under the urge of his virility, went where it sufficed to pay to get what he wanted. Rejected and despised, he went to women who were also rejected and despised.

* Thadée Natanson.

Gauguin had gone to Tahiti (he was there at this very time) for many reasons, but also because of the complete freedom of the senses that might be enjoyed there in a state of nature. The neighbourhood of the Gare Saint-Lazare and of the Place de l'Opéra were Lautrec's antipodes.

During these years, the arts had made heroines of prostitutes: Huysmans had published *Marthe, Histoire d'une Fille* in 1876; Édmond de Goncourt *La Fille Élisa* in 1887; Zola *Nana* in 1880; Maupassant *La Maison Tellier* in 1881. Constantin Guys, Félicien Rops and Degas had made numerous drawings of scenes in brothels.* Van Gogh had worked in them and so had Émile Bernard and Raffaëlli. Accustomed to living naked, these women did not pose like professional models. 'Models always look as if they were stuffed,' said Lautrec; 'these women are alive. I wouldn't dare pay them to pose for me, yet God knows they're worth it. They stretch themselves out on divans like animals . . . they're so lacking in pretention, you know!'

The same lack of pretention also put him at his ease as a man for, whenever he went among people unused to his appearance—which he did as rarely as possible—Lautrec would surprise expressions of either pity or amusement.

Lautrec had nothing of that sort to fear in the brothels. Accustomed to the most curious aberrations, the women, living as they did on that other face of the world, where man abandoned himself to his instincts, where all that was usually so carefully concealed was admitted and paraded, were not in the least surprised by the painter. He was just a little man of monstrous appearance and insatiable appetites, no more extraordinary than many others, and certainly much less so than many of the perverts who, on quitting these twilit rooms, resumed an appearance of complete normality once in the street outside.

Nothing could surprise them. That he was a descendant of the Counts of Toulouse and an artist who was already becoming known meant nothing to them. The social hierarchy had no importance here. Lautrec's unhappiness fused with theirs and created an atmosphere

---

* About seventy of these drawings were destroyed, 'out of a sentiment of piety' (to quote the phrase of some commentators), by Degas' brother at the artist's death.

of reciprocal tenderness, of which they, like himself, were normally deprived.

'They have good hearts; good manners come from the heart. That's enough for me,' said Lautrec. He was Monsieur Henri, who would caress the hand you abandoned to him for an hour at a time.

These women were not used to consideration. In their cloistered, carefully regulated existence, subjected to an almost military discipline —rise at ten, care of the body, luncheon at eleven, a satisfying dinner at five-thirty (the day's work began about eight), supper at two o'clock in the morning—they fulfilled the most passive and humiliating role possible to a human being. They were merely objects awaiting a customer: objects that were selected, used, paid for and then returned. But for Lautrec they were lovers.

Here he could at least enjoy an illusion of the affection he so much needed.

Having been adopted by these women, he wandered through the closed and shuttered house, tapping the parquet with his little stick and singing out of tune. He shared their meals, presiding over them with the madame of the house. (Each woman had her appointed place in accordance with seniority.) He added sweetmeats, patés and fine wines to the menu. (But the women lacked his knowledge of vintages. 'They know nothing about it. It's laughable, eh?') He remembered the dates of their birthdays and bought them presents. He played cards with them during their leisure hours, he listened to their confidences, drafted their letters, and consoled them when they were unhappy.

They seemed always sad, and laughed only when they were drunk; but he knew how to bring a fugitive smile to their lips. He knew what they lacked, because he lacked it himself: a sense of human identity. And he set about giving it to them, receiving it back in return.

'Astonished but moved,'* the women submitted to his caresses, touched by his politeness, his delicacy and his voice that became so tender when he talked to them. It was all illusion; he had to pay, and obey the rules, but somehow it seemed to be taking place in some other world.

* Thadée Natanson.

Lautrec made a note of the days the women had off from the establishment he frequented. He invited them to his studio, gave them meals in restaurants or took them to the circus. And they behaved with as much propriety as women of the fashionable world.

One of his favourite models from the Rue d'Amboise was called Mireille. She used a great deal of make-up and peroxided her hair till it was egg-yellow. One day, she came to his studio with a tuppenny bunch of violets.

She gave them to him with a shy grace, so the painter told Gauzi. He was not used to such attentions and was touched.

'I had never suspected such delicate feeling in a woman of that sort,' he admitted.

These were the only women who could bring a little tenderness into his life. He put the bunch of violets into a glass of water, and showed them to his visitors with all the emotion of a boy of sixteen suffering from calf-love.

Lautrec became a part of these women's lives. He knew their little secrets, the jealousies that divided them and set one against another, sometimes so sharply that madame, the 'marquise,' had to call them to order: 'Now then, Mesdames, where do you think you are?' He was admitted everywhere and at any moment; he entered their rooms, watched them washing and dressing, surprised them in their morning sleep, when their faces without make-up were gaunt and pale; his eyes half-closed, he observed from the depths of a chair their Lesbian gambols and delighted in the intimacy of this atmosphere redolent of the *odore di femina*.

Welcomed, cherished and fondled, he purred with pleasure.

'A brothel! All right, a brothel! I don't feel nearly so at home anywhere else.'

When depression weighed heavily on his spirit, he returned to these women who, like himself, had something to kill in their lives.

He would sniff and say: 'At last, I've found women who suit me.'

*   *   *

Lautrec watched, drew and painted. Yet his canvases have neither romanticism nor vulgarity; he avoided the equivocal and the lewd

The following identification of the family group opposite has been made by Mademoiselle Mary Tapié de Céleyran, of the Château du Bosc.
1. Emmanuel Tapié de Céleyran, cousin germain du peintre. 2. Madame Pascal, née Cécile de St-Aubin, tante à la mode de Bretagne du peintre. 3. Adèle Tapié de Céleyran, Comtesse de Toulouse-Lautrec, mère du peintre. 4. Amédée Tapié de Céleyran (mon grand-père), oncle du peintre. 5. Louis Pascal, cousin du peintre. 6. Le Comte des Cordes, allié de la famille. 7. Mon père Raoul Tapié de Céleyran, cousin germain du peintre. 8. Madame Amédie Tapié de Céleyran, née Alix de Toulouse-Lautrec (ma grand-mère) tante du peintre. 9. Madame Raoul Tapié de Céleyran (ma mère). 10. Germaine Tapié de Céleyran, depuis Comtesse d'Anselme, cousine germaine du peintre. 11. Geneviève Tapié de Céleyran, cousine germaine du peintre. 12. Gabrielle d'Imbert du Bosc, La Comtesse Raymond de Toulouse, grand-mère paternelle du peintre. 13. Louise d'Imbert du Bosc, Madame Léonce Tapié de Céleyran, grand-mère maternelle du peintre. 14. Beatrix Tapié de Céleyran, cousine germaine du peintre. 15. Madame Emmanuel Tapié de Céleyran, cousine du peintre. 17. Henri de Toulouse-Lautrec. 18. Marie Tapié de Céleyran, cousine germaine du peintre. 19. Le bull-dog 'Tuck' dont nous avons deux portraits par Toulouse-Lautrec. 20. Alexis Tapié de Céleyran, cousin germain du peintre. 21. Olivier Tapié de Céleyran, cousin germain du peintre.

Family group at the Château du Bosc (1895) [See key on facing page]

Lautrec at his easel (c. 1890)

Toulouse-Lautrec at Villeneuve-sur-Yonne. Painting by Édouard Vuillard (1898)

Shooting party. Lautrec with Grenier, Dr Bourges and others

Lautrec 'fishing

as much as he did the sentimental. He felt too close to this world to indulge, like Constantin Guys, in anecdote or a wink of complicity. He had too much lucidity to conceal the reality from himself.

He was like a surgeon operating. With his short-sighted eyes, he explored, analysed, and recorded frankly and pitilessly what he saw.

But he did not record only the defects; he could find a certain freshness too, discern innocence behind degradation.

His works were documents only incidentally; they were in no sense records of prostitution. In the first instance, they were works of art, but they were also, in their own way, a plea. Lautrec disassociated these women from their profession because he wanted to paint them as he would have painted any other women and with the same implacable truth. He could then state with all the greater firmness that no one in the world had the right to make anyone an outcast.

* * *

The *patronne* of the house in the Rue d'Amboise, Mlle Blanche d'Eg—, who prided herself on her taste in art (her house was one of those to which artists went to celebrate their success after a private view), asked Lautrec to decorate her big salon.

The house in the Rue d'Amboise was seventeenth century; it still had fine *boiseries* of the Louis XV period. Lautrec set to work. With the help of a housepainter and a pupil of Puvis de Chavannes, he filled the panels of the salon with sixteen designs each nearly six feet high. Against a pale yellow background, he painted flowers, leaves, garlands and sixteen oval medallions containing portraits of the girls, all in rococo style.

But he had not abandoned the outside world. While working on these decorations, he was also designing a third poster. It had been commissioned by Jehan Sarrazin, a curious bohemian of the Butte who had opened, at 75 Rue des Martyrs, a new *boîte*, the Divan Japonais.

'A propagator of the olive among the peoples of the north' (for so he referred to himself), Jehan Sarrazin had for a long while past been wandering about the bars of Montmartre with a bucket on his

F

arm, from which he offered connoisseurs a dozen olives wrapped in a poem for five sous. Then, though he had not given up his bucket, he had started the Divan. It had a low, narrow room, furnished and decorated in the currently fashionable Japanese style. Its billiard tables were painted blue and red, the ceiling gold and the chairs lacquered in black; while the customers were served by waitresses dressed in kimonos. The 'poet of the olives' showed considerable perspicacity in finding new attractions. A year before, he had been particularly lucky in engaging a singer, Yvette Guilbert, who had largely contributed to the success of his establishment.

After difficult beginnings, Yvette Guilbert was making a name for herself. Her rather extraordinary figure was beginning to be known: she was tall, thin and flat-chested with a cap of red hair and 'an unending neck.' Her very long arms were gloved to the shoulders and her eyes made up to look very round. She sang between ten and eleven every night at the Divan Japonais to a public that included many painters and writers. Her voice was harsh and she sang songs of a somewhat acid flavour, such as *Les Vierges*, which was regularly demanded three or four times an evening.

> *Ce sont des abricots pas mûrs.*
> *Elles ont peu de charmes, mais ils sont durs,*
>   *Pour sûr!*
>   *Les Vierges!*

Yvette Guilbert's personality must have attracted Lautrec. Yet curiously enough he all but left her out of his poster for the Divan, contenting himself with sketching her in a corner of it, whilst giving the greatest prominence to Jane Avril, who was merely a spectator.

It was a remarkably balanced composition and an undoubted masterpiece. Bruant also commissioned a poster of himself. He had just accepted an offer from Ducarre, the manager of the Ambassadeurs on the Champs-Élysées, and was getting five thousand francs a month to appear in this café-concert.

The movement which was drawing Lautrec away from Montmartre was a general one. Montmartre had reached the height of its fame, but the consequence was disintegration. The stars who had given the Butte its fame were in demand elsewhere. After the 'Ambass,' Bruant left for a long tour of the provinces and Algeria. Oller, seeing how things were going, founded the Jardin de Paris on the Champs-Élysées as a branch of the Moulin Rouge. Every night, after the Moulin had closed, he took his dancers and customers there in brakes, the horses trotting and the whips cracking in an ostentatious procession.

Ducarre of the Ambassadeurs was a little old man without any education and with 'all the appearance of a guest at a poor wedding.'* He was not a great admirer of Lautrec's talent and argued about the artist's fee, finally agreeing to a sum which would hardly cover the cost of printing. This meanness irritated Lautrec. 'As far as I'm concerned, I've done my work for nothing,' he wrote to Bruant. 'It's a pity they should have taken advantage of our good relations to do me down. We must try to be more prudent another time.'

Unfortunately, Lautrec was not at the end of his disagreements with Ducarre. Having seen a sketch of the poster, Ducarre pretended to accept it but secretly asked an artist called Lévy to do another. When Bruant heard what was happening, he lost his temper and declared that, if his friend's work was not used, he would refuse to sing. Ducarre protested that Lévy's poster was so pretty! 'You can hang it in the lavatories,' said Bruant. Ducarre gave way, and Lautrec's poster was soon on the walls of the capital. However, it did not please everyone.

'Who will deliver us from the likeness of Aristide Bruant?' wrote a contributor to *La Vie Parisienne*. 'You can't go anywhere without finding yourself face to face with him. It has been said that M. Bruant is an artist . . . How can he consent to appear on the walls side by side with the Bec Auer and the Oriflamme. He must suffer from such propinquity . . . And does he really need to have recourse to the vulgar means of advertising used by sellers of bicycles and sewing-machines?'†

* * *

* Yvette Guilbert.
† This same year, Lautrec drew a second poster for Bruant, when the singer went to the Eldorado.

Commissions for Lautrec now came rapidly.* Through Joyant, Boussod et Valadon commissioned him to do two coloured lithographs.

Long held in little esteem and used mostly for purely commercial purposes, lithography was only gradually recovering its artistic prestige. However, some of Lautrec's friends, notably Charles Maurin, Adolphe Albert and the sculptor Carabin, were much attracted to it. On their advice, he set to work, excited at the prospect of a new medium.

His efforts (Lautrec painted sketches for his lithographs on cardboard, as he did for his posters) soon bore fruit and, in October, Boussod et Valadon were able to put on sale, at twenty francs, two admirable plates: *La Goulue et sa Soeur* and *L'Anglais au Moulin Rouge*.

This success encouraged him to persevere; he developed a passion for lithography as he had done for the poster, and soon agreed to collaborate with André Marty, the publisher, who was intending to publish the first number of a periodical devoted to engraving, called *L'Estampe originale*,† in March 1893.

Lautrec's two lithographs were pulled at Edward Ancourt's excellent printing firm at 83 Rue du Faubourg-Saint-Denis. The painter at once made friends with one of the old workmen, Père Cotelle, who knew all the tricks of the trade and greatly helped him in his task. Père Cotelle was well-known in art-printing circles, particularly because of his hat: a filthy felt skull-cap with which he lovingly greased the stones.‡

Asked to make a lithograph for the cover of *L'Estampe originale* Lautrec gave public expression of his gratitude to the old artisan: he drew him in shirt-sleeves, spectacles on nose, turning the wheel of

---

* He painted some thirty works in 1892.

† 'Unlike its predecessors,' said the prospectus, 'the collection will not be limited to one form of engraving, nor to engravings of one colour. Every kind will be represented, engravings in polychrome will be side by side with engravings in bistre, sanguine or black.' Among the artists who promised to contribute with Lautrec were Anquetin, Émile Bernard, Bonnard, Carabin, Eugène Carrière, Chéret, Maurice Denis, Gauguin, Charles Maurin, Pissarro, Puvis de Chavannes, Raffaëlli, Rachou, Odilon Redon, Renoir, Vuillard, Whistler and Willette.

‡ 'In this he was merely following an old tradition, which all good working lithographers still practice.' (Maurice Joyant.)

his hand-press, while beside him Jane Avril—the painter's homage to a dancer who was a friend of the arts—was examining a proof.

Lautrec was now going about Paris more frequently. In the autumn, he took some of his friends to the Folies Bergère, where an American dancer, Loïe Fuller, was arousing the enthusiasm of the crowd. Indeed the dances she created were received with a sort of frenzy.

In the darkened hall Loïe Fuller would come on to the stage like an apparition, her long robes swirling in rhythmic undulations under the coloured spot-lights. Hers was an ethereal, iridescent dance of spirals and arabesques or, again, of a great butterfly with variegated wings.

Lautrec promptly fell under her sway—'the Samothrace side,' he announced delightedly—and he soon started painting 'the nymph of the luminous fountains.' He also made a lithograph of her: it was in black, but he added colour with a wad of cotton-wool and powdered every proof with gold.*

There was another performance in central Paris that attracted Lautrec's attention: the *Ballet de Papa Chrysanthème*, a Japanese fantasy produced in November by the Nouveau Cirque in the Rue Saint-Honoré.

Founded by Oller in 1886, the Nouveau Cirque was a meeting place for all elegant Paris and was, so affirmed the serious *Journal des Débats*, 'the eighth wonder of the world.' The year before, it had already inspired Lautrec to paint *La Clownesse aux cinq plastrons*. The *Ballet de Papa Chrysanthème* aroused his interest once again. The ring of the Nouveau Cirque, owing to a clever piece of machinery, could be transformed into a swimming-pool. On this occasion, the swimming-pool was strewn with water-lilies. Dressed in imitation of Loïe Fuller, the dancers, led by the Fairy of the Lake, appeared amid coloured lights to take their places round the pool among the reeds.

Lautrec painted this ballet twice.

*   *   *

The moment had arrived when Lautrec might think of holding a one-man exhibition of his work.

He was now twenty-eight and had already produced more than three

* This lithograph was published by Marty in 1893.

hundred paintings, posters and lithographs, not to mention innumerable drawings. But he still looked on himself as an amateur, receiving compliments with some embarrassment.

Joyant, however, was prepared to place the gallery in the Boulevard Montmartre at his disposal. It was finally agreed between them that an exhibition should be held at the beginning of 1893, in January and February. Nevertheless, feeling in need of support, Lautrec asked Charles Maurin to share the honours with him.

Lautrec hung some thirty works in Joyant's gallery, including his pictures of the Moulin-de-la-Galette and of the Moulin Rouge, as well as his posters and lithographs. The exhibition was very well noticed. 'It is a long time since we have met an artist as gifted as M. de Toulouse-Lautrec,' wrote Roger Marx in *Le Rapide*,* 'and perhaps his authority derives from the integration of his faculties; I mean the integration of his analytical penetration with the brilliance of his method of expression. In his cruel and implacable observation, he resembles Huysmans, de Becque and all those others who are able to depict a human being's innate character on the mask of his outward appearance.'

The majority of the critics agreed with this judgment. Gustave Geffroy, who knew Lautrec well, since they both attended gastronomic dinners† in the Restaurant Drouant in the Place Gaillon, wrote in *La Justice*,‡ that the painter 'showed himself more or less expert in expressing the upsurge of innate individuality...'

This remark enormously amused Lautrec who, from then on, was always exclaiming: 'Oh, life, life! Oh, the upsurge of innate horror in a night-club!'

Even *Le Temps*, which was not much given to joking, complimented him: 'Toulouse-Lautrec, my friend, you are hard and cynical about our species... You sing the epic of the mob by showing its ulcers as they are. You're a knowing fellow, my friend!'§

But the one opinion about which Lautrec was anxious was that of Degas. He sent him a personal invitation. One night, Degas came,

* February 13, 1893.
† These took place on Fridays and were attended by such people as Monet, Rodin, Raffaëlli, Carabin, Joyant, Clemenceau and Edmond de Goncourt.
‡ February 15, 1893.
§ February 4, 1893.

wrapped in a cloak. He examined each picture for a long time. He hummed to himself, but uttered never a word. Lautrec waited anxiously. Degas finished his tour of the room and started down the corkscrew staircase that led to the basement. He was on the point of disappearing, only his head and shoulders were still above the floor, when he stopped and turned: 'Well, Lautrec,' he said, 'it's clear you're one of us!'

Lautrec was delighted.*

And Lautrec had good reason to be pleased. His fame was increasing. He was exhibiting at the same time as the 'XX' in Brussels, at an exhibition of posters in the Musée Communal at Ixelles and at the second Salon of the Association Pour l'Art at Anvers. His notices at all these were equally good. Young foreign artists, such as the Belgian Evenepoel, came to ask his advice.

Lautrec's success naturally had its counterpart. Raffaëlli remarked angrily that he had invented the method of light touches on cardboard. His family was taking increasingly greater umbrage at his notoriety and, finally, contrary to the usual custom of the Cercle Volney, where everyone was free to exhibit what he liked, this year Lautrec's work was refused. It was a portrait of a woman painted in Père Forest's

---

* Reported by Joyant. But Degas' remark was much less laudatory than Lautrec and Joyant imagined—and than has since been thought. For, indeed, of the two exhibitors of 1893, the great artist in Degas' eyes was not Lautrec but Maurin. When a collector, Henry Laurent, told him of his intention to buy Lautrecs, Degas said: 'Buy Maurins! Lautrec has a great deal of talent, but he's merely the painter of a period; he will be the Gavarni of his time. As far as I'm concerned, there are only two painters that count, Ingres and Maurin.' Trusting Degas' judgment, Henry Laurent ignored the Lautrecs and formed a collection of Maurins. During the next few years, he acquired several hundreds, always with Degas' approbation and, on each of his visits, Degas continued to express the greatest possible admiration for Maurin. Pointing to the *Femme qui rit* and the *Femme au Corset*: 'You could put them next to Rembrandt,' he said, 'they'd stand up to him.' Moreover, Degas was not always kind about Lautrec. In his splenetic way, he said some cruel things about his junior. Perhaps he felt a certain jealousy and displeasure that Lautrec should have borrowed much from him and have treated subjects he probably considered as his own. 'The gentleman's wearing trousers that are too big for him,' he once said wickedly. In 1916, he said disgustedly of Lautrec's work to Sylvain Bonmariage: 'It all stinks of the pox.' It was hardly a kindly judgment from an artist for whom brothels had also served as a field of observation and who, as a misogynist, must certainly have behaved far less 'humanly' in them than had Lautrec.

garden. In a rage, Lautrec sent in his resignation, and went to collect his canvas. He took it in a cab to Le Barc de Boutteville, who suggested putting up a notice saying: 'Refused by the Cercle Volney.' But to this Lautrec would not consent.

He also had trouble with the police. Towards the end of 1892 another exhibition took place at Le Barc's to which Lautrec, Bonnard, Vuillard, Maurice Denis and Gauguin sent pictures. Le Barc put one of Lautrec's in his window. It was of two women in bed, and there could be no doubt about what they were because their hair was cut short.* The commissaire of police for the district ordered the dealer to remove the picture.

These affronts, however, did not weigh very heavily on Lautrec; and if he rejoiced in his success less than he should have done, it was for quite another reason: Bourges was getting married and, naturally, the two friends were to cease living together.

However independent Lautrec might be, he needed a refuge in which to find an element of quiet and rest. Seeing his bewilderment, his mother came to Paris and took a flat in the Rue de Douai. Perhaps she hoped to wean her son from his life of debauchery and excess— too much alcohol, too many women and also too much work.

But though his mother's affection was as precious to him as it had ever been, the Lautrec of 1893 could no longer swallow its protective quietude. Though mother and son still loved each other, they no longer understood each other. 'Incomprehension,' 'incompatibility of temperament,' 'misunderstandings'; these were the words that came to the minds of Lautrec's friends.† His mother wanted him to be what he never could be; and he, on his side, could tolerate neither reproaches nor advice.

Lautrec snapped his fingers at all counsel and reproach. Priests, who were friends of the family, lectured him from time to time. 'I

* At that time short hair was 'an undoubted sign of reprehensible morals'. (Francis Jourdain.)

† These are in fact the words used by Joyant, who perfectly understood Lautrec's feelings at this time. 'After his death,' he wrote, 'a charming young woman of his own world said: "I would have taken charge of Lautrec; I think I could have saved him by marrying him . . ." ' 'Why didn't you do it while there was still time?' exclaimed Joyant. 'Wasn't he famous enough?'

can do anything I like,' he lisped mockingly, 'since Mama keeps nuns
in our old castle of Boussagues,* whose principle duty it is to pray
for the salvation of my soul, as they go running up and down the keep
like frogs in a glass bowl!' To a priest who persisted, he said bitterly in a
sarcastic tone: 'Oh yes, Abbé, don't worry, I'm digging my grave
with my cock.'

Deprived of the amenity of Bourges' flat, he went from time to
time to dine with his mother, in those quiet, respectable rooms that
shone with polish and smelt of lavender, and where the white net
curtains hung so immaculately. As for the rest: 'I shall set up my tent
in a brothel,' he said.

* A small feudal estate in the Hérault.

Women

PART THREE

[1893—1897]

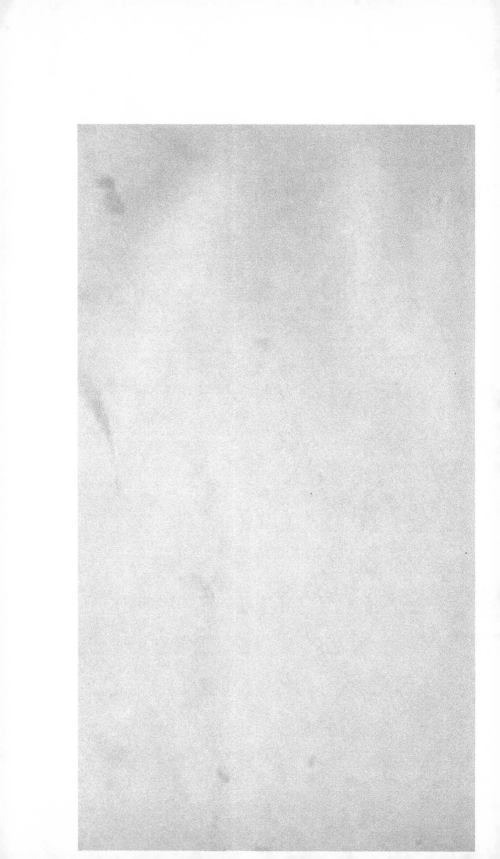

CHAPTER ONE

The Rue des Moulins

'Under the blankets, you no longer feel your wretchedness,'
a Marseille prostitute told us grandly. (You sometimes feel
another sort of wretchedness though. But that's not the
question.)

MONTHERLANT

LAUTREC's life was an impetuous and unceasing frenzy of activity.
It was like an *ignis fatuus*, like burning tow. His intellect and his emotions
were in a state of incessant excitement. Since he had separated from
Bourges, his disease had gone untreated, and in consequence may
treacherously have fanned his vitality into flame.

His companions in pleasure wondered how he ever found the time
to work. And those who were aware of his feverish production
wondered when he ever found the time to amuse himself. When he
travelled he summarily insisted that his friends accompany him.
He took Joyant off to London, and Guibert to Bordeaux where,
rather than go to a hotel, they stayed in a brothel in the Rue de Pessac.
From now on, these houses were always to serve Lautrec for hotels.
In Paris he obliged Dethomas to stay with him in the Rue d'Amboise
or in the Rue Joubert.

He was working more busily than ever in these houses but he did
not confine himself to them. He sought out subject matter in other
places too. Péan, now retired, had founded the Hôpital International
at his own expense, and Lautrec made sketches there, still fascinated
by the surgeon who 'rummaged in stomachs as if he were looking in
his pocket for change.'

He was constantly suggesting some new excursion to his friends.
'We should go and see *her*,' he said one day. 'Who?' 'Not a word!' he
whispered, a finger to his big mouth. They followed him from street
to street, while from time to time he turned round, waved a finger and

173

murmured: 'A mystery!' Clambering painfully up to the fifth floor of an old house in the Rue de Douai, the painter stopped, breathless, and declared: 'She's more famous than the President of the Republic!' and tapped at an attic door.

The door opened and an old woman with a face bloated with drink led the visitors into her filthy room. Who was this old hag to whom Lautrec brought sweets, and who earned an exiguous livelihood playing a guitar and making a monkey dance on the terraces of the cafés in the Place Pigalle? It was La Glu—Victorine Meurent—who, thirty years before, had posed for Manet's *Olympia*.

Lautrec's curiosity was insatiable. Everything stimulated his wonder and excitement and, in spite of drinking to excess, he remained as greedy as ever. He habitually overate, and searched for an increasingly complex and fastidious cuisine to stimulate his jaded palate. He knew every restaurant in Paris and its speciality, loved officiating at the stove himself, found time to invent recipes, and delighted in marrying, with exquisite taste, the wines to the food. Cooking, like painting, is an art; and Lautrec lavished the same care upon it.

But he could joke about it too. After watching a boxing match at the Nouveau Cirque between a negro and a kangaroo, he invited his friends to come and eat a kangaroo with him. He placed before them an Ouessant sheep, garnished with a cow's tail and a pocket in which he had placed a mouse, and to prevent his friends drinking water, he put goldfish in the water-jugs.

At the end of these nights, when the early workers were beginning to make their way through the deserted streets, Lautrec, after a last drink, would hoist himself into a cab and often fall asleep in it before reaching his destination. If a cabby thought it proper to awaken him Lautrec would tell him furiously to 'mind his own business,' and would go back to sleep again.

The cab would remain standing there; from time to time the horse would paw the cobbles; the quarters and the half hours would ring out from the churches; dawn would break and when Lautrec awoke he would sigh and look up at the shuttered windows of the houses. Should he go to bed? No. He had slept enough! He would give the cabby the address of the Ancourt printing works.

There the workmen became accustomed to seeing him appear in the grey light of early morning, often before the works had opened. Having drunk a glass of white wine or a glass of old marc in the bar on the corner, he would greet everyone in the workroom, make a joke or two and perch himself on a stool. Then turning up the sleeves of his evening coat he would set to work on one of the lithographic stones.

He would start on a new work or retouch one that was ready for pulling, adding tone to the surface with a toothbrush that now never left his pocket. Utterly captivated by the art of lithography, and having grasped its possibilities from the very first, he devoted all his thought, enthusiasm and love to it. Pursuing his designs through every stage, he helped the workmen, chose the paper and ink, supervised the proofs, knowing exactly what he wanted and going ruthlessly into every detail, tearing up the pulls that did not satisfy him, signing and numbering the rest, and destroying the stone once the printing had been completed.

At the end of the previous year, Lautrec had become friendly with an artist, Henri-Gabriel Ibels, who was both a great lover of lithography and an enthusiastic frequenter of cafés-concerts. The two men had much in common. Lautrec was delighted with Ibels' humour, and the resourceful dodges he thought up to acquire a little money. Ibels had succeeded in persuading the music publisher, Georges Ondet, to have his songs illustrated by 'real' artists rather than by merely commercial ones.

Ondet, who lived in the Ancourt house, published not only the works of Théodore Botrel and of Xanroff, but also those of Désiré Dihau. Introduced to Ondet by Ibels, Lautrec was delighted to be able to apply his passion for lithography while putting his talent at the service of Dihau. He enjoyed himself designing covers for several songs: *Ta Bouche, Nuit blanche, Pour toi!* among them. A hundred advance copies were pulled separately and sold by Kleinmann, the publisher of engravings.

Lautrec missed no opportunity of this kind. When the Indépendants gave a banquet, he made a lithograph for the menu, drawing a milliner of the Faubourg Montmartre arranging hats in her shop. This milliner was, in fact, Renée Vert, who was very soon (in September 1893) to marry his friend Adolphe Albert and for whom Lautrec, by way of amusement, occasionally designed models for hats.*

This menu was no doubt a little token of gratitude to his friend Dodo—as Lautrec affectionately called Adolphe Albert—who as secretary of the Painters-Engravers had seen to it that he was invited to exhibit in the fifth exhibition of the group in April. Lautrec submitted a dozen engravings. At the same time he was making seven illustrations for an article by Geffroy which was to appear in July in *Le Plaisir à Paris: Les Restaurants et les Cafés-Concerts des Champs-Élysées*, and was also busy with a series of lithographs devoted to the café-concert, which *L'Estampe originale* was also to publish in July. This edition was to consist of twenty-two lithographs in black and Lautrec and Ibels were to share the task between them.

To make their sketches, Lautrec and Ibels went to the Petit-Casino, to the Scala in the Boulevard de Strasbourg or to the Ambassadeurs, which was usually frequented by a rowdy public which went there deliberately 'to make a noise.' While daylight lasted Lautrec worked in his studio or at home (he said that painting portraits rested him), then he would shuffle off to the cafés-concerts with his sketchbook to draw the comic actors and the entertainers: Paula Brebion who sang soldier's songs while performing contortions; Edmée Lescot, who dressed as an Englishwoman to sing *Lingaling* or as an Alpine shepherdess to yodel; Mme Abdala, who was terrifyingly thin and appallingly ugly, and whose speciality was pulling faces, squinting or twisting up her mouth as she sang; and the fat Caudieux, with the 'large corporation to which he was cordial' who aroused the enthusiasm of the crowds at the Petit-Casino with his great success:

* Renée Vert has often been confused with another milliner, Mlle Le Margouin, with whom Lautrec later made friends. Renée Vert had had a son by her first husband, who had died, and I had the good fortune to meet him. Dr Louis Chouqet, as he now is, was kind enough to give me the benefit of his recollections and to allow me to see various family papers and documents. I was able to check a number of details. Lautrec had already been friendly with Renée Vert for a long time. In 1888, the milliner appeared with Adolphe Albert, La Goulue, Claudon and others in an illustration Lautrec made for *Paris Illustré* (March 10), *Bal Masqué*, and in the sketch for it the artist painted on canvas.

Une, deux, trois, zut!
Une, deux, trois, zut!
Et tintintin,
Vive le Quartier Latin! . . .

His eyes full of images and his pockets full of sketches, Lautrec
wandered through the streets, going from light to light, from port
to gin and vermouth ('You must drink it in a tumbler, half gin, half
vermouth. And you needn't be afraid of getting drunk! The vermouth
destroys the effect of the gin,' he asserted), from brandy to absinthe
('Have another drink?' 'Can't you see I'm drunk?' 'No,' Lautrec
replied, 'because I'm beginning to be drunk too'), from the last light
to the first cab, where he would fall asleep, snoring and dribbling.
Restored by a glass or two of cheap brandy, he would awake refreshed
and ready for business at the lithographer's. Making his 'button hook'
ring out on the floor, he would call for his stones, and with an incredible
sureness of hand and eye would sketch in the features of those he
had selected as subjects for his eleven plates for the *Cafés-Concerts* series.
Of course, he included Jane Avril and Bruant, even Ducarre, the
manager of the 'Ambass,' and Yvette Guilbert to whom he was now
becoming more attracted.

This lithographic debauch did not however seduce Lautrec from
his paintings or from his posters. On the contrary, he jumped at every
opportunity for making new ones. He solicited dancers and singers as
models, frequently meeting with a rebuff from some who did not think
his work sufficiently flattering.

He had hoped Loïe Fuller would commission him to do a poster;
but she preferred second-rate commercial artists. In his disappointment,
he stopped going to see her at the Folies-Bergère.

Jane Avril, at least, had great confidence in him. She was to appear
at the Jardin de Paris in June, and it was to him she went for her poster.

The Jardin de Paris had quickly become one of the most popular
places of revelry in the capital. Oller provided his customers with a
great variety of attractions; he had succeeded in amalgamating a
café-concert, a dance-hall, a circus, a shooting-range, a bar, a slide,
stomach-dancers and fortune-tellers. The quadrilles of the Moulin

Rouge were all the rage, and one night La Goulue, kicking her leg above her head, had not been afraid to knock off the Prince of Wales's hat. 'Hullo, Wales, are you paying for the champagne?'

Lautrec designed a poster for Jane Avril that was in perfect keeping with the extravagance of this establishment. It shows the sad-faced dancer raising her 'packet of linen' to reveal a black-stockinged leg while in the foreground the huge finger-board of a double-bass seems almost to be alive.

'Oh, life! life!' lisped Lautrec, with a glint of mockery in his eye.

*   *   *

Lautrec had never missed the fancy-dress balls given by the *Courrier français* (for one of them, two years before, the 'Mystic Ball,' he had disguised himself as a choir-boy, with a chimney-sweep's broom in his hand instead of an aspersorium), and was naturally among the two or three thousand who attended the Quat'z-Arts Ball in February.

This ball, given by the students of the École des Beaux-Arts, was a recent innovation. The first, held in 1892, had taken place without incident. The second, this year, was organised by Jules Roques at the Moulin Rouge. Its highlight was a procession of half-naked models who were carried in, to a rolling of drums, on shields, in baskets of flowers or in palanquins, representing Olympian goddesses, slave girls, 'roses stripped of their leaves,' women of the Bronze Age or Oriental princesses, such as Cleopatra, the queen of the procession, whose single garment was a belt of sequins.

But there were some complaints from the prudish and five days later, Senator Bérenger, President of the League against Licence in the Streets, laid an information and proceedings were instituted. The case was called in June.

Lautrec was present in court, where he saw La Goulue playing an unexpected part. When a commissaire of police ironically remarked that he had witnessed even more outrageous scenes at the Opéra ball, La Goulue, pretending to be gravely shocked, gave evidence to the effect that she had been utterly scandalised by the spectacle of such nudity. Lautrec, delighted by her hilarious evidence, later made a lithograph of the scene: *La Goule devant le tribunal.*

In spite of a good deal of laughter, the accused were sentenced on June 30 to a fine of one hundred francs with benefit of the First Offenders Act. It was a farcical case. But the whole affair ended disastrously. On July 1, the students of the Beaux-Arts set off in procession to hoot Bérenger. The police charged the crowd with batons and in the brawl a perfectly peaceful citizen was killed on the terrace of the Café d'Harcourt, in the Place de la Sorbonne. The demonstration became a riot, barricades were erected in the Latin Quarter and the Government brought in troops from outside Paris. Quiet was not restored till July 6.

To some extent, the climate of the period explains this sudden outburst of violence. The anarchists were creating terror and during 1892 many bombs had burst in Paris, in blocks of flats, in restaurants, in barracks and in the offices of the Compagnie des Mines de Carmaux, whose workmen had been on strike for some time. Ravachol had been guillotined. The anarchists denounced the Government with increasing virulence in their newspapers.

Moreover, they claimed Lautrec as more or less one of themselves. 'Here's a chap who's got sand in the belly,' wrote *Le Père Peinard*, 'both Lautrec's drawing and colour make no bones—they're simple, direct and true to life. He just sets down big simple areas of black, white and red—that's his form. No one can equal him at catching the likeness of the decadent rich sitting in restaurants or cafés with prostitutes, who are prepared to love them at a price. *La Goulue, Reine de Joie, Le Divan Japonais* and a pub-keeper, called Bruant, twice—that's all Lautrec's done by way of posters. But they're good, sound stuff and they leave the fools, who have no ideas except conventional ones, up the creek!'

Lautrec was, however, a royalist who thought monarchy 'a means of reducing the power of the civil service over the daily life of the citizen,' and, although he moved among artists and intellectuals, many of whom admitted the attraction libertarian theories had for them, he avoided any discussion of politics. These theories corresponded to a mental outlook existing at that time; the modern-minded defended them; snobs took them up. Lautrec himself had become friendly with a group of literary men who held daring views, often lightly tinged with anarchism; this was the circle of the *Revue blanche*, which the brothers Natanson had founded two years before in the Rue des Martyrs.

Lautrec immediately felt at home with them. Alexandre and Thadée Natanson were of Polish origin and had made their mark in literary and theatrical circles. They lived in the grand manner and were overflowing with both ideas and money. They discerned with an almost infallible flair all that was best and most characteristic of the dying century; they supported Mallarmé, Ibsen and the young painters, Bonnard, Vuillard, Roussel, Maurice Denis and Vallotton, who had given themselves the name of Nabis; in February, the *Revue blanche* published an article in praise of Lautrec's exhibition at the Boussod et Valadon Gallery.

Thadée was, perhaps, the more remarkable of the two. He was a big man, who ate enormously, and because of his generosity and his luxurious and expensive tastes, which were in accord with his vitality and his enthusiasms, he was known as 'The Magnificent.' A man with many irons in the fire, he was very knowledgeable in matters of art, and had a lively intelligence, which was however inclined to lean towards Utopian dreams. He was at once subtle and impulsive. If he was childish in some ways, he also had a touch of genius: but it was an undisciplined genius which was too often astray among the clouds. He had married a very young girl (she was fifteen years and three months old at the time) of splendid and irresistible beauty, who to some extent shared his dreams. Misia, who numbered among her ancestors a Russian prince and a Belgian musician of talent, was as capricious as Lautrec who, needless to say, was secretly in love with her. She was a brilliant pianist and lived in a world of unreality in which her whims were her only law. On getting married she had spent on 'a fairy trousseau' the whole of the three hundred thousand francs of her dowry.*

Lautrec was immediately adopted and made much of by the Natansons. He would, of course, contribute to the *Revue blanche* (in the meantime he asked Misia to sit for the cover of a song by Dihau, *Sagesse*),

* In her *Memoirs* Misia herself admits to spending this considerable sum—the equivalent of some £40,000 today. Most of it at Watrugant in Brussels.

and he made friends with some of the writers who contributed, in particular with Tristan Bernard, a man of gay, sceptical humour, who loved his food and wine, and would gently shake his long, Assyrian beard with pleasure over an epigram or a dish; and with Romain Coolus.

Coolus, who had a musketeer's beard, a huge forehead and dark velvety eyes, was four years older than Lautrec. No one could have been more attached to his own independence, yet Lautrec intrigued him. By alternately demanding and cajolling, Lautrec soon made him his devoted follower. He nicknamed him Colette; and coaxed him to follow him everywhere, even into brothels. Since Lautrec could paint in them, there was no reason why Colette should not be able to write in them. 'One's comfortable there,' he said, 'and they are the only places where people still know how to polish shoes.' He introduced his friends: 'This is Paulette. She's sweet, isn't she? . . . We're in love . . . Stay! Look at her breasts! No, I shan't touch them . . . And just look at that shoulder. No, no, stay there! We're in love. Don't laugh . . . Hasn't she got a bottom like a little empress? You can't help loving her . . . You can't help it . . . eh?' Coolus soon had his desk in the house where Lautrec had his easel.

Coolus was passionately fond of the theatre. He deplored the fact that Lautrec did not go there more often, since he was sure that the painter would find interesting subjects for his pencil and brush. Lautrec was somewhat reluctantly persuaded. When *Femmes savantes* was revived in September, the painter was in a stall at the Comédie-Française.

He was completely captivated, as he had been by dance-halls, circuses and cafés-concerts. As elsewhere, the performance for him was in the auditorium as well as on the stage. The Comédie-Française seemed to him an inexhaustible mine of material. He delighted in its rather old-fashioned atmosphere and claret-coloured seats, the dignity of the box-openers in their little bonnets, the exaggeratedly accented diction of the actors and actresses, the devout attitude of the elderly subscribers. He immediately set about making lithographs of various scenes and the actors, among them Leloir and Moreno, in *Les Femmes savantes*, Bartet and Mounet-Sully in *Antigone*.

From now on he went regularly to the theatre, the Comédie-Française, the Variétés, the Théâtre-Libre and the Renaissance. And, at the same time he designed three posters in succession, one for Caudieux, another for Bruant (*Aristide Bruant dans son cabaret,*) and another to publicise a serial, *Au pied de l'échafaud,* which was to appear in *Le Matin*.

In November, Georges Darien, the author, was about to launch with the aid of Ibels and the collaboration of Anquetin, Vuillard and Willette, an illustrated weekly, called *L'Escarmouche*. Lautrec suggested to him a series of lithographs on the entertainments of the day, and twelve were published before this ephemeral periodical disappeared in January.

In one of these lithographs, for which he returned to the Moulin Rouge to sketch, Lautrec ironically drew his father sitting at a table on the promenade above the legend: 'A tough! A real tough!' 'My father has never revelled except on coffee and milk,' he remarked impertinently.

Borrowing Goya's 'I saw this' from *Los Desastres de la Guerra,* Lautrec used it as an epigraph to his lithographs in *L'Escarmouche*.

Goya's exclamation was one of horror. Lautrec's a cry of triumph.

'Life is almost an enchantment,' his friend Vincent used to say in spite of his anguish and misery,* and Lautrec echoed it.

*   *   *

In Brussels Octave Maus had dissolved the Société des 'XX' and substituted for it another group, which was to break still more daringly with the past: the Libre Esthétique.

The first exhibition of the new group was held at the beginning of 1894. Maus invited several French artists and writers to the private

---

* Lautrec's work during the year 1893 included some fifty paintings (of which just under twenty were of brothels), nearly forty lithographs and four posters. Of the lithographs for *L'Escarmouche* may be mentioned *Mademoiselle Lender et Brasseur aux Variétés, Mademoiselle Lender et Baron, Répétition générale aux Folies-Bergère* (Émilienne d'Alençon and Mariquita), *Sarah Bernhardt dans* Phèdre, *Au Moulin Rouge: l'Union franco-russe* (the end of the year review), *Antoine dans* L'Inquiétude, and *Madame Caron dans* Faust. The three last appeared in January 1894.

view including Lautrec, who had sent only posters and lithographs.

He took the opportunity to show the friends who accompanied him the pictures he most admired in the Royal Museum, the Van Eycks and the Cranachs, the Frans Hals, the Memlings and the Quentin Metsys. Tyrannical as ever, he insisted that they should look only at what he wanted to see, and only at the end of a long visit, during which they all had to stand for some considerable time in front of Breughel's *Massacre of the Innocents*, was he prevailed on to permit his victims a favour: 'And now, before we go, gentlemen, you may, if you wish, cast an eye on the Jordaens, but don't linger.'

In his eyes, only a few pictures counted, but they counted supremely. For an hour on end he could stand, 'his chin leaning on the round rail,'* before Cranach's portrait of Doctor Johann Schoner without growing tired of looking at it. 'It's magnificent!' he cried. 'As fine as the panel of a carriage!'

The old city, the neighbourhood of Saint-Gudule, and the romantic little streets delighted him no less, and he would go for long drives in a landau before going to sample the specialities of some famous restaurant, Le Gigot de Mouton or L'Étoile, or to pay a visit to an explorer who was suffering from some mysterious disease in the hospital, and who had a most extraordinary yellow complexion!

Lautrec managed to extract the most from his tortured life. 'Life is splendid!' he often declared. If some of his friends, Tapié, for example, or Joyant, or Gauzi, or the understanding Thadée Natanson, were not deceived, many others were taken in by his impetuous boisterousness. Few men seemed happier. He spread a sort of careless gaiety wherever he went. No one could have been a better companion. Not only was he forgiven all his petulance and his caprices, but people sought out his company. They laughed with his laughter, and were thirsty with his thirst. He was full of zest.

In a Belgian restaurant he would be delighted to observe some stout woman's appetite, as she sat alone at a table, a whole line of glasses in front of her, busily devouring her fish and her snipe cooked in champagne; at the frontier he would argue with the customs officers over his right to bring through 'a quantity of Hollands gin or Dutch

* Francis Jourdain.

beer'*; as he emerged from a Parisian crowd he would declare: 'In
the symphony of human odours, the sharp smell of the navel—and I
know about this!—holds the same place as the triangle in an orchestra!';
he would furiously apply his stick to a journalist who, for a joke, had
been rash enough to seize him by the elbows and lift him off the
ground; he would report some new discovery: 'Do you know
what I've just found in the Rue Lepic? It's absolutely fabulous. On
the wall of the *pissoir*, some poor chap has written with extraordinary
care: "My wife insults me, scratche me (without an "s"), deceive
me (also without an "s")," then straight off without a spelling mistake:
"but the more she makes me suffer, the more I love her." Pretty
splendid, isn't it? Rather sweet? . . .' It was difficult to believe that
there lay behind his enthusiasms anything other than a tremendous
joy of life.

One night, the Natansons asked him to dine with a few friends and
afterwards do a round of the night haunts. That night, unusually,
Lautrec spoke little and drank not at all. Thadée Natanson noticed
how taciturn he was and wondered what sorrow was oppressing him.
They went from night-club to night-club without succeeding in cheer-
ing the painter who seemed 'appallingly melancholy.' At last, they
had to separate and go home. A cold dawn was breaking. Lautrec
was twirling his stick and standing on the edge of the pavement, as
if he could not make up his mind where to go next. Anxious and
concerned, Thadée Natanson, for his part, hoped Lautrec would go
to a brothel and forget his depression in the company of the girls.
Then a woman in the party suddenly insisted that Lautrec should have
luncheon with her next day—she had a surprise for him, she said—
and she refused to leave him till he had promised to come.

'What else could one do?' she said later to the Natansons. 'He looked
so mortally sad that I was afraid of leaving him there all by himself . . .
I felt that I must try at any cost to give him some reason to go on living
till midday tomorrow.'

But even in the consoling retreat of the brothels, Lautrec had his
disappointments. Mireille, the woman from the Rue d'Amboise
who had one day brought him a tuppenny bunch of violets, had,

* Joyant.

against his advice, been persuaded by a white-slave trafficker that
two or three years in the Argentine would make her fortune. She had
refused to listen to Lautrec and had gone off to Buenos Aires. 'None
of those who go like that ever come back,' said Lautrec sadly.

He stopped going to the Rue d'Amboise; and, since a new and
extremely luxurious house had recently been opened at 24,* Rue des
Moulins, in the neighbourhood of the Bibliothèque Nationale, he
established himself there.

This particular house had in a very short time acquired a European
renown. It offered its customers every possible convenience, from
the most exquisite to the most eccentric. Even women, principally
rich foreigners, did not disdain to tour its salons and luxurious rooms.
There were carved and basket-work beds, beds with testers, Gothic
beds, Louis XIII, XV and XVI beds standing in superbly decorated
rooms that were furnished with bibelots, statuettes, caryatides and
carved candlesticks, while their walls were panelled or hung with
satin, tapestries or mirrors. One of these beds whose great head-board
bore the figure of a naked woman in relief, stood in a room where not
only the walls but the ceiling was one huge mirror. A Second Empire
bed, in the shape of a shell, stood on a parquet floor that was designed
to resemble the waves of the sea. There were not only ducal rooms but
Chinese rooms and the great salon, decorated in the Moorish style,
with arched, heavily carved doorways, resembled the interior of a
mosque.

Lautrec soon made himself at home there. Mme Baron and her
daughter Paulette, (Mlle Popo), whom she passed off as her sister,
Marcelle, Rolande, Mlle. Pois-Vert, who had borrowed her name
from Outamaro's prints, Lucie Bellenger, Elsa la Viennoise, a slender
Austrian with a milk-white complexion, were from now on both his
models and his consolers.

He became their spoilt child and ruled the house as he had ruled
in the Rue d'Amboise. Whether at meals, in the salon or the rooms,
he was completely at home. Behind the closed shutters, Lautrec became
Monsieur Henri, the Painter—or the Coffee-Pot—the prince of an

---

* Today, No. 6. The furnishings of this house were sold by public auction on
October 30, 1946, 'owing to cessation of business.'

assembly of women. 'He made the greedy eat, the thirsty drink and
the gay laugh.' And always he arrived with his arms laden with huge
bunches of flowers, which filled the women with childish delight. They
gratified him sexually; but they did more than that, they gave him
tenderness, 'a sweet that cannot be bought.' 'On Sundays,' he said, 'the
women play dice with me,' and during their idle hours, he made
them dance together to a mechanical piano. Were they not as beautiful
in their light veils as the Graces of Botticelli's *Primavera*?

Sex had become for Lautrec a simple matter. If a man ever existed
without complexes, it was certainly the 'Little Priapus.' But despite
his assumption of knowingness, Lautrec was astonished by much of
what he saw. He was discovering, not without a certain satisfaction
that was, in a sense, a form of revenge, just how depraved man could
be. Everything in love's domain, where he himself had only hunted
as a poacher, interested him. The atmosphere of love intoxicated him.
Perversities moved him to exclaim: 'How ingenious. How monstrous!'

With grave delight he manipulated the whips and the cat-o'-nine-
tails, and the other instruments of the 'torture' chamber, where stood
a cross and a pillory. This perfectly organised house could provide its
clients with women disguised as brides, nuns or nurses, and indeed with
negresses. A certain eccentric gentleman, Lautrec recounted, lisping
with delight, came each week 'to try on dolls' hats.' One of the women
was the sales-girl. 'This little hat,' she would say, shaking the bonnet
strings, 'this little hat, Madame, suits you to perfection,' and the
customer drooled with pleasure.'*

Lautrec painted some twenty scenes of the intimate life of this world
behind the shutters.

Once its doors were shut, the brothel recovered a sort of bourgeois
calm, an 'almost family'† routine; and the laundry-man, who had a
paralysed face, would deliver a parcel of linen to the door-keeper,
while the women hummed sentimental songs or wrote to their boy-
friends. It was this quiet, monotonous existence that Lautrec depicted.
But sometimes he turned to a harsher world for his material. Having
entered by chance a brothel of the very lowest category, he recorded

---

* Recorded by Thadée Natanson.
† Joyant.

his stay with a terrible picture, *Monsieur, Madame et leur petit chien*, in which the brothel-keeping couple, with their toad-like faces, are bestiality itself. And he painted the women, their shifts raised, queuing up for the medical inspection; or drew scenes that were questionable to say the least (*En haut de l'escalier de la Rue des Moulins: On monte!* for instance) and some that were frankly pornographic.* But, in general, it would be difficult to tell, if one did not happen to know, what environment had furnished Lautrec with his models.

He watched the women's faces as they slept. He contemplated them all with love, whether they still had a girlish air about them or were already weary, haggard and used up. How often 'could one choose one's life?'

In soft warm colours, Lautrec was painting a big canvas in which he was summarising his observations. It was of the salon in the Rue des Moulins, with its huge sofa and group of waiting women. He caught them in this room, with its tall fluted columns, in a timeless stillness as if under a spell of enchartment.

Lautrec's audacity had no limits now. He had never concealed the fact that he frequented these places. And now he paraded it. If asked for his address, he would give that of the Rue des Moulins. It was easy to find: the house was 'clearly numbered.' At a gala night at the Opéra, he had no inhibitions about appearing in a box with Marie-Victoire Denis, the mistress of the establishment, and one or two of its inmates.

But he was absorbing increasing quantities of alcohol and his nervous irritation increased. He was often bitter and sometimes aggressive. To a man about town, whose marriage was not exemplary, and who indignantly reproached him for going to such places, Lautrec replied with scathing insolence, shouting so that the whole café could hear: 'By God, I suppose you prefer to keep a brothel at home!' On another occasion, at a party in the Rue de la Faisanderie, when his host asked him if he were enjoying himself, Lautrec pointed to the ladies with their low-cut dresses and bare shoulders, their necks

---

* There exist a certain number of works by Lautrec, though they are comparatively rare, which would be difficult to exhibit. They are mostly in private collections.

gleaming with precious stones, and declared, 'Enjoying myself! Divinely, my dear chap! One might think one was in a brothel.'

His jokes were often wry and sarcastic. When the great picture dealer, Durand-Ruel, suggested holding an exhibition of his lithographs,* Lautrec gave him an appointment at his studio—in the Rue des Moulins. His delight at the dealer's bewilderment, when he received him among the women precisely as he might have done among the family portraits in the state rooms of Le Bosc or Malromé, was at once childish and satanic. And his joy was much increased when he learnt that the dealer's coachman had absolutely refused to wait outside No. 24, and in outraged dignity had moved his horses away to stand outside the house of a respectable notary.

*   *   *

Crushed by the competition of the Moulin Rouge, the Élysée-Montmartre had closed down. Rodolphe Salis had sold his Chat Noir. Bruant, who had made a fortune and had recently married a singer from the Opéra-Comique, Mathilde Tarquini d'Or, was thinking only of retiring to his native village, Courtenay, where he had bought the château. In the meantime, the *Revue blanche* had left the Rue des Martyrs and had gone to the Rue Laffitte. And, finally, Joseph Oller had founded a new music-hall, the Olympia, in the Boulevard des Capucines. Lautrec's Montmartre was dying.

Lautrec, though he made a few lithographs for Kleinmann of the Moulin Rouge, was now mostly concerned with the entertainments of central Paris; he drew Marcelle Lender in *Madame Satan*, Réjane and Galipaux in *Madame Sans-Gêne*, Lugné-Poe and Berthe Bady in *Au-dessus des Forces humaines* and in *L'Image*, Brandès and Le Bargy in *Cabotins*, and Brandès and Leloir in the same play. This last play belonged to the repertoire of the Comédie-Française, which moreover inspired Lautrec to paint a big canvas: a full length portrait of his cousin Tapié walking nonchalantly down one of the gangways.

In April, the Théâtre-Libre produced *Le Missionnaire* by Marcel Luguet. Lautrec made one of his best lithographs for the programme, *La Loge au mascaron doré*, in which Charles Conder appears sitting

* It took place from May 5 to 12.

next to a woman who is watching the stage through opera-glasses. He also made a lithograph for the menu of a dinner given by Adrien Hébrard, the editor of *Le Temps*, and designed some more posters: *Bruant au Mirliton; Sescau photographe; L'Artisan moderne*, which was an advertisement for a line of *objets d'art* that the editor of *L'Estampe originale*, André Marty, was putting on the market; *Confetti*, a poster for a London manufacturer who specialised in its production; and *Babylone d'Allemagne*, a bookseller's poster for Victor Joze's latest novel.

At the same time, Lautrec was discovering new stars, the Scottish singer, Cissy Loftus, the English dancer, Ida Heath, and above all Polaire, an attractive little Algerian. He made some striking portraits of this girl who, as *La Vie Parisienne* wrote, 'sings with her legs, recites with her arms and emphasises with the rest of her.'

But above all Lautrec was attracted to Yvette Guilbert. In March, continuing his series of illustrations for songs, he made a lithograph for the cover of *Éros Vanné* by Maurice Donnay, which 'the Sarah Bernhardt of the fortifications' was singing at the Scala:

> *Elles ne sont pas prolifiques,*
> *Mes unions, évidemment.*
> *J'assiste aux amours saphiques*
> *Des femmes qui n'ont point d'amants . . .*

Yvette Guilbert fascinated Lautrec and as always when he fell in love with a model, he studied her exhaustively. She had the 'profile of a gutter-snipe swan' and 'sang of revelry with a funereal air.' Every model of whom he made drawings, paintings or lithographs had something in common: he drew them into his own universe. There was no difficulty with Yvette Guilbert. She was his type.

With charcoal, paint and lithographic pencil, he laboured to reveal her personality; he ransacked her body like an inquisitor.

For Lautrec, Yvette Guilbert occupied the same place in the café-concert as had La Goulue in the dance-halls of Montmartre. She personified the café-concert as La Goulue had incarnated the quadrilles. Lautrec wanted to design a poster for her. He sketched one in charcoal, reinforced it with colour and sent it to her.

The singer, who made the most of her unpromising appearance, was not particularly vain. Basically, she was more attracted than repelled by Lautrec's talent. She was disturbed by the latent force in the dwarf which communicated such a penetrating power of analysis to his hand. It was clearly no ordinary man who had drawn the sketch, and she was tempted to accept it. But her advisers intervened. The singer must not accept so crude a distortion! So she refused Lautrec's offer, alleging that her poster for next winter was already ordered. 'It will have to be for another time,' she wrote to him. 'But, for the love of God, don't make me so appallingly ugly! Just a little less! . . . Several people who came to my house uttered cries of horror when they saw your coloured sketch . . . God knows, everyone cannot see its value as a work of art!'

Lautrec did not consider himself defeated. He planned to publish an album of lithographs entirely devoted to the singer and for which Gustave Geffroy would write a preface. One morning, together with Maurice Donnay, he went to call on Yvette Guilbert in the Avenue de Villiers. She now met him for the first time.* 'A puppet,' the maid exclaimed as she hurried to warn her mistress of the unexpected visitor. And Yvette Guilbert was herself taken aback.

She could find nothing to say at sight of the 'huge, dark head, the red face and black beard, the greasy, oily skin, the nose broad enough for two faces, and a mouth that gashed the face from cheek to cheek, with huge, violet-rose lips, that were at once flat and flaccid.

'At last, I looked Lautrec straight in the eyes. Oh, how fine, large, richly warm and astonishingly, luminously bright they were! I kept on gazing into them, and suddenly Lautrec became aware of it and took his spectacles off. He knew his one magnificent feature and he offered it to me with all his generosity. And his gesture showed me his ludicrous, dwarfish, little hand, which was square and attached to extraordinarily short, marionettish arms. Maurice Donnay said: "Here you are; I've brought Lautrec to luncheon with you, he wants to make sketches of you."'

---

* In her memoirs (*La Chanson de ma Vie*), Yvette Guilbert gives the date of this meeting as 1895. This is an error.

Yvette never forgot that meal: Lautrec's chin some eight inches above the cloth, the food being engulfed in that appalling mouth, 'each movement of chewing inciting the saliva on his enormous lips. When the fish with a *rémoulade* sauce appeared, there was an extraordinary splashing.'

But, as usual, Lautrec's simplicity and charm soon took effect. To those who loved Lautrec, said Thadée Natanson quite rightly, 'it required enormous effort to see him as he appeared to the rest of the world.'

That first meeting was followed by many others, and by many sittings. Lautrec carried his equipment to the Avenue de Villiers and drew the singer endlessly. One day, looking through some of his sketches, Yvette, somewhat irritated in spite of herself, said: 'Really, you have a genius for depicting deformity!' Wounded to the quick, the painter said acidly: 'But, of course!'

Their meetings were often stormy. It was as if Lautrec delighted in irritating the singer. 'Oh, love, love!' he would cry. 'You can sing it in every tone of voice, Yvette, but hold your nose my dear . . . Oh, hold your nose! . . . If you sang *Le Désir*, we should understand each other, and be amused by the different forms it takes . . . But love, my poor Yvette! . . . Love! *It doesn't exist!*'

He lisped the phrase between his teeth. 'But what about the heart, Lautrec? What about that?' 'The heart? The heart has nothing to do with love.' He laughed, remembering perhaps the remark made by his distant ancestor to the Duchess de la Trémoille: 'The heart! How can an intelligent woman confuse the heart with mere matters of copulation?' 'But, my dear Yvette, men loved by beautiful women having nothing but vice in eye, mouth, hands and heart . . .' He grew excited and was almost shouting, his face contorted 'by an infernal, sorrowful smile.' 'And what about the women! . . . Look at their faces!' He opened a sketch-book, pointed to the drawings: 'Look, these are lovers and their beloveds. Look at that!' He laughed: 'Eh? Look at the faces of those Romeos and Juliets!' And he roared with laughter.

He laughed, too, when Yvette suggested that he hid himself in brothels to escape his creditors. Not at all, he lived there simply because he liked it; there was no other reason at all! He liked to see 'prostitution palpitating.' No one guessed what beauty there was in ugliness, always and everywhere; but he could see it and went in search of it. He was the friend and confidant of the 'poor creatures who were the servants of love;' he knew their 'sentimental sufferings.' They would have been worthy of the brush of a Benozzo Gozzoli because they were so beautiful.

Quivering with emotion he went back to his paper, covering it with strong, nervous lines.

*   *   *

The *Yvette Guilbert* album was published by André Marty at the end of August. It had sixteen plates.

The singer's first reaction was favourable. 'I'm delighted, absolutely delighted! And, believe me, I'm most grateful to you.' But, as had already happened over the poster, Yvette Guilbert's friends cooled her enthusiasm. Her mother went so far as to suggest she should bring an action against Lautrec 'for defamation.' The writer, Jean Lorrain, a made-up, scented and be-ringed sybarite, who had helped her at the start of her career and hated Lautrec, threatened never to see her again because she had 'agreed to be drawn by that little man who,' he said, 'has reproduced you in goose droppings' (the plates had been printed in green). Nevertheless, Yvette Guilbert signed the hundred copies of the edition.

The praise with which the press greeted the book (one of these articles was by Clemenceau in *La Justice*) completely reconciled her to her harsh portraitist. She invited him, together with Geffroy, to her Vaux estate, near Meulan. All three of them went for a boating party on the Seine. While the two men rowed in top hats, Yvette handled the rudder lines. 'I had the luck to be guided by a star,' said Lautrec.

A little while later, when Arsène Alexandre had founded *Le Rire*, Lautrec published in it a new drawing of Yvette Guilbert (singing *Linger Longer Loo*). 'The singer,' said the newspaper, 'was on the eve of her departure for London. But, knowing that Toulouse-Lautrec had been commissioned to draw a portrait of her for *Le Rire*, she

[OPPOSITE] Lautrec aged thirty-two

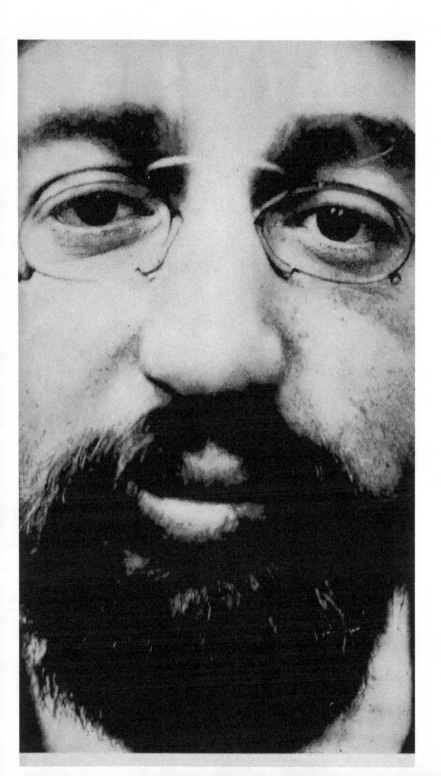

The brothel in the Rue d'Amboise (c. 1893)

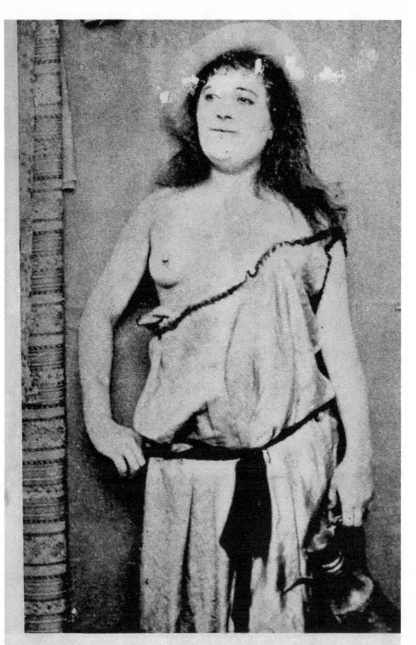

'Mireille', Lautrec's favourite model among the girls of the Rue d'Amboise (*c.* 1893)

(*above*) Lautrec and a
model in his studio at
rue Caulaincourt (1895)

Lautrec and Model in the
studio of Maxime
Dethomas

Lautrec at Malromé
(*c.* 1896)

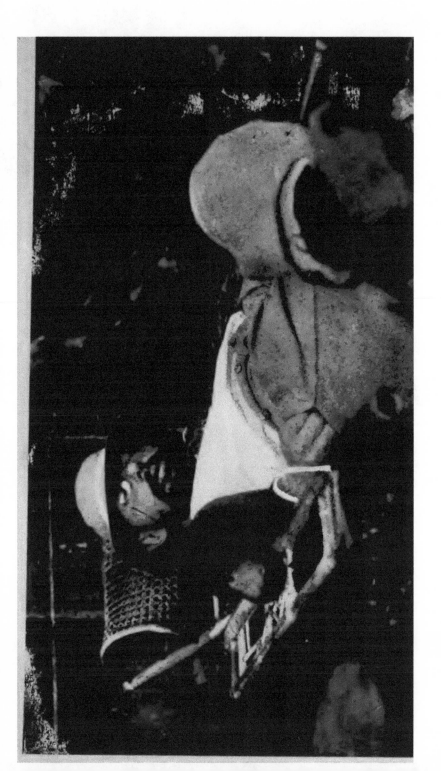

Lautrec swimming in the Bas:

l'Arcachon from the yacht *Le Cocorico*

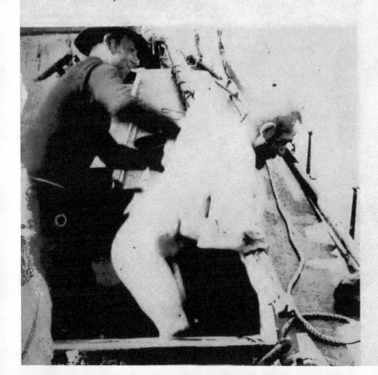

not only agreed, but insisted on giving him a sitting and singing this charming song for him alone.'*

* The following details are given by J. Adhémar: 'A special pull in black was offered as a prize by the paper, on February 16, 1895, to the winner of a competition. M. Guibaud, the winner, does not seem to have collected it.' Besides lithographs, posters and drawings, there are about forty-five paintings by Lautrec for 1894 (about thirty of which were inspired by brothels).

[OPPOSITE] Lautrec and Paul Guibert (c. 1892)

CHAPTER TWO

The Passenger from No. 54

Il y a une heure bête
Où il faut dormir.
Il y a aussi la fête
Où il faut jouir.
CHARLES CROS

DURING the last few months of 1894, the anarchists had been more active. Explosions had shaken France, and one bomb, for which Vaillant was responsible, had burst in the Palais Bourbon itself. The anarchists had replied to the guillotining of Vaillant by setting off bombs in the Hôtel Terminus, in the church of the Madeleine and in the Restaurant Foyot where the Senators ate. And Caserio had assassinated President Carnot at Lyons because he had refused to reprieve these three associates.

Paris was living in terror of bombs. Police precautions became daily more stringent and when one day a telegram from Count Alphonse was delivered to the concierge of the Cité du Retiro: SAVE THE GRAND DUKE! the Préfecture were mobilised and the police brought into action. It transpired, however that this was no aristocrat in danger, but a great eagle-owl Count Alphonse had forgotten to remove from his Paris flat when leaving for Albi.

The police during the general alarm had arrested and interrogated a large number of suspects. In the spring, twenty-five of them, including a number of intellectuals who had naïvely taken sides with the ruffians, were prosecuted on the grounds of being 'an association of male-factors.' Among the accused was a civil servant from the Ministry of War, who was also well-known as founder of *La Revue Indépendante* and author of a pamphlet on the Impressionists. His name was Félix Fénéon.

Thadée Natanson, who was a barrister at the Paris bar, successfully undertook his defence, and when the case came to an end on August

12, Fénéon was released. Since he had been dismissed from the Ministry, the Natansons gave him a job as assistant editor of *La Revue blanche*.

Fénéon at once attracted Lautrec's interest. He was a curiously reserved man some three years older than the painter, who was now thirty. Tall, with a thin face and a sparse, curly beard, he was inclined to dress rather eccentrically in red gloves and a cape with huge checks. He spoke in slow, carefully modulated phrases: 'What view do you take of your health? Is it satisfactory? Would some refreshment among lights and leisurely talk be agreeable to you? We offer you our company, if it would not be displeasing to you.'

During the trial, Fénéon's replies to the President of the Court had created a sensation. With a completely impassive face, he had answered the questions with such charm and courtesy that it was difficult not to excuse him for any possible insolence that might be implied.*

Careful to keep in the background, discreet almost to the point of mania ('I only like working indirectly'), preferring to advise and encourage others rather than write himself, Fénéon was devoted to the arts, and possessed a profound and unusually informed under-standing of painting. He not only attracted Lautrec by his unusual personality, but also by the knowledge he had of his art.

In January, 1895, the Théâtre de l'Oeuvre staged a play by Victor Barrucand, *Le Chariot de terre cuite*. Lautrec, together with another artist, Valtat, painted the décor.† He also designed the programme in which he portrayed Fénéon riding on an elephant. He gave the critic

* 'Detonators have been found in your desk; where did they come from?' 'My father picked them up in the street.' 'How do you explain the fact that detonators can be found in the street?' 'The magistrate asked me why I didn't throw them out of the window instead of taking them to the Ministry. You can see how detonators might be found in the street.' 'Your father wouldn't have kept such things. He was employed by the Bank of France and clearly had no use for them.' 'Indeed, I don't think he had any use for them, no more than his son, who was employed at the Ministry of War . . .' 'You said that you did not think that the detonators were explosives. But M. Giraud has made experiments establishing the fact that they are dangerous.' 'That proves I was wrong.' 'You know that mercury can be used to make a dangerous explosive, fulminate of mercury?' 'It is also used for making barometers.' ·

† 'The programme announced a décor by Toulouse-Lautrec,' wrote Jean Lorrain, 'I preferred to go away.'

the features of the Buddha, a comparison he often liked to make. It was not his best lithograph. And to this may well be due the fact that Fénéon advised Lautrec to devote less of his time to lithography and more to painting.

But Fénéon was wrong if he thought Lautrec would follow anyone's advice.

At the end of 1894, Lautrec had made friends with another writer on the *Revue blanche*, Jules Renard, the author of *Poil de Carotte*. The two men were bound to get on well. They were both the same age and had much in common. Renard's searching glance, which 'seemed to undress your soul,'* was that of a man perpetually on the look out for the slightest hint of insincerity and he recorded his thoughts and reactions in his *Journal* with acid lucidity.

'A little blacksmith in spectacles,' he wrote of Lautrec after their first meeting in November. 'His smallness is painful at first, but then he becomes very lively and pleasant, producing grunts between his phrases that raise his lips as the wind does those bags for keeping out draughts at a door.' Lautrec's charm soon had the same effect on Renard as it had on Yvette Guilbert and Fénéon. 'The more one sees of him,' said Renard a little later, 'the taller he grows. In the end he assumes a stature above the average.'

But the similarities between Lautrec and Renard were more superficial than profound. Renard suffered from lack of recognition and worried about the limited sales of his works. His anxieties were the day-to-day frustrations of a writer and bore little relation to Lautrec's personal tragedy. But there was one bond between them: their common liking for animals. Renard was writing a book about his observations of animals, his *Histoires naturelles*. Lautrec thought he might illustrate it, and made the suggestion to Renard.

Like his friend Maurin, Lautrec often went to the zoo. He never grew tired of watching the antics of the monkeys—'ludicrous and lubricious'—the parrots and penguins—'They walk like me! Marvellous! Eh! What?'

But the project of the *Histoires naturelles* was shelved for the time being.

* Jean-Jacques Bernard.

In the meantime Lautrec was seen more and more in the company of writers. In the late afternoon, accompanied by Tapié, he would go to the cafés in the neighbourhood of the Opéra or the Madeleine, to the Cosmopolitan in the Rue Scribe, to Weber's or to the Irish and American Bar in the Rue Royale.

Weber's, at that time, was patronised by writers, painters, musicians and explorers who liked to meet there for an apéritif. Lautrec was always delighted at the sight of the big room crowded with distinguished people sitting at little mahogany-coloured tables, among which Charles, the waiter, glided so agilely and attentively.

Polaire, who smiled 'as if she had drunk the juice of an unripe lemon,'* would be there with the monacled poet Moréas; Debussy, smoking thin, Turkish cigarettes; Forain, whose laugh would roll like thunder and dominate the hubbub of conversation; and also Willy, Georges Feydeau, Jean de Tinan, Caran d'Ache, Paul Souday and Léon Daudet.

Joyant, Ibels, Maxime Dethomas and Paul Leclercq, another friend from *La Revue blanche*, would often join Lautrec at his table where, over a glass of port, he would draw, eat gruyère fondue, play poker-dice for the drinks (a special privilege, for gambling, like smoking a pipe, was forbidden at Weber's), and make outrageous observations. 'You have a pretty wit, Monsieur de Toulouse-Lautrec,' someone remarked one day. 'Monsieur,' Lautrec replied, his eyes sparkling, 'my family has done nothing for centuries. Without wit, I'd be an utter fool.'

But there were too many social-climbers at Weber's, people who came there simply to be seen ('and to write about it afterwards,' said the painter sarcastically), and Lautrec much preferred the Irish and American Bar, which had opened close by. He treated it as his own particular fief and, should an unfortunate customer walk in whose face he happened to dislike, Lautrec would irritably call Achille, the proprietor, and insist that the fellow be 'deliberately ill-served so that it would never occur to him to come back.'†

Lautrec liked the intimacy of the narrow bar, where the customers

* Colette.
† Paul Leclercq.

were herded along the wall at a single row of tables; the English bar counter with its gleaming, polished mahogany rail ('Admirable, eh? ... It's as fine as a Rembrandt!') behind which Ralph, who was half-Chinese and half-Redskin, prepared 'night-cups,' 'rainbow-cups' and an infinite variety of cocktails. The ordinary customers here were racing men: trainers, stable lads and jockeys, most of whom were English, and coachmen from the great houses (among whom was M. de Rothschild's corpulent Tom) waiting for their masters to finish dining in the neighbourhood. Presiding over them all was fat Achille, who addressed Lautrec as 'Monsieur le Vicomte Marquis' while serving him mint-juleps and Welsh rarebits (a word which he pronounced in his Vaudois accent as *raebit*).

And when Footit and Chocolat, clowns from the Nouveau-Cirque, arrived, Lautrec would make room for them beside him.

Apparently unwearied by the performance they had just given, Footit and Chocolat would often dance and sing 'to the sound of a banjo and a mandolin, played by an Englishwoman and her son, whose father had been a Texan mulatto.'* Chocolat was a Negro from Bilbao. In the circus ring, dressed in a red suit, he played the oaf, received resounding buffets, and could arouse roars of laughter simply by declaring: 'Chocolat, that's me!' But at Achille's, free of his role, the dunce revealed a man of subtlety and intelligence. Lautrec made endless drawings of the two clowns and published two lithographs of them in *Le Rire*.

At the beginning of 1895, Lautrec brought two new customers to the Irish and American Bar, the English dancer May Milton, who was the inseparable friend of Jane Avril, and the Irish singer May Belfort.

He had seen May Belfort when he had gone one evening to the Décadents in the Rue Fontaine. Dressed in a long, Kate Greenaway dress, and a child's bonnet tied under her chin with ribbons, she cuddled a cat and sang with a childish lisp:

> *I've got a little cat,*
> *I'm very fond of that ...*

* Joyant.

'I took her in hand,' Lautrec said.

This rather delicate-looking girl, 'with eyelids of a Chinese rose,' had strange tastes. Her chaste appearance, her 'celestial air,' were deceptive. She was intrigued by the repugnant and doted on toads, crabs, snakes and scorpions.

The equivocal charm of this curious 'child' had its effect on Lautrec. He lavished attentions on 'the orchid,' as he called her (Joyant called her 'the frog.') One day, in his studio, he kissed her; she fled disgusted. Lautrec smelt of garlic.

Though May Belfort refused to become his mistress, she at least agreed to sit for him. Lautrec painted five portraits of her, published several lithographs and, when she was engaged to sing at the Petit Casino, he designed a poster for her—in a splendid crimson which 'made a bright and triumphant splash of colour on the walls of Paris.'*

A third poster was commissioned by *La Revue blanche*, but this time Lautrec chose for his subject the 'radiant and sibylline Misia Natanson in a fur bolero, a muff, a veil and a huge hat crowned with green feathers.'

But the beautiful Misia protested that the painter had distorted her face. 'Lautrec, why do you always make women so ugly?' Misia asked. 'Because they are,' the painter replied.

Lautrec was becoming more irascible these days. His drinking, the nervous exhaustion due to his wildly prodigal way of life, his lack of sleep and relaxation, were beginning to affect his nerves and aggravate his peculiarities. He would switch from laughter to deep depression and exasperation. He would crush a person's fingers when he shook hands and perhaps insult him. His friends could pass over these incidents. But others, like the actress Réjane, of whom he said (her breath stank) 'That woman's like the Schlingothard tunnel,' never forgot their resentment. But he continued to think affectionately of his friends, of Forain, for instance: 'I'd like him to be hard up . . . I'd send him some money . . . But he would not have to know about it, or he'd tell me to go to hell.' But the way he spoke became more abrupt every day, betraying his irritation.

His conversation became elliptical and laced with expressions that

* Joyant.

were understood only by the initiated; the others were clearly not worthy of 'ramereaux aux olives';* and so much the worse for those who complained, for the 'ouax rababaou' (Lautrec was imitating the furious yapping of a small dog), for 'you mustn't give jam to a policeman.'

Lautrec was soaked in alcohol and in a continual state of intoxication. As Thadée Natanson remarked, the hairs of his moustache had little time to dry. Yet although he was rarely drunk in the full sense of the word, it was said that even the smell of a cocktail could suffice to restore him to the 'magic enchantment of alcohol.'†

There was, however, one day, and only one, on which Lautrec drank sparingly. In February, Alexandre Natanson gave a great party in his house at 60, Avenue du Bois-de-Boulogne to celebrate the completion of ten fresco panels by Vuillard. Lautrec undertook the organisation of the party. He designed a lithograph for the invitation on which was written boldly in English: 'American and other drinks.' He then had several rooms emptied of their furniture, replaced it with chairs and stools, set up a bar, removed the pictures from the walls and put up advertisements for liqueurs and apéritifs.

When Natanson's guests arrived—and there were three hundred of them—they were not a little surprised to see Lautrec fulfilling the functions of a barman. For the occasion, he had the top of his head shaved and his beard trimmed into two little tufts and under his short white jacket he was wearing a waistcoat made from the Stars and Stripes

---

* 'Ramereaux aux olives' (pigeons with olives) was one of Lautrec's favourite dishes; he had taken great trouble about the recipe, which he had acquired from a pastry-cook in the Rue de Bourgogne, and gave it only to his favourite guests. Here, as a curiosity, is the painter's recipe (Maurice Joyant quoted it, together with a few others, in his work on gastronomy, *La Cuisine de M. Momo, célibataire*):

'Take young pigeons, draw them and stuff them with beef, veal and sausage meat, spiced with aromatic pepper, nutmeg and sliced truffles. String them and fry them lightly in a stewpan, then put butter, bacon, shallots, onions in a casserole and make a light sauce with flour; add salt, pepper, herbs, put in the pigeons, cover with good stock. Leave to simmer gently, with the casserole covered, for about an hour. During the last twenty minutes, add green, well-soaked, stoned olives and a glass of brandy. Let it braise well and reduce. Arrange the pigeons in a dish surrounded by the olives and covered with the strained sauce which should be thick.'

† Thadée Natanson.

of an American flag. His assistant was Maxime Dethomas, chosen from among his friends, not because he knew how to make cocktails, but because he was enormously tall: the contrast lent a touch of the absurd which delighted Lautrec. Dwarfed by the stature of his assistant, Lautrec looked like a grotesque puppet in his curious garb and, emphasised by his hairless cheeks, his lips seemed even more swollen and monstrous than usual.

He worked all night long behind his bar, which was laden with bottles, blocks of ice, lemons, plates of sandwiches, salted almonds, and chipped potatoes, sardonically inventing an endless variety of violently intoxicating mixtures. His intention was clearly to make the flower of letters and the arts drunk.

He succeeded only too well. Silent and unresting—he later asserted that he had served over two thousand drinks—he mixed his potions, watched for their effect, judging the moment when some dignified and self-important personage was tottering and one last murderous drink would finish him off.

Few escaped the ravages of barman Lautrec's cocktails who, to increase his victims' thirsts, had cooked salty sardines in a silver chafing dish with Hollands and port.

Many of the less wise were already being carried snoring to the beds and sofas in the neighbouring rooms (happily provided by the 'organiser'). One drunk, who had reached the stage where he had confidence in his own strength, offered to fight the athletic Alphonse Allais, who promptly knocked him down. Glass in hand, Fénéon was fearlessly stumbling in pursuit of Stéphane Mallarmé who, refusing to 'empty the disquieting goblet,'* was fleeing through the rooms. Vuillard's bald head was turning red. Sescau was playing his banjo and singing nostalgically: '*Une petite anguille, un beau matin d'été . . .*' Lugné-Poe stumbled into the walls, muttering in a cavernous voice: 'Let's go to work!'

* Francis Jourdain. He and Thadée Natanson give the best accounts of this party. 'The gaiety of everyone was authentic,' he wrote. 'I am not quite sure, however, that, when I went home in the dawn with "Gros n'arbre", I had not to overcome a sort of vague sadness. Perhaps I did not quite know what to call this orgy . . . "The Fontanges side?" . . . "the sniveldrop side?" . . . Lautrec had none of these melancholy uncertainties.'

The guests were falling like ninepins. Bonnard, normally so sober, dozed and muttered as if in a dream—a painter's dream—: 'I want a pink one.' The demand was immediately satisfied.

Behind his bar, delighted but silent—'Don't speak to the man at the wheel'—Lautrec continued his tireless shaking of cocktails, contemplating the field of massacre with a twinkle in his eye.

The Natansons' party was unlikely to be forgotten.

There were bodies lying all over the place: some snoring, some hiccoughing, some beating on the walls. The rooms stank like a tannery.

At dawn, discarding his barman's napkin, Lautrec left the Avenue du Bois and disappeared happily into the frosty morning. It had been a good night's work.

> *Ah! Je comprends que l'on jalouse*
> *En barman ton profil grec,*
> *Extraordinaire Toulouse-*
> *Lautrec!**

In his studio in the Rue Tourlaque, Lautrec continued to work on his big picture of the salon in the Rue des Moulins.

Artistically speaking, this was an epilogue. He had painted over fifty pictures of the world of prostitutes and he assembled in this one canvas the essence of his experience in the brothels.

Six women figure in this monumental work. One of them, in long wine-coloured draperies, her red hair falling in a little fringe across her forehead and temples, is perhaps the most penetrating study Lautrec ever painted.

This canvas was preceded by an unusually detailed study in pastel of the same dimensions;† evidence of the importance Lautrec attached to this work. From now on, he was only rarely to paint scenes of this nature: he had said what he had to say about prostitutes.

At this time there was a certain slowing down in his production compared to the exceptionally fruitful months which had just elapsed. While he had painted some fifty pictures in 1893, and some forty-five

---

* Verses sent to the painter by Romain Coolus the day after the party.
† They are both almost exactly 47 ins. × 52 ins.

in 1894, there were no more than thirty-five in 1895. Nevertheless, he was still working intensively. He illustrated new songs by Dihau, stories by Coolus, a menu for Sescau (in which, between the 'roast lamb' and the 'vegetables,' appeared 'foies gras de l'oïe Fullerr'), designed a lithograph for the cover of a play by Tristan Bernard, *Les Pieds nickelés*, and another for the final album of *L'Estampe originale*, which was once more a portrait of Misia Natanson.

Lautrec's dexterity was remarkable. His touch was so sure that he could draw directly on to a lithographic stone without a preliminary sketch. He was now preparing a series of thirteen lithographs, portraits of actors and actresses, for publication in May. A series, it must be admitted, that was less happy than his previous attempts in this genre; he so distorted the features of his subjects that it is not easy to determine their identity.

However, it is difficult to suppose that he was showing signs of creative exhaustion. On the contrary, he was finding time to experiment with new techniques. In the workshop of Muller the potter, at Ivry, Lautrec supervised the making of a ceramic tea-tray as a surprise for Yvette Guilbert; before it went into the kiln he had ironically inscribed beneath her portrait Yvette's criticism of the drawing which had served him for model: 'Little monster! This is a horror!'

Such things naturally took up a great deal of Lautrec's painting time. But there was interference from a more pernicious quarter. His dipsomania was leading him to abandon his brushes more frequently. Alcohol not only upset his nervous equanimity, but it wasted hour after hour. The time spent in bars was paid for by masterpieces that would never leave his brush.

At this moment Lautrec developed a great passion for the actress Marcelle Lender, whose grace, distinction and dresses 'of an exquisite richness and taste,'* so highly praised by the gossip writers, had already attracted his attention; and he had drawn her performances in some of his lithographs. Since February, she had been playing at the Variétés, in *Chilpéric*, an operetta set in the period of the Merovingians. It was one of those comic operas which had been so much in fashion since Offenbach, and whose gaiety Lautrec enjoyed. Marcelle, playing the

* *Le Rire*, February 16, 1895.

part of Queen Galswinthe, danced a fandango and a bolero with admirable elegance during the course of the entertainment. Excited by her performance, Lautrec dragged Coolus off to the theatre twenty nights running, and sat each time in the same stall on the left of the front row, sketching ceaselessly.

When Romain Coolus, rather bored, asked Lautrec 'why he wanted to cram him night after night with these far from mysterious lyrics,' the painter replied that he attended the performances merely to see Lender's back. 'Look at it,' he said; 'you can rarely see anything so magnificent. Lender's back is sumptuous.'

Lautrec made lithograph after lithograph of her: *Lender dansant*, *Lender de dos*, *Lender de face*, *Lender saluant*, *Lender en buste*. When the German review *Pan* commissioned one from him, he was bold enough to design a *Marcelle Lender* in eight colours.

In his studio, Lautrec had begun work on a large canvas, *Marcelle Lender dans Chilpéric, dansant le boléro*, in which his note-taking at the theatre finally bore fruit.

Lender was accustomed to have supper after the performance in the Café Viel on the Boulevards. One night* Lautrec arrived there with Jules Renard and the proprietor of the *Matin*, Alfred Edwards, and sat down opposite his model. His manner embarrassed her. He paid her no compliments and his attitude was almost hostile. The theatre? The circus and the cafés-concerts were much more amusing. To the waiter who enquired what he wanted, Lautrec replied: 'A sour herring.' There were no sour herrings at the Viel! Very well, he would have some ham and a dish of gherkins. 'And tell the wine waiter to hurry up. I'm thirsty!' Lautrec devoured the gherkins and drank a bottle of burgundy, constantly raising his glass to his lips and emptying it at a gulp.

He joked and told dirty stories. He made no attempt to sketch Lender but looked at her so insistently that she was put out of countenance. He met her three times at supper and on each occasion behaved in the same way. From then on Lautrec was constantly hanging round the actress, who was intrigued but entirely failed to understand the reason for his persistence; she did not realise that all Lautrec was

* The memories of Marcelle Lender, quoted by Sylvain Bonmariage.

interested in 'was her gargoyle.' One day, he sent her a bunch of white roses and asked for a special meeting. He lunched with her, and later joined her in her dressing-room. He said no word about the painting on which he was engaged and was back in his stall in the front row during the performance, his sharp eyes fixed on his prey.

A few weeks later, the picture which was the result of this intensive and detailed investigation was finished.

Lautrec may have thought of making the actress a present of it. Unfortunately, Marcelle Lender, in common with most women (Jane Avril and Polaire were exceptions), did not think much of his art which, she felt, lacked the graces of gallantry.* Instead Lautrec offered his canvas to Paul Leclercq who, however, refused to deprive the painter of this masterly work.

*   *   *

If Coolus had awakened Lautrec's interest in the world of the theatre, Tristan Bernard revealed to him the world of cycling.

Editor of the *Journal des Vélocipédistes* and sporting director of the two Paris Vélodromes (the Vélodrome Buffalo at the Porte de Neuilly and the Vélodrome de la Seine at Levallois-Perret), Tristan Bernard was one of the most famous figures in French sporting circles.

With the invention of the pneumatic tyre a little before 1890, cycling had leapt into fashion. Every class of society had gone crazy about the bicycle. In the Bois, the Prince de Sagan and General de Galliffet (in full dress uniform) pedalled among the carriages. Nor were women less keen to practice the 'pretty sport.' Their skirts replaced by Zouave trousers—the 'third sex,' the newspapers called them— went riding through the suburbs and the countryside.† Advertisements such as the following appeared in the press: 'Lady cyclist, 45, desires marriage with gentleman owning a bicycle.'‡ The newspapers were

---

* 'That horrible man!' she once cried to a friend who was praising Lautrec's talent. Then she went on: 'He's very fond of me . . . But, as far as the portrait's concerned, you can have it.' (Reported by Albert Flament, in *Le Bal du Pré Catelan*).

† There were soon so many of them in Paris that the Prefect of Police forbade women to wear cycling trousers within the confines of the capital.

‡ Quoted by J. Adhémar.

regularly publishing articles on the 'little queen'; but they were not enough for the 'cyclo-maniacs,' whose passion brought specialised periodicals into existence, such as that edited by Tristan Bernard.

The first races had been held as early as the latter part of the Second Empire, and they were extremely popular. Clubmen and pretty women filled the seats of the vélodromes, where the races were held to the din of noisy orchestras.

Wearing knickerbockers and a bowler hat, Tristan Bernard presided over the meetings. He had little difficulty in persuading Lautrec to attend them. Lautrec was delighted with Bernard's knowledge of athletics and the turf, and the fact that he could recite without a single error or omission the family tree of any thoroughbred, whether on the flat or on the steeplechase course 'with the certainty,' said Paul Leclercq, 'of a professor of history detailing the genealogy of the Capets.'

Bernard introduced Lautrec to the great champions and their trainers and to the representatives of the firms whose machines were competing. Nearly every Sunday, the painter was to be seen among the officials on the lawns beside the tracks and, more often still, in the competitors' enclosure.

He took very little interest in the results of the races. What delighted him was the sight of physical activity.

Followed by Tapié, he wandered here and there, losing no detail of the spectacle and, from time to time, he would stop to point out some strapping young man: 'He's splendid!' he would say. Then, always ready to grasp the odd or the peculiar, he would exclaim: 'He looks like a sole, he's got both eyes the same side of his nose.'

In the competitors' enclosure, he showed the same enthusiasm and excitement as he did for the prowess of a dancer or an acrobat. Like these, the cyclists personified movement, physical vigour and bodily fitness: experiences Lautrec could only enjoy at secondhand.

Among those who attracted his particular attention were the gaunt cyclist Zimmerman, 'The American Flyer,' who, although he looked so clumsy when walking, seemed to burn up the track the moment he was in the saddle, and was the champion of the two thousand metres race; or Jimmy Michael, the little Welshman with the obstinate face, who lapped indefatigably at twenty-five miles an hour while chewing a toothpick.

Lautrec soon made lithographs of these two stars of the track: Zimmerman with his machine, and Michael standing beside Simpson, the bicycle manufacturer.

The painter made particular friends with the riders and staff of the Simpson 'stable,' among them the firm's French representative, Louis Bouglé, a man of considerable culture and breeding, and with the trainer, Warburton, who was nicknamed 'Choppy.'

Lautrec was never tired of praising 'Choppy' and talked of almost no one else. He advised all his friends to place themselves in the trainer's care. They could not fail to derive benefit from it. Could there be anything better for one's health than sport? It was a pity that he himself could not set the example. In his enthusiasm, he bought a rowing-machine and, determined to get fit (it did not, of course, occur to him to drink less or go to bed earlier), he spent many hours rowing in his studio, wearing a sailor's hat and a scarlet flannel shirt.*

He boasted a good deal of this physical training—no visitor to the studio was exempted from performing on the rowing-machine under Lautrec's critical eye—but the enthusiasm lasted, as one might suppose, only a very short time, and the machine soon joined the chaos of litter in the studio.

*   *   *

Having put on a great deal of weight, verging indeed on the obese, La Goulue had left the Moulin Rouge. A still-born child had hastened her decline.

Of the dancers of yesterday, there remained practically none but Grille d'Égout. Rayon d'Or had married a gold prospector from Alaska. La Macarona had fallen ill and been operated on by Péan. Nini Patte en l'Air had retired to establish in the Rue Frochot (under the respectable but assumed name of Madame Veuve Monnier), a school of dancing, which was giving a start to the new 'chahuteuses', such as

---

* 'A neighbour, who was unable to understand the peculiar and regular noise,' recorded Paul Leclercq, 'told various people in the district that Toulouse-Lautrec had acquired the curious eccentricity of kneading flour and baking his own bread'

Cigarette, La Tourterelle and Églantine. As for Valentin le Désossé, he was now only an old, superannuated entertainer, nostalgically frequenting the Moulin Rouge. He looked, said Jane Avril, like a 'worn-out Don Quixote.' He rarely danced: 'I come to a dance-hall as an amateur and a good bourgeois on Thursdays and Sundays. I have a private income, I am a property owner, and I keep my carriage. Mention the name of Valentin le Désossé in the École Militare district and my concierge and my coachman will reply: "Not known here!" I am M. Renaudin, a retired wine merchant from the Rue Coquillière and the agent for my brother, a suburban notary, and that's how it is! I let rooms to officers and return their greetings in the Bois when they pass in their phaetons . . . The girls of the Moulin can no longer dance! The best of them is perhaps Cha-U-Kao; but she's not up to my standard. There was only one dancer: La Goulue . . .'

La Goulue had made a lot of money at the height of her success. Oller had given her a contract for as much as three thousand seven hundred and fifty francs a week.* And she had not entirely wasted it. When she gave up quadrilles, she had set herself up with a fairground booth and, with five or six assistants, appeared in a gaudy oriental dress to perform stomach dances, which she euphemistically called 'the Dances of the Dancing-Girls' (but whose tendency, so a chronicler remarked, was 'clearly expressed'). Decorations of some kind, she thought, would help to attract customers to her show. She remembered Lautrec, and early in April she asked his help.

April 6, 1895

My dear Friend,

I shall come to see you on Monday, April 8, at two o'clock in the afternoon. My booth will be at Trône;† I've got a pitch on the left of the entrance; it's a very good place and I shall be very glad if you have the time to paint me something; perhaps you will let me know where I should buy the canvases, and I'll let you have them the same day.

La Goulue.

---

* About £600 a week today.
† The Trône Fair, on the Place de La Nation (formerly Place du Trône).

Lautrec had always wanted to undertake large-scale decorations. He could not expect to be given the walls of a public building as yet. But he had already decorated the Ancelin inn at Villiers-sur-Morin and, more recently, the salon in the Rue d'Amboise. A fairground booth? Well, why not? Besides, he would be delighted to oblige La Goulue, who had been so intimately linked with his life as a painter.

From the Trône Fair, La Goulue was going to move to Neuilly, where the annual fair opened in the Avenue on June 16—'La Fête à Neuneu'—where the 'prettiest hussies' and the 'most distinguished libertines' went to flirt, to shoot at little pink pigs and eat 'unspeakable sweets at ninepence a pound.'* Lautrec promised to deliver to La Goulue her décor in time for the fair: two huge canvases, approximately nine feet square, in which he would show her dancing at the Moulin Rouge with Valentin le Désossé, and today 'as a dancing girl,' kicking her legs up before a crowd of spectators, among whom would figure not only himself, but Tapié, Guibert, Sescau, Jane Avril and Fénéon.

He set to work, but was soon interrupted. Joyant was going to London to meet Whistler and Lautrec went with him for the trip.

Lautrec rarely missed an opportunity of going to England. He enjoyed every moment of his brief visits across the Channel, as well as the crossing in a paddle-steamer, especially if the sea was rough. He loved the streets of London and delighted in visits to the National Gallery and the British Museum. He was intrigued by the sad-faced drinkers in the pubs (which miraculously removed his desire to drink); in the piles of fish at Sweetings in Cheapside; in porterhouse steaks at the Criterion or the Horseshoe, which 'you eat like a cake';† in the basement of Liberty's 'where by electric light, young sales-girls show you fairy-like stuffs and tissues, which have made the fame of this house.'‡

Lautrec knew many people in London. His friend Charles Conder, who had left Paris the year before, now lived there and they wandered the streets together. Lautrec wanted to see everything (except the 'sights' listed in the guide books, of which he had a horror).

* *Fin de siècle* June 23, 1895 and June 25, 1896.
† ‡ Joyant

Conder belonged to that group of painters and writers who gravitated about Oscar Wilde. But 1895 was a tragic year for the poet they admired. Wilde had been arrested on April 5. The first trial had opened at the Old Bailey on the 26th, but the jury disagreed and Wilde was released on bail, pending a re-trial. One evening, Conder took Lautrec to call on the writer.

With 'a sort of horror,'* the painter observed the man who only yesterday had occupied one of the most distinguished positions in the literary world, but was now pilloried as a criminal and shortly to suffer imprisonment and exile. Nevertheless, he was still braving the deep-seated puritanism of the English and believed he would be acquitted.

Wilde refused to sit for Lautrec. But Lautrec was not going to let the opportunity pass. He was certainly indignant, indeed horrified, by the treatment meted out to Wilde. But he was not altogether in sympathy with him. For if anyone was Lautrec's complete antithesis, it was Oscar Wilde, the poet whom Whistler designated as 'the artist one must not be,' with his aestheticism, his studied attitudes and his paradoxes, affectations and languors. ('I am sad because half the world does not believe in God, and the other half does not believe in me.')

Though Wilde refused to sit for him, Lautrec charged his memory at that meeting. He was so impressed by Wilde's extraordinary personality that he forgot nothing: the flaccid cheeks, the sallow skin, the fair hair smoothed flat against the skull, the small contemptuous eyes sunk in the unhealthy fat of the lids above and the swollen bags beneath.

As soon as he got back to Paris, where the Wilde affair was making a considerable stir in artistic circles,† Lautrec published (in *La Revue blanche* on May 15) a pen drawing of the poet in the witness box. Then he painted a rapid portrait in oils which was brutally frank in its simplicity. And resuming his decorations for La Goulue's booth,

---

* Joyant.
† 'Wilde has been punished because he thought he was living in Renaissance Italy, or in Greece at the time of Socrates,' wrote Henri de Régnier in *La Revue blanche*.

Lautrec included Wilde among the spectators watching the dancing girls.

When the fair opened at Neuilly, La Goulue was able to appear on the stage in front of the painter's panels. They at once aroused a great deal of attention.

'The two panels are having a wild success!' exclaimed the critic of the *Fin de Siècle*, who called them 'extraordinary illuminations.' 'They are,' commented *La Vie parisienne*, 'gigantic jokes on the part of Toulouse-Lautrec, that immensely eccentric painter, who has amused himself by indulging in the popular art which is both sordid and vicious; it's a panorama of the chahut, a huge symbolic distortion of the popular dance-hall! It's an unbelievable design in shrieking colours, but it's very amusing, and with singular irony the artist has painted Oscar Wilde in the foreground! Oh, how good it is to see someone flouting the public!'

This decoration, a homage from the painter to the dancer, was in fact a farewell.

For one splendid and ephemeral moment La Goulue and Lautrec had been the essence of Montmartre, which was now living merely on the prestige it had acquired at the time of the wild quadrilles, the songs of Bruant and the showmanship of Salis.* But that moment was now past. 'No luck!' said an elegantly dressed man in front of La Goulue's booth. 'Yesterday, we saw a tiny expanse of her thigh!'

It was a derisory echo of the cry, 'Higher, La Goulue! Higher!' which had so excited the Moulin Rouge in the past.

> *Moulin-Rouge, Moulin-Rouge,*
> *Pour qui mouds-tu, Moulin-Rouge?*
> *Pour la mort ou pour l'amour?*

On the stage of her booth, La Goulue went through the routine of her 'Moorish' dances. It was almost ten years to the day since she had made her début in Montmartre. After the show the painter saluted her with his accustomed gesture, his 'little stick' raised in the air as if he were presenting arms. They never saw each other again.

---

* When Salis died in 1897, the Chat Noir had already been closed down for some months.

As for La Goulue, she fell on increasingly hard times. After 'a few weary appearances at the Jardin de Paris' as a dancing girl, she became a wrestler, and then a lion-tamer (she had become monstrous, 'fat enough,' wrote Jean Lorrain, 'to split open the tights she wore'); she bought two leopards, four old and anaemic lions, a hyaena and a melancholy bear. And these animals, though they were under-nourished, absorbed the rest of her savings. At a fair in Rouen, one of the beasts tore off a child's arm. When the last animal was either dead or sold, La Goulue was completely ruined.

Reduced to indigence, she returned to Montmartre where, in rags, she sold flowers, sweets and oranges at the doors of the night-clubs and of the Moulin Rouge. She drank. 'I'm a good girl,' she would mutter; 'it's life that's been bad, not me!'

In 1914, on the occasion of a great retrospective exhibition of Lautrec's work which he had organised, and in which were included the panels from the Neuilly booth, Joyant had the idea of inviting her. He thought she might make a come-back. 'But,' he wrote, 'faced with a huge, amorphous woman, a real pachyderm, who could hardly remember the painter, whom she called Toudouze, mixing him up with the man who made pretty portraits,' he had to abandon the idea of resurrecting her. 'There are pilgrimages which one must not make again after twenty years.'

In 1915, a fire destroyed part of the Moulin Rouge. From time to time, La Goulue would stop in front of the hoarding to gaze through the chinks at the ruins of the ancient temple of her fame. After the war, she appeared in fairs again.

Pierre Lazareff records that, in about 1925, he saw her in a booth decorated with a great sign: 'Here is the celebrated Goulue of the Moulin Rouge dance-hall.' 'A showman was trying to attract the crowd by telling them bits of the dancer's past history . . . It was a mockery. The curtain revealed a fat woman in worn finery, her flesh too abundant, her smile hideous . . . And this woman, whom even our curiosity could not distract from her vice, was drinking a litre of coarse red wine from the bottle as she sat in a corner of the booth on a deal packing-case. When she had finished the wine, and smacked her lips with satisfaction, she wiped her mouth with the back of her hand and spat on the ground, roaring with laughter . . . We tried to make her talk: "Those were good times, eh? You remember?" In a thick voice, chuckling between her words, she said: "Of course I remember, what do you think! What a lot of girls there were, and the fun and games, that was something!" It was impossible to get any more out of her; we tried, but it was no good.'

Later, La Goulue served for some time as a servant in a brothel before ending up, half rag-picker, half beggar, on a piece of waste land at Saint Ouen. She lived in a wretched caravan, with a dog called Rigolo, her one and ultimate consolation.

Of her old life, her only relic was a piece of lace, a vestige of one of those exciting petticoats, of which she had 'made a curtain which was grey with dust.' She fell ill and was taken to the Lariboisière Hospital in January 1929; there she died on the 30th, at about sixty years of age.

Before dying, she asked for the offices of a priest: 'Father, will God forgive me? I am La Goulue.'

That very year, the panels Lautrec had painted for her went to the Luxembourg.

They also have a history. In about 1900, La Goulue, who was hard up, sold them to a collector, Dr Viau.

In the Viau sale, in 1907, they were knocked down for 5,200 francs. They then passed from collection to collection, went to Scandinavia, and later returned to Paris. In 1926 they belonged to a dealer who, thinking it would be easier to find buyers for smaller pictures, had no hesitation in cutting them up into eight large pieces and many smaller ones. A number of art critics protested violently against this vandalism and they were finally restored to their original state. In 1929 they were bought by the Beaux-Arts for 400,000 francs. Transferred to the Louvre in 1947, they are now in the Jeu de Paume.

*   *   *

Lautrec did not linger in Paris. He could no longer stay still. Hardly had the fair at 'Neuneu' begun when he went off to the Channel coast. He needed a 'refit,' he said.

Wearing a flat cap with the jacket and brass buttons of a captain of the Merchant Marine, he hobbled about the harbour of Granville or the streets of Dinard, protected from insult by the faithful Dethomas; or he would swim. On the beach, wearing a sailor's striped jersey, he adopted comical attitudes ('I'm being a lion') for Maurice Guibert to photograph. Sometimes, in his studio in the Rue Tourlaque, he would dig a mask out of his mass of belongings and put it on: 'Do you think it's all right, suits me? . . . Doesn't make me any uglier? . . . Merely changes me!' Poor Lautrec.

He was due to go into the south-west this summer, and, with his passion for the sea, decided, rather than cross France by train, to sail from Le Havre in a Worms steamship on the Dakar Line and go round the coast to Bordeaux. Guibert accompanied him on the voyage.

He embarked in the *Chili*. There were very few passengers on board. Lautrec at once decided to take things in hand. Before leaving, he had bought cases of good wines, port and olive oil. The voyage turned into a gastronomic cruise. He soon made himself at home in the galley and insisted that the ship should call in at the Breton fishing ports, so that he might buy fresh fish and lobsters. Lautrec provided the crew with sumptuous meals, 'bourrides bordelaises' and 'homards à l'armoricaine.' Cutting up his lobsters, shallots and herbs, thickening sauces, seasoning, spicing, adding tomato sauce, flavouring his dishes with brandy or white wine, he was kept very busy.

The voyage seemed all too short. On arrival at Bordeaux, Lautrec noticed for the first time a woman passenger. So absorbed had he been in his cooking, he had paid little attention to anything else. He took one look at her and was enraptured.

Lying gracefully in a deck chair, a little straw boater tilted over her forehead, she was gazing into the distance as if lost in a dream. She seemed to him exquisitely charming and attractive. Her fair hair was pulled back into a silky bun. Her delicate profile stood out against the shadow cast by an awning. Who could the radiant creature be?

'The passenger from No. 54'* was the wife of a colonial civil servant and on her way out to join her husband in Sénégal.

Lautrec was perfectly aware that there was no chance whatever of this beautiful girl responding to his advances. But that did not

* This would seem to be the number of her cabin.

matter. He would cancel his plans and continue the voyage with her, abandon himself to the delicious dream of believing that the impossible was possible.

Guibert, though used to Lautrec's sudden impulses, did not for a moment believe he intended to put such a scheme into practice—until the *Chili* actually raised anchor and sailed from Bordeaux. They were embarked for Lisbon. For once, Guibert protested. This time Lautrec had gone too far. He was determined to put a stop to the escapade as soon as he could, which would be in Portugal.

Meanwhile, completely indifferent to Guibert's recriminations, Lautrec was on deck, sketching the 'passenger from No. 54.'

He drew this dream figure, this image of the 'sweetness of life,' with a gentle hand.

*   *   *

When they reached Lisbon, Lautrec pointed out to Guibert the pleasures of elephant shooting, and assured him that 'the danger of being eaten by cannibals was an indispensable stimulus to the delights of an expedition.'* Guibert resolutely refused to give way: he had no wish to go to Dakar, and he would not go. Guibert prevailed and they disembarked at Lisbon, but not before Lautrec had arranged that the captain should send a cable to Paris from Sénégal announcing their safe arrival in Africa.

From Lisbon, Lautrec and Guibert went to Madrid. The painter visited the Prado and was lost in wonder at the Velasquez and the Goyas. But, deprived of his romantic dream, he strayed into the streets of the prostitutes, the Calle del Gato and the Calle de las Infantas, which were lined with whitewashed houses and dazzling in the July sun. Hands beckoned from behind the vermilion, yellow or orange blinds. Black heads of hair decorated with blood-red flowers called from the windows, "Caballero! Caballero!" On the walls of the salons were pictures of toreros.

Then, suddenly, Lautrec grew tired and bored. These streets were too filthy. There was too much soliciting of custom; even the police were pimps. The dirt, the servility, the crude venality disgusted him. He fled from Madrid, having taken an insurmountable dislike to the

* Schaub-Koch.

painted Carmens, their flamboyant ornaments and the carnations they wore in their hair. Having gone on to Toledo, where El Greco's *Burial of the Conde d'Orgaz* afforded him one last excitement, he took the Bordeaux train with Guibert.*

In the Rue de Pessac in Bordeaux, he returned to French brothels with undisguised pleasure. He made pen and ink drawings of the women and amused himself with a number of pornographic sketches, for which Guibert was the principal model.

Lautrec finished this peripatetic summer at Taussat and Malromé. He drew and painted a little, but spent most of the time resting.

At Malromé, at the summer's end, he would sit in a big basket chair dreaming through the warm, peaceful evenings. More than likely his thoughts were of the women of the Rue de Pessac and the Rue des Moulins, of the prostitutes of Madrid, of the hubbub of mechanical pianos or the noise of castanets, and of the 'passenger from No. 54'; of the women he had desired and never obtained, and of the love of which he had known only a parody. But they were coming in from riding now and the horses were neighing in the park. He sat up, sipped his absinthe, and his eyes clouded.

Picking a frog off the grass, and putting it into his mouth, he let it jump from between his lips.

---

* On the authority of Joyant, this journey to Lisbon and Madrid has generally been dated 1896. But, on the one hand, the 'passenger from No. 54' inspired Lautrec to design a poster which was exhibited in February 1896 at the Libre Esthétique in Brussels; and, on the other, there is a drawing by Lautrec, dated August 1895, entitled: *Dans le train de Madrid à Bordeaux.*

CHAPTER THREE

Auto—da—Fé

We must overdrive ourselves so as to live quickly and die sooner.

JULES RENARD: *Journal*

ONE day in 1894, Count Alphonse alighted from a goods truck at Albi station. To the horror of his brother Charles, he was dressed only in bathing drawers. On his back was an osier basket containing a cormorant, above which, somewhat perilously balanced, was a cage containing a great eagle-owl. The weather was very hot, and Count Alphonse had removed his clothes during the journey and thrown them on to the line. They were too tight, he explained.

Since this memorable arrival, he had been living with his birds in the tower of the Hôtel du Bosc in Albi. The Templar, as he was called, amused the town with his eccentricities. His shirt tails flapping, an old felt hat on his head and espadrilles on his feet, he fished with his cormorant in the Tarn. He had taken a particular dislike to bridges and never used them now. He either swam across rivers or, if the weather was cold, used fords which he sometimes had to walk a long way to find.

His relations with his brother were somewhat distant and his food and that of his birds was hauled up in a basket to his window by a pulley: if he wanted to communicate with Charles, he did so through the post:

My dear Friend,

Our father and mother were unfortunate in their choice of a Christian name for you. They ought to have realised that some people would find it impossible to call you 'mon cher Charles' because the words sound disagreeable to the ear.

I am not, however, writing to you to deplore our parents' inadvertence, far from it, but to tell you that, though I can just understand

217

why your coachman mistakes that screw of yours for a horse, I find it quite intolerable that he should mistake a rat for a mouse. I gave him orders to supply me with mice for my eagle-owl, and he sends me nothing but rats. My eagle-owl is not a native of Thuringia, where his congeners eat anything; he first saw the day, or rather the night, in Périgord, a district where both man and beast are used to eating well. Please tell Léon to put mice in my basket from now on.

Your affectionate brother,

A.*

The eccentricities of his 'affectionate brother' were not much to Charles's taste. But his nephew's paintings were even more reprehensible. His daubs were offensive to both morality and religion.

One Sunday in 1895, Charles summoned a few friends to the courtyard of the Hôtel du Bosc as witnesses and then solemnly proceeded to burn eight of his nephew's canvases on a fire of vine twigs. 'This filth shall no longer dishonour my house,' he declared.

Lautrec, so it appears, accepted the auto-da-fé philosophically enough. He was amused that Uncle Charles should have thought it necessary to have witnesses: 'a pork butcher and a chair-mender,' he said.†

Was it indifference towards his own work? More likely a certain weariness. For he felt at times that painting had replaced nothing for him. What use was it? He said: 'It won't give me back my legs; I paint for lack of anything better . . .' Yet such disillusioned remarks were contradicted by his feverish activity, by his urgent need to record what his eyes saw and the joy that came from doing so. But the melancholy which engendered them was always present, like a

* Quoted by Franz Toussaint: *Sentiments distingués*.
† Marie Tapié de Céleyran contests in *Notre Oncle Lautrec* that these canvases were burnt. 'There are,' she writes, 'things too foolish to be recorded, and Lautrec hated fools.' I record the event as it is reported by Franz Toussaint (*op. cit.*). He was the son of Colonel Toussaint who, together with M. de Laportalière and Charles de Montazet, was one of the witnesses. Franz Toussaint mentions other names too. Though invited to be present, certain notables had refused, in particular Julien de Lagonde, editor of the *Nouvelliste*, and Gustave de Lapanouse. Lautrec's own comment was recorded by Paul Leclercq who, in his memoirs (*Autour de Toulouse-Lautrec*), also reports this affair. He says that Lautrec himself had told him about it and had made the above comment.

subterranean stream whose flowing can from time to time be heard. Some works of art are like monstrous parasitic growths that proliferate on their creator, living on what they take from him and giving nothing in return except the pride of having nourished them. What was the use?

What did a few canvases burnt at Albi matter? And what did the rebuff administered by MM. Detaille, Gérome and Vibert matter? These three were the judges of a competition organised that September by the Boussod et Valadon Gallery to select a poster for the American publication of Professor Sloane's *Histoire de Napoléon I*. Lautrec's entry was turned down. The painter then sent his sketch to Frédéric Masson, a specialist in Napoleonic studies. It was not well received. 'Violet was the stigma of decadence,' he said and those, like Lautrec, who dared to use it in their work 'were anarchists who ought to be shot.'* But what did all this matter? Lautrec was not the man to linger over a disappointment. His tragedy lay deeper.

He returned to work, pleasure and intoxication. He continued his round of Weber's, the Rue des Moulins, bars and brothels, cocktails and prostitutes. And during the winter he completed a big canvas: *Tristan Bernard au Vélodrome Buffalo* which, to some extent, did for bicycling what *Marcelle Lender dansant le boléro* had done for the theatre. Lautrec's experiences were now beginning to crystalise very quickly. He made lithographs of scenes at the Folies-Bergère and at the Palais de Glace, of Lender in *Le Fils de l'Arétin*, of his memories of London, of the singer Anna Held, of the double programme of Wilde's *Salomé* and Coolus' *Raphaël*, which the Théâtre de l'Oeuvre produced in February; and he designed a poster for a serial, *Le Tocsin*, for the *Dépêche de Toulouse*. He was also designing another poster for the Salon des Cent for the following April, in which he depicted 'the passenger from No. 54' in elegant and subtle colours. Then he went back to the prostitutes. At one time, on the suggestion of Joyant, he thought of illustrating Édmond de Goncourt's *La Fille Élisa* and he even made a few drawings and water-colour sketches in the margins of a copy. But, in the end, he preferred to dedicate an album of his own making to the women of the brothels.

* Recorded by Joyant.

This album was to consist of ten plates, under the simple title of
La Fille. However, Lautrec soon changed this title to one which summed
up his attitude towards the world of prostitution: *Elles*. In the vocabulary of the period, the word *'elles'* meant simply 'women' in general
and without distinctions. By choosing this title, Lautrec was stating that,
as far as he was concerned, there was no difference between prostitutes
and other women.*

In this series of lithographs he included Cha-U-Kao, the only
dancer remaining at the Moulin Rouge whom Valentin le Désossé
had praised for her talent. She appeared also in Oller's establishment,
the Nouveau-Cirque, as a woman clown. Lautrec had drawn her
once before, waltzing in the arms of another woman.† During these
months he made many more studies of her in her baggy trousers,
huge yellow ruff and high white wig, tied with yellow ribbon.

Lautrec's interest in Cha-U-Kao was linked with his increasing
attraction to Lesbians. 'Monsieur Henri' was not only a favourite in
the Rue des Moulins, but had become an assiduous frequenter of
La Souris, a bar in the Rue Bréda‡ near the Place Pigalle. There a
group of women, isolated by a common inclination, met and were
'quite at home.'§ The proprietress, Madame Palmyre, sat enthroned
behind her counter. She was a large woman, with a generous heart and
a harsh exterior, who had certain characteristics in common with her
little bulldog, Bouboule. Chéri-Bouboule was a remarkable dog.
He hated the whole tribe of women and, hideously jealous of his
mistress's favours, frequently bit the calves of the customers.

Men who sometimes strayed into this specialised bar did not linger
long. They were quickly put out of countenance by the 'little messieurs,'
with their too-smooth cheeks and 'their strictly masculine jackets and

---

* Jean Adhémar, who has noted this implication of Lautrec's title, remarks that
the painter's outlook was shared by some of his friends. From the *Mémoires d' un
Jeune Homme rangé* by Tristan Bernard, he quotes this significant sentence:
'Lying on the divan, Daniel watched a rather stout woman going to and fro in
the room, who, if it had not been for the extreme scantiness of her costume,
might have been taken for a diligent housewife, so quickly and surely did she
deal with jugs and buckets.'

† *Les deux Valseuses*.
‡ Today Rue Henri-Monnier.
§ Leclercq.

stiff collars.'* Lautrec, however, enjoyed the atmosphere. Women and love in any form fascinated him, wherever he encountered them.

Here at La Souris—'La Touris,' as he pronounced it—he mingled with his accustomed ease among these women, some of whom were strapping and manly types with short hair and high stocks, while others were languorously and exaggeratedly feminine and dressed in the brightest of colours. 'Wearing their vice like flowers in their hats.'†

Couples fondled, or quarrelled. Some played cards, some dice, and they all chattered. They all smoked too. The ashtrays overflowed with the lipstick-stained butts of Turkish cigarettes and even big cigars. To the odours of alcohol, musk, amber and patchouli were added the ether and morphine of the drug-addicts.

'Find me,' said Lautrec, 'a more foolish woman than she who is the woman of another.' Watching and drawing, he was in his element. And flattered by his attention, the customers of La Souris were happy to sit for him. They asked his advice and came to him with their differences. They welcomed him into their circle, and he became part of the establishment.

But frequenting La Souris did not entirely satisfy Lautrec's taste for perversion. From time to time he organised 'lascivious spectacles . . sapphic occasions.'‡ And on one occasion he took a Lesbian, nick-named Le Crapaud, from La Souris to a brothel in the Rue de Mirome-nil. There he threw her into the arms of the other women and, as 'a passionate spectator,'§ watched their gambols.

*   *   *

While Lautrec was temporarily diverting himself with these fancies, Joyant was preparing another big exhibition of his works for January 1896.

For the last two years, Joyant had been associated with a specialist in chromo-lithography named Michel Manzi, who also worked for Boussod et Valadon. Together they arranged Lautrec's exhibition in a little eighteenth century house shaded by acacias, belonging to the Gallery. It was at 9 Rue Forest.

* Leclercq.
† Warnod.
‡ § Schaub-Koch.

The exhibition was to bring together a representative selection of paintings, posters and lithographs. There were, however, no paintings of brothels displayed for the delectation of the ordinary visitor. To avoid unnecessary scandal and useless argument 'about subjects and themes,'* Lautrec refused to allow them to be shown to the general public. He insisted that they be hung apart in two little rooms on the first floor, their walls 'hung with strawberry and green velvet and their furniture covered in yellow.'† He pocketed the keys of these rooms, intending to permit only certain privileged people to enter them, people he thought worthy of *ramereaux aux olives*.

This secretiveness naturally attracted the curious to the Rue Forest. But Lautrec was inexorable. 'Nothing to sell,' he said to the excited dealers.

And he was undoubtedly right, for the exhibition, although lacking the more audacious works,‡ created a considerable stir, and aroused accusations of cynicism and obscenity: and to such an extent, that Gustave Geffroy published in *Le Journal* a long notice in defence of the painter he admired. 'Those who make the journey to the Rue Forest,' he wrote, 'will not regret their trouble, if they care for direct observation, brilliance of design and a harmony of light in rich and subtle colour.' Replying to accusations that had been made against the painter, he went so far as to defend the works Lautrec had reserved. Cynicism? Obscenity? 'I can record no such impression,' he declared. 'Concern for the truth is master here, stronger than all the curious meanings read into them by the beholder. Without the use of fantasy or nightmare, by a simple refusal to lie and a determination to state the whole truth, Lautrec has created terrifying works, projected a cruel light on to some of the hells of misery and vice that are sheltered behind the façade of our civilisation. Never were low cunning, passive stupidity, animality and also, which is even sadder still, the suggestion that so many of these women with ingenuous faces might have lived happy, regular, simple lives, never has all this been expressed with such clarity and with such quiet bitterness . . .'

The exhibition in the Rue Forest was decisive proof of the quality

* † Joyant.
‡ They are today mostly in the museum at Albi.

and importance of Lautrec's work. His paintings and drawings began to be in demand. Further evidence of this lay in the fact that forgeries were already in circulation (the year before the painter had had some fakes seized). Could a great collector, such as the banker Isaac de Camondo, avoid having at least one Lautrec in his collection? He hesitated. Ultimately, he decided to buy one of the portraits of Cha-U-Kao for 500 francs.*

Isaac de Camondo, a collector of greater ostentation than certainty of taste, was at home in the Rue Gluck every Sunday, when his guests had the opportunity to examine his innumerable works of art, his collections of Japanese prints and paintings by Manet, Monet and Degas. One Sunday, Lautrec went to the banker's house and was disgusted to find two splendid canvases by Manet hanging in a bathroom. 'The pig!' he exclaimed.

A pair of stockings was lying on the tiled floor. The painter picked them up, rolled them into a ball and sniffed them, his eyes closed.

'The pig!' he said. 'He uses the bidet in front of the *Lola* and the *Fifre* . . .'†

*   *   *

At the end of January, Lautrec left Paris again. With Guibert, who at one of the last exhibitions of the Indépendants (he painted in his spare time) had referred to himself as 'the pupil of God and Toulouse-Lautrec,' he went to Le Havre and embarked in the *Chili*. But this time the travellers journeyed no further than Bordeaux.

Lautrec spent a short time at Arcachon, and then went off to Brussels with Joyant to attend the private view of the Salon de la Libre Esthétique.

His contribution this year consisted of four posters, all of women, May Milton, May Belfort, Misia and the 'Passenger from No. 54,' and they attracted little attention.

---

* Approximately £80 today. This portrait went to the Louvre in 1914 with Camondo's gift. It is to be remembered, by way of comparison, that at the sale of Père Tanguy, in June, 1894, a painting by Van Gogh went for 30 francs and that at the celebrated Cézanne exhibition at Vollard's, which had been held at the end of 1895, a few weeks before Lautrec's, Cézanne's works were sold for between 10 and 700 francs.

† Recorded by Thadée Natanson. Lautrec's portrait of Cha-U-Kao was also, according to Joyant, relegated to a bathroom.

During his stay in Belgium, Henry Van de Velde, an ardent supporter of 'art nouveau,' invited Lautrec to lunch at his house, which he had recently finished building. The house, which was in the Brussels suburb of Uccle, was called the Bluemenwaf, and had been conceived entirely as a piece of decoration, and the emphasis on colour harmony had been carried almost to the point of eccentricity. It had been applied to everything and, indeed, to everyone including Madame Van de Velde, whose fairness was set off by a crushed-strawberry dress. Even gastronomy had been sacrificed to appearance and the dishes were designed to flatter the eye rather than the palate—yellow eggs on violet plates, red beans on green ones.

Lautrec was delighted. 'Incredible, eh!' he said to Joyant as they left, then added: 'But in the final analysis only the bathrooms, the lavatories and the nursery [which were painted glossy white] quite come off.'*

Nevertheless, on his return to Paris, Lautrec proceeded to make certain alterations to the Rue Tourlaque in the 'art nouveau' style. This style bore a certain relationship to his own researches into design and rhythm, and to the curvilinear element found in a number of his works. For the Japanese had influenced the theoreticians of 'art nouveau' as much as they had Lautrec.

Stuffs from Liberty, cane furniture and green garden tables gave his studio a new look. And to add to the décor, he painted some *Modèles au repos*. Rather unexpectedly he depicted all these women from the back, either sitting on the floor or lying on a sofa. They were works of tender and melancholy gravity.

By this, his thirty-first year, Lautrec's output had begun to follow a constant downward curve. In 1896, he painted only two dozen pictures: he had produced double that number three years before. Now he worked only by fits and starts, for he was more frequently under the influence of alcohol. Boast as he might: 'What? If I was drunk, no one would know it . . .' it was, unfortunately, becoming only too obvious.

* As M. G. Dortu, Madeleine Grillaert and Jean Adhémar have already pointed out in their work, *Toulouse-Lautrec en Belgique*, this visit to Van de Velde must have taken place, not in 1894 as Joyant stated, but in 1896: the Bluemenwaf was only finished in that year.

Lautrec and his mother at the Château de Malromé (1899)

Lautrec at Mont Saint-Michel

Lautrec on the train (*c.* 1897)

Lautrec with his mother at Malromé (1899)

Summer 1899. One of the last known photographs of Lautrec

His friends were alarmed and distressed and tried to restrain him. But he was difficult to control. The least criticism, the most friendly advice, infuriated him. The slightest thing could send him into a fury and he scarcely required a reason for it. No one could forecast what the reactions of 'this being of lightning and sun' would be to either people or events.

One Sunday in March, Joyant took Lautrec to Camondo's to meet the ex-King of Serbia, Milan, who wanted to buy a picture from him. From the moment they got inside the house it was evident a storm was brewing. Lautrec, on a sudden whim, thrust the footman aside and walked into the banker's reception rooms with his bowler hat still on his head and a scarf untidily round his neck. As soon as he found himself in the presence of the ex-King, Lautrec grew excitable and clearly intended to amuse himself at his expense. When Milan asked him if he were descended from the Counts of Toulouse who had so distinguished themselves during the early crusades, Lautrec replied impertinently: 'I should think so, sir. We took Jerusalem in 1100 and Constantinople afterwards,' and then, though he had never boasted of his family's age before, he attacked the fallen sovereign: 'After all, you're nothing but an Obrenovitch!' Milan quickly changed the subject. 'My son, King Alexander,' he said, 'is very interested in the arts, he's very fond of painting.' 'What sort of painting?' Lautrec interrupted. 'I bet it's good!'

Alarmed by the turn the conversation was taking, Camondo begged Joyant to try and prevent a scandal, and Joyant succeeded with some difficulty in interrupting Lautrec and dragging him away. He had 'suddenly become completely unmanageable' and, as soon as they were outside in the street, he repeated obstinately: 'Takovo! Obrenovitch! Karageorgevitch! At bottom, they're only swineherds! It's only yesterday that the whole lot of them weren't even wearing trousers but the fustanella!'*

* Recorded by Joyant. 'A little while later,' says Joyant, 'at an exhibition of Lautrec's works, King Milan bought, at a higher price than any paid before, *La Clownesse* which, after the days of massacre and pillage of the Konak of Belgrade, when King Alexander and the Queen of Serbia lost their lives, ended up in a celebrated collection in Switzerland.' This was one of the portraits of Cha-U-Kao (Oscar Reinhart collection, Winterthur).

H

His nerves raw, the painter continued to pursue his wild life. During this month of May, he quite suddenly became excited and interested by the world of the law. There were two celebrated cases taking place at this time; that of the financier, Arton, who was accused of having distributed among members of parliament a million and a half gold francs to suppress the Panama scandal, and that of various people accused of getting money by false pretences out of Max Lebaudy, the 'Petit Sucrier,' who was heir to a colossal fortune.

Lautrec was not much interested in the moral or political side of these cases. It was their human and perhaps their theatrical aspect which attracted him. As far as he was concerned the Courts of Justice were equivalent to the theatre. They afforded a spectacle and an opportunity to observe human behaviour: that, for instance of Arton, who appeared completely unruffled before the court, and whom Lautrec considered with admiration as 'a sort of artist, a man who had placed all his faculties of invention at the service of his crimes.'*

But this enthusiasm for the legal world was short-lived. After making a few drawings and lithographs Lautrec lost interest. He still went to the theatre, particularly to the Opéra; but even the theatre was losing its attraction for him. In a state of exhaustion, he would often fall asleep in his seat. One night, his head fell on his neighbour's shoulder. The neighbour shook him and Lautrec woke up murmuring politely by way of excuse: 'It's country-house life!' Lautrec turned his attention more to the auditorium and behind-the-scene activities than to the stage itself. He painted the stage-hands at the Opéra and made a lithograph of a box during a performance of *Faust*. He made use of the Opéra ball to paint Dethomas. It was a fine portrait and perfectly fulfilled his intentions: 'I shall paint you immobile in a place of pleasure,' he had said to his friend.

He still went to the Vélodromes, but the painting he had made of Tristan Bernard on the race-track of the Buffalo was to remain his one important work inspired by sport. However, Bouglé—known in the trade by his English nickname of Spoke—commissioned him to do a poster for the Simpson Company. To follow up this proposal, Lautrec, always ready to travel, went with the 'Englishman from

* Francis Jourdain.

Orléans' to London, where the company's racing-cyclists were to take part in some publicity events. On his return, he submitted the poster. Unfortunately Bouglé had to reject it: Lautrec, in his drawing of the racing-cyclist Michael, had put the pedals of his bicycle in the wrong place. The painter had hastily to design a second poster.*

Besides his work on lithographs, Lautrec was still devoting a good deal of time to posters. He made one for the American publication, *The Chap Book*, in which he depicted the Irish and American Bar; another for *La Vache enragée*, an illustrated magazine published by Willette, and another for an American ink manufacturer (*Au concert*), in which Tapié and Misia appeared. And, finally, *La Troupe de Mademoiselle Églantine*, a poster for Jane Avril and three other dancers, Églantine, Cléopâtre and Gazelle, who had been given an engagement by the Palace Theatre in London.

It seems probable that even poster designing was beginning to bore Lautrec. Thadée Natanson felt this one day when, catching sight of a spoiled proof on which had been printed only two large red spots and a smaller one, Lautrec had sarcastically declared that it was magnificent, and had insisted that Thadée should provide the large misprinted sheet with a handsome frame—which Thadée nobly did.

Thadée Natanson had bought an attractive country-house at Villeneuve-sur-Yonne, an old posting-inn to which the staff of the *Revue blanche* went for holidays during the summer. Lautrec was naturally invited to stay and he went there in the spring.

The Natansons did their best to limit Lautrec's drinking. All temptation was removed: there were no spirits in the house and wine only was served at meals. Curiously enough, Lautrec appeared to submit willingly to this régime. He relaxed, bathed happily in the Yonne and went on boating parties. On searching the attics of the old inn, he discovered a collection of ancient clothes and hats, and excitedly dressed up in them, frolicking about the lawns, his 'little stick' to the fore, imitating the buzzing of bees with pouted lips. With Cipa Godebski, Misia's half-brother, he jokingly discussed compiling a book of aphorisms, *Le Célibataire*, of which it was surprising that even a

* The sketch refused by the Simpson Company is called *Cycle Michaël*.

single line was written: 'One really regrets being a bachelor only in the country.' And he busied himself on a portrait of Cipa. The Natansons felt that they were on the way to curing Lautrec of his insatiable appetite for drink.

Unfortunately, there was a little door at the end of the garden. And from time to time Lautrec furtively disappeared through it on his way to a nearby inn.

*   *   *

The album, *Elles*, was published at the end of April.

Till now, Lautrec's lithographs had not been particularly sought after by collectors. Moreover, he had printed them only in small editions, ten, twenty-five, thirty, sometimes fifty, but rarely more. Kleinmann, who had published them fairly frequently during the last three years, had undoubtedly been courageous; and Gustave Pellet, the publisher of *Elles*, was no less so. The sale of the album would not be helped this time by the popularity of an Yvette Guilbert or by actors and singers of the cafés-concerts. *Elles* would have to make its own way, and in spite of its subject. In its conception and treatment, it was bound to be much less saleable than the genteel pornography thrown on the market by astute businessmen, such as the *Levers et Couchers des Parisiennes*.

Gustave Pellet had a liking for the arts. He came from a family that had lost all its money—his mother had invented the elastic corset— and this grumbling Savoyard, whom his friends had nicknamed 'Pain d'Épice' because of his yellow complexion, had set himself up at the age of thirty as a bookseller on the quays of the Seine, primarily to dispose of the collection of rare books he had formed as a young man. Then he had taken to publishing, and had found himself an office in an old stable at 9 Quai Voltaire. It was probably his friend Maurin who had advised him to publish the work of Lautrec.

The painter and his publisher exhibited the series of plates at the Salon des Cent, which had just opened at 31 Rue Bonaparte, and for which Lautrec had designed a poster reminiscent of the 'Passenger from No. 54.' Printed on paper watermarked with their names, the album was published in a limited edition of a hundred copies which Lautrec had signed and Pellet initialled and stamped.

It was a failure. In spite of eulogistic reviews and the curiosity it aroused—Maurice Barrès, looking through the album, made the comment: 'Lautrec ought to be subsidised by parents to inspire young people with a horror of illicit relations'—the collectors were not interested. In June, Ambroise Vollard, Cézanne's dealer, put the album on show with no better results. *Elles'* lack of success persisted and, ultimately, Pellet resigned himself to selling the plates separately, whenever he could persuade a customer to buy one.*

*   *   *

In July, Lautrec was at Taussat on the Bassin d'Arcachon. He had hired a villa and, from morning till night, he set about 'refitting' himself. He was in great need of it.

When he was not more or less naked, he wore a blue jersey and red woollen trousers, which he turned up to his knees. He went boating with fishermen or yachting with his friends. Sitting cross-legged at the helm and giving orders to the crew, he sailed 'in utter happiness' for whole days at a time.

He planned long voyages; to Japan for instance, of which he had always dreamed. But who would go with him when even Guibert had refused to go as far as Dakar?

At Taussat, Lautrec caused almost as much astonishment as did Count Alphonse at Albi. Shaking their heads, the good people of the district cast disapproving glances at the dwarf as he waddled along the beach with Tom, his cormorant, following along behind on a lead. Lautrec fished with Tom in the Bassin. He took him everywhere, even into the cafés, where he ordered absinthe for the bird. 'He's got a taste for it,' Lautrec said.

When he was not either in the sea or on it, he hunted praying-mantis among the dunes, and he sent pairs of them to Viande Crue (Lautrec's nickname for the sculptor Carabin). 'Look after them carefully,' he wrote. 'We'll organise fights between them in Paris. It'll be a triumph!'

---

* The portrait of Cha-U-Kao was to prove one of the most sought-after lithographs of this series and to be snapped up by collectors. Even today, it is one of the most frequently reproduced of all Lautrec's works.

In the evening, disguised as a Muezzin, he went to the highest window in his villa and called the faithful—Guibert and the friends who were on holiday with him—to prayer.

Guibert accompanied Lautrec to Bordeaux when the painter set off, as he said, 'to soak myself in the family'—the women in the Rue de Pessac. But the expeditions to Bordeaux were not entirely limited to visiting brothels. They went from bar to bar. One night, after a tour of the cabarets, Lautrec and a few of his friends landed up at the Café de Bordeaux, on the Place de la Comédie. It was about to close. This, Lautrec declared, was an excellent reason for finishing off the ends of the bottles; to mix together the remains of the brandy, rum, absinthe, vermouth, chartreuse and any other spirit that happened to be at hand. Lautrec himself took charge of the shakers, poured the mixture into large glasses and baptised it 'the earthquake.'

'I must admit,' noted one of the company subjected to this 'cocktail,'* 'that, after an evening during which one had already drunk a good deal, one was glad to get to bed after such a nightcap.'

Lautrec had not touched a paint-brush since he had arrived at Taussat. He was having a complete rest. Nevertheless, wishing 'to enclose his villa and isolate it from his neighbours,' he set to work painting screens to put round the house. It is more than likely that he gave his curious neighbours something to think about and that his designs were, to say the least, pornographic. However, according to Lautrec, his canvases 'looked very well out of doors.'†

The inhabitants of Taussat were less than pleased and Lautrec's neighbours certainly had to look the other way. His landlady took offence and complained to the authorities: 'The tenant in my house, at 207 Chalet de la Plage, has placed between himself and the passage which serves the tenants of the villas in front, a screen of rough canvas, daubed with designs which I won't bring myself to mention . . . It is not permissible for every tenant to erect anything he pleases in the locality . . . particularly when these screens are adorned with such unsuitable pictures that decent and respectable parents must shelter their children from them . . .'

* Achille Astre.
† These paintings have disappeared.

But Lautrec hardly concerned himself with their opinions.* On the other hand, he was very much hurt when, either by mistake or, more likely out of malice, his cormorant was killed. As Tom was walking in the sunshine outside the villa, someone shot him.

Lautrec remained about three months in the Bordelais and shortly before leaving he won a race in the Arcachon regatta, sailing a friend's yacht.

* * *

Lautrec returned to Paris and his winter quarters in the Autumn to discover that a widespread movement, a 'League for the Moralising of the Masses' by 'beautiful and pure' posters, had been founded. There were to be no more posters displaying 'scanty clothing.' Something more edifying was required: Saint Geneviève keeping an eye on the innocence of little girls, for instance. Lautrec jeered at these projects, which people were ingenuous enough to think he might assist. They could hardly expect from him such 'moral posters' as those at which *Le Rire*, and other publications, were jibing, of which one illustrated the paternal advice: 'Young people, don't go home too late.'

Lautrec mockingly attended some of the League's meetings, and politely invited the 'preaching friars' to a big dinner at which there were quantities of food, drink, flowers and women. And when these 'lay sacristans,' these 'prophets in feathered hats,' who wanted 'to bring art within the reach of cabmen,' were well and truly drunk, he wished them good night with 'sadistic'† pleasure and made his way to the Rue des Moulins.

He now drank so much during the course of a night that he often became completely incapable, and Dethomas or Coolus, who never left him these days, would have to take him home.

But drinking seemed to have little effect on Lautrec's vitality and, apart from taking up a good deal of his time, it in no way diminished his talent. In his better moments, Lautrec was the same as ever, full of good humour and wit. One night at Weber's, hearing two regular customers boasting how fast they could run, he cried 'Let's have a

---

* There is no information as to how the dispute ended.
† The word is Joyant's.

competition!' and organised a race up the Champs-Élysées from the Obelisk in the Place de la Concorde to the Arc de Triomphe. 'Uttering bird-like cries,'* he followed the competitors with Tapié and a few others in an open cab.

But at his worst moments, no one could do anything with him. Purple with anger, he would scream insults and furiously shake his stick. And he was far from beautiful in his anger. Nevertheless, his friends preferred his anger to seeing him, as they so frequently did, overcome with drink and exhaustion, collapsed on a café bench, snoring, drooling and hideous. Francis Jourdain saw him in this state one night at La Souris, among a crowd of women dressed in men's clothes. 'It was a distressing sight. Saliva trickled down the thin cord of his pince-nez and fell drop by drop on to his waistcoat.'

And yet Lautrec could be up and about at dawn the next morning. While his friends were still sleeping, he would already be at work, either at Stern's, the new printer of his lithographs, or in the Rue des Moulins, drawing the sleeping girls with a winged hand.

His work finished, he would go to see Joyant and radiantly show him what he had done: 'A masterly drawing, Monsieur, captured at dawn!'

*   *   *

In December, he made several lithographs for menus, one of which, *Le Menu du Crocodile*, records a brief visit to the châteaux of the Loire, which he made together with Joyant, Tapié, Guibert and two or three other friends during the festival of All Saints.

They went to Blois, Amboise and Chambord. During this excursion Lautrec and Joyant hoisted themselves up to the top of one of the towers of the Château d'Amboise. As they gazed out over the wide, peaceful landscape of the Loire valley and the bronze-coloured river beneath the cloudy sky, Joyant committed 'the imprudence' of telling Lautrec that 'landscape counted for something in painting after all,' that a Monet would be tempted by these velvety greys, yellows and soft blues. But Lautrec's old rancour against nature—the nature which had 'betrayed' him—at once flowed out in imprecations against the painters who served it. 'Only the figure exists!' he replied in sudden

* Leclercq.

exasperation. Landscape? It should be no more than an accessory. Pure landscape painters? They were nothing but coarse brutes! Corot, Millet, Manet, Renoir and Whistler were great only because of their figure painting. 'By abandoning the figure, Monet showed he was capable of anything!'

In his lithograph, the *Crocodile*, Lautrec took for his theme the story of Marie de Medici's escape from Blois, when imprisoned there by her son Louis XIII. Guibert, wearing a nightshirt and holding a candle, is seen carrying off the naked Queen under the eyes of Tapié, in the guise of 'a Hokusai monster,' while Joyant is a crocodile and Lautrec a frog-like draughtsman.

He was also working on other lithographs of his friends. While Dethomas, 'Lautrec's faithful companion on his journeys into brothel-country,'* had figured the previous June in a somewhat curious posture in one of his friend's works called *Débauche*, Tapié now figured as a motorist in cap, goggles and goatskins, a representative of those eccentrics who had recently appeared in the streets driving noisy, infernal machines. How stoic Tapié was! His tyrannical cousin had insisted that he 'have a frockcoat tailored from a billiard cloth.'† And Tapié did so.

Still preoccupied with his studies of theatre audiences, in January, 1897, Lautrec had sent Pellet, 'the intrepid publisher,' as he called him, one of his best lithographs, *La Grande Loge*, of which he had previously made a painting. Two women and a man are listening to a play. The man wearing a top-hat, sprawling, puffy-faced and apathetic, is Rothschild's coachman, Tom; of the two women, one probably came from the Rue des Moulins, the other, looking very dignified, is Mme Brazier—Mme Armande to her friends.

Mme Armande had recently bought a bar, Le Hanneton, at 75 Rue Pigalle. Under her management it was beginning to compete with La Souris.

Mme Armande was a one-eyed ex-prostitute, who had at last done with men. She reigned at her counter, straight-backed and glum; and when her women customers entered the establishment, they went

---

* Claude Roger-Marx.
† Thadée Natanson.

to embrace her and receive a kiss of welcome before sitting down. Lautrec was one of the very few representatives of the enemy sex to frequent Le Hanneton. And Armande la Borgne, whom Lautrec had nicknamed La Gambetta in memory of the one-eyed politician, treated him with maternal affection. He painted her as Juno and also in 'her hideous nudity.'*

Nevertheless, Lautrec still preferred La Souris and in the spring he went to live there. 'Listen . . . to see them make love, what? The technique of tenderness . . .' Perhaps, as Thadée Natanson said, these women attracted him because they 'love each other more deeply than men can love them'—and as no one had ever loved Lautrec.

At this time, he made a lithograph which referred to the scandal of the hour, the adulterous love of the Princess de Caraman-Chimay and a gipsy. He placed the two lovers side by side, 'a delicious bird, a marvel of the aristocratic way of life,' and the 'olive-skinned, almost negroid, sad, appalling Rigo, who looked like Theodora's circus charioteer.'† He called this coloured plate, which was published by Pellet, *Idylle princière*.

Lautrec also painted a few portraits. But his work did not always please his sitters. Henri Nocq, the engraver, considered his portrait 'spiteful in the extreme.' As for that of M. de Lauradour, Joyant saw in it merely the portrait of a top-hat, a beard and a briar pipe. True, Lautrec had painted M. de Lauradour because he had a splendid red beard and wore his top-hat like no one else, but also because of an encounter which had delighted Lautrec, and which had proved M. de Lauradour to be 'even more insulting than Bruant.' As Lautrec and M. de Lauradour were crossing the Pont Caulaincourt one afternoon, they met Bruant, who asked the painter who was 'the pipe-smoking fellow who stank of Eau de Javel'. M. de Lauradour went for him as no one, in the whole of Bruant's career, had ever attacked him, and with a splendour of resounding epithet. Lautrec was delighted at the spectacle of this splendid beard pouring the insults of a fishwife over the disconcerted Bruant.

Lautrec's production continued to decrease. He made only fifteen

* Schaub-Koch.
† Louis Thomas.

paintings this year, 1897; and his lithographs were also fewer. At last alcohol seemed to be blunting his creative faculties. For long periods he scarcely bothered to work. From time to time his friends pointed out 'living Lautrecs,' a prostitute with a beaky nose, 'a bald and greedy diner, his tongue licking the shell of every oyster he swallowed to the mother of pearl.'* Lautrec would look, and then, with a certain melancholy in his voice, say: 'Too splendid! Can't deal with that!'

In their endeavour to stop Lautrec drinking, his friends suggested journeys and expeditions, anything to take him away from the Paris brothels and bars. Joyant took him to Crotoy, in the Somme estuary, and there, 'confined to the boat and to his ration, at least during the hours at sea, he did not drink.'† And Dethomas suggested a journey to Holland where they could hire a boat and sail through the canals. Lautrec agreed.

To begin with all went well. The two friends went to Haarlem to look at the paintings by Frans Hals, which were to be Lautrec's only pleasant memory of the Low Countries. He also wanted to see the famous butter-market at Middleburg on the island of Walcheren. They arrived too late. Lautrec said it did not matter—they would just wait a week. But on the day of the market, when Dethomas went below to wake the painter in his cabin, Lautrec refused to get up. The whole piquancy of the affair lay in having been bored stiff in a provincial town for a week. 'I don't care a damn about the butter-market! And now we can go! Cast off!'‡

The voyage came to an early end. Lautrec had had enough of it. He was infuriated by the importunate curiosity of the Dutch peasants. He could not walk twenty yards in peace. While out with Dethomas on the island of Walcheren, some children began to follow them. They were laughing and joking and their numbers increased rapidly. Furious, Lautrec asked Dethomas to 'pitch into them.' But Dethomas refused. He tried to calm Lautrec, who was getting violently angry. They eventually discovered that the children had mistaken the two

---

* Thadée Natanson.
† Joyant.
‡ Francis Jourdain.

Frenchmen for performers in a circus which advertised a giant who played with a dwarf 'like a ball, throwing him into the air and catching him, while hanging from one foot.'

The explanation was not calculated to please Lautrec. He wanted no more of Holland. He loathed the country. They went back to Paris.

*   *   *

The self-controlled Lautrec of the past, who had concealed his distress behind a quip, had disappeared. No doubt there were moments when he was still in evidence, but they were becoming increasingly rare.

His behaviour was more than ever marked by irritation, ungovernable anger, and a certain wildness. His eccentricity was becoming comparable to that of his father, and he was liable to fall heavily asleep anywhere and at any time; for two minutes or for two hours. His restlessness was no longer due to excessive vitality. Alcohol and the disease he had caught from Rosa la Rouge, which had been completely neglected during the last four years, were corroding and undermining him. The brilliance of his eyes was growing dull. He was becoming pasty-faced and had little appetite for food.

His friends were anxious. But what could they do? Lautrec was becoming more intractable and more difficult to manage every day. Bourges, who published his *Hygiène de Syphilitique* this very year, advised a long cruise; it would afford, so the doctor thought, 'a sedative, tonic and restorative treatment.' Lautrec might once again consider the idea of going to Japan.

In May, while everyone was wondering what to do about him, Lautrec took the lease of a studio on the first floor of a house in the Avenue Frochot, a charming district with little gardens, which lay not far from the Rue de Douai, where Countess Adèle had her apartment. Had Lautrec found this studio on his own initiative, or had someone tactfully succeeded in making him go to live nearer his mother? Countess Adèle—she was now nearly fifty-six and was, said Paul Leclerq, 'an old lady with pretty hands who went to mass every day'— could certainly look after her son more easily there, particularly if he fell ill.

But if Lautrec was moving closer to the Rue de Douai and his 'poor sainted mother,' he was also closer to the Rue Bréda and La Souris, and to the Rue Pigalle and Le Hanneton. And this may well have been the reason for his move.

As soon as he had redecorated his new studio in the 'art nouveau' style, Lautrec invited his friends and acquaintances to a house-warming party. On the invitation card, he drew himself as an animal-tamer, spurs on his heels and a whip in his hand, facing a cow with a swollen udder: 'Henri de Toulouse-Lautrec will be much flattered if you will accept a glass of milk on Saturday, May 15, at about half-past three in the afternoon.'

The invitation was, of course, an ironic one. Although there was every kind of milk food and cheese, together with brown bread, cherries and strawberries, on the 'modern style' table in the studio, which was decorated with cornflowers and daisies, Lautrec had taken the precaution of engaging a barman to make proper cocktails.*

Two details are worth recording here. Curiously enough, Lautrec made a mistake in his address on the invitation card, giving the number of his studio as 5, instead of 15, Avenue Frochot. And when Lautrec left the Rue Tourlaque, he casually abandoned 'to the concierge to do as he liked with' an incredible number of pictures, eighty-seven in fact.†

* *L'Invitation à une tasse de lait* has often been dated 1900. But an article which appeared in *La Vie parisienne* of May 22, 1897, to which attention was first drawn by Jean Adhémar, not only gives an account of the party, but incidentally describes the lithograph.

† These pictures had a lamentable fate. The concierge gave some thirty to the tenant who succeeded Lautrec, a Dr Billard, and the remainder to café proprietors in the district in exchange for a few glasses of wine.

The doctor's servant used the stretchers of Lautrec's pictures for kindling and the canvases for mops. When some twenty had been destroyed in this way, she came to the conclusion that the rest would be very useful to stop up holes in her house in Savoy. And this she did.

In the end, one canvas only survived. Dr Billard had, for no apparent reason, preserved it. In 1914, when giving these facts to a reporter from *L'Éclair*, he had to admit that even this canvas had escaped his grasp. 'One of my patients,' he explained, 'traded it with me in exchange for a little memento which I still preserve to remind myself that I did not deserve the fortune that had fallen into my hands, for I was both blind and deaf.' And the doctor added sadly, 'My only Lautrec, the survivor of the eighty-seven, which I exchanged for a daub worth perhaps forty sous, has since been sold for 8,000 francs.'

It was a curiously casual act. When someone expressed surprise, he replied: 'It's of no importance!'

When Lautrec had first thrown himself into the ungrateful task of becoming a painter, he had thought that by hard work he might perhaps become a great artist, and that he would find in art his compensation for living. But can one ever tell if one is a great artist? We cannot see ourselves with other people's eyes. And does being a great artist make for happiness?

One Friday night, when Lautrec, Anquetin and a few old friends from the Cormon studio were on their way to the Rat Mort to dine, they met Degas in the Rue de Douai. 'Ah, I'm delighted to see you!' exclaimed Degas, addressing Lautrec. 'I've just come from Durand-Ruel. They showed me your work. It's quite excellent. It has style and character! I congratulate you. I'm very pleased to have seen your things. They're magnificent! Work hard! You've got a splendid talent . .' Then he broke off and went away. The friends walked on in silence. Lautrec, astounded at this rare and sudden praise from Degas, was moved to tears. When they had gone a hundred yards or so, he turned to Anquetin: 'Do you think he meant what he said?' But Anquetin, as certain of his own genius as ever, replied in his superior way: 'Do you mean to say you didn't see he was making a fool of you!' One of Lautrec's friends indignantly took Anquetin to task, but the cruel reply had shaken Lautrec: he was never able to believe in Degas' praise.*

The first work Lautrec undertook in his new studio was a portrait of Paul Leclercq. 'The work of leading up!' he said with a wink, as he did about almost everything from an attempt at seduction to the preliminaries for a painting. But the work of 'leading up' went on for ever. For four or five consecutive weeks, Leclercq went to sit in one of the big wicker-work chairs in the studio. Lautrec, a green felt hat pulled over his eyes, so as 'to concentrate the light and avoid the shadows,'† sat at his easel, stared at his model, applied two or three touches of paint, sang a dirty song, then put his brush down, got to his feet, and said: 'That's enough work!...The weather's too fine!...'

* Recorded by Jeanès.
† Leclercq.

And he would lead Leclercq off on a round of the cafés.

'I remember very well,' wrote Paul Leclercq, 'that in all I sat only for two or three hours.'

It seemed as though the years of fruitful experience were over. His long sessions at La Souris gave rise only to a few lithographs, of which one was of Madame Palmyre's bulldog.

This dog's head delighted Lautrec at thirty-two as much as it would have done as a boy. He now began to recapitulate. He returned to the theme of brothels, and made lithographs, with a delicacy he had perhaps never shown before, of Elsa la Viennoise, a woman of the Rue des Moulins. He also remembered the Moulin Rouge, where he had not been for months, and made a lithograph of a scene from one of his old pictures.

But, indeed, his nostalgia went farther back than the Moulin Rouge. It led him to Le Bosc and the enchantments of childhood and youth. Horses and carriages began to haunt him again as they had fifteen years earlier. When Vollard commissioned a coloured lithograph from him for one of his *Albums des Peintres-Graveurs*,* Lautrec returned to one of his early subjects and designed the *Charrette anglaise*, a work astonishingly full of movement.

At this time, Lautrec painted several nudes of red-haired women, either on all fours on a bed or standing in front of a mirror. They are depressing, bitter, almost painful works. There is a graveyard smell about the bodies of these women whose 'flesh is marbled in red and green.'†

*   *   *

He spent part of the summer of 1897 at Villeneuve-sur-Yonne with the Natansons. He made two paintings of Misia, first reading a book,

---

* Vollard writes in his *Souvenirs:* 'When I came home one evening, my servant said: "A little while ago, a funny little man came to the door. I told him M. Vollard was not in. And, when I asked his name, he made no reply, but picked up a piece of charcoal that was lying about and drew on the back of this canvas that's turned to the wall a funny little figure. Then he went away." Bonnard, at that time, was working on a decoration for my dining-room and, on the back of one of his sketches, Lautrec had left me a drawing of himself as a visiting card.'

† J. Lassaigne

then at her piano. He would ask Misia to play the same piece over and over again. It was Beethoven's *Ruins of Athens.* 'Oh, those splendid *Ruins!* Play the *Ruins* again, Misia!'

Misia and Lautrec often went to lie in the garden and played a game that enchanted them both. Misia sat on the grass, her back against a tree. She read, or pretended to, while Lautrec tickled the soles of her feet with a paintbrush. He discovered there, so he said, 'imaginary landscapes.' The game went on for hours.

There were many women who never knew how much Lautrec loved them.

*   *   *

One morning, at Villeneuve, the Natansons were horrified at the sound of shots coming from Lautrec's room.

They found him lying on his bed and shooting at a spider making a web on the opposite wall.

The Dog in Spectacles

PART FOUR
[1897—1901]

CHAPTER ONE

Madrid-les-Bains

Don't expect me this evening, for tonight will be dark and sleepless.

GÉRARD DE NERVAL: *Dernière lettre.*

IN a bar in the Rue Volney, an American general would tell anyone who would listen to him, and with all the enthusiasm of a proselyte, how he had been cured of alcoholism. Of his own accord, he had submitted to treatment in a clinic and was now content to sip lemon-squash whereas previously he had drunk whisky all day long.

'Magnificent, eh?' Lautrec said, in astonishment at so much will-power. Out of admiration for the American, he went frequently to this bar. Could it be that he was on the point of following his example? His friends began to hope so, and Lautrec went so far as to consider the idea of spending some time in a clinic. For a while, he gave up cocktails and drank only port.

It is probable that there was a reason for this sudden change of attitude, for it was at this time that Lautrec fell in love with one of his young relations, Aline, a young girl who had just come out of a convent. He believed that she was not altogether indifferent to him. Unhappily the girl's father forbade any such ideas* and Lautrec returned to his drinking. As Joyant remarked, one might have thought he was bent on his own destruction. At the beginning of 1898, in a letter to Robert de Montcabrier, a distant cousin, whom he was helping with advice, Lautrec spoke bitterly of 'the horrible profession of being a painter.'† In January, at the suggestion of Maurin, he experimented with the technique of dry-point, but after nine attempts,‡

* Recollections of Aline Séré de Rivière, recorded by Francis Rico.

† Joyant catalogues only fourteen paintings for 1898.

‡ Among them were portraits of Maurin, Tristan Bernard, Francis Jourdain and Henry Somme. Of the Maurin dry-point, Lautrec said to Francis Jourdain, when sending him a copy: 'The only really successful thing about this portrait is that he resembles William Morris.'

which were not particularly successful, for he had bought plates from the first dealer he happened to come across, he lost interest. Gauzi, whom he had not seen for some time, came to his studio one day. 'I had the impression,' said Gauzi, 'that I was in a picture store. Everything was in order, the canvases neatly stacked along the walls, but there was no picture on the easel; I was in a desert.'

In the rare moments when he was working, Lautrec continued to relive his past and deal with old themes. Four years earlier, he had published the album on Yvette Guilbert; he now made a second (with no more than eight lithographs this time) for an English publishing house. Yvette Guilbert was now a singer of international fame. Eight years earlier, he had painted a portrait of Mlle Dihau at the piano; and now he painted the old woman, who had grown a little heavier, giving a singing lesson.

And, finally, while Clemenceau's book, *Au Pied de Sinai*, was about to be published with drawings Lautrec had made of Russian and Polish Jews, studied in the Tournelle district, he was at last able to fulfil his wish to illustrate Jules Renard's *Histoires naturelles*. This was his main task for the year 1898.*

Lautrec had become friendly with one of his neighbours, Edmond Calmèse, who ran a livery stable at 10, Rue Fontaine-Saint-Georges. He spent hours in the stables and coach-houses, as he had done at Le Bosc in the past. 'To think men of letters dare talk about sport!' he said. And when he was asked whether there was anything he regretted not having enjoyed in life, he replied curtly: 'The horse.'

Lautrec was in search of models for the *Histoires naturelles*. From Isle-Adam he ordered a toad, which was sent to him in a hat box and remained his guest till it escaped into the Avenue Frochot. For other models, he went daily to the zoo in the Bois de Boulogne. He was inspired by a Himalayan wild sheep for the ram.

For his journeys to the Bois, Lautrec hired a governess-cart from Calmèse drawn by 'a pony with a round, sharp eye and as a fat sausage,'

* The *Histoires naturelles*, of which a hundred copies were printed, appeared in 1899. It had no success, and was ultimately remaindered by the publishers. Today, it is much sought after. A copy was sold at the Galerie Charpentier in Paris for 1,490,000 francs (14,900 N.F.) in 1959.

called Philibert, whom he spoilt abominably. He often went round by the Champs-Élysées to pick up Paul Leclercq at his house. The two friends would go off to the zoo together to see the painter's favourite animals, in particular the ant-eater and the armadillo, who appeared to appreciate his visits. Lautrec would sit on a camp-stool in front of their cages, and their greetings were 'a tender exchange of affection.'*

The expeditions to the zoo were not, unfortunately, limited to visiting the animals: the cart stopped at every café in the Bois.

Lautrec's drunkenness had now become terrifying. At times, he lost all dignity. When invited out to dinner, he was likely to insult an unknown guest who displeased him or overwhelm with embarrassing attentions a woman 'who happened to attract him only too much.'†

One night, when dining with friends, he completely forgot himself and set about attracting the attention of the young maid. Whenever she carried a dish into the room, he sang an obscene song and, suddenly, noticing a stain on her apron, he said: 'So yours are black, are they?' Drunkenly obstinate, he constantly repeated the question, seized her apron, pulled it off, and clasped hold of her. She screamed and the host had to interfere. Lautrec stumbled off to collapse in a chair in the library.‡

His friends wondered anxiously how it was all going to end; but Lautrec seemed unconcerned.

At this time, Little Tich was appearing at the Folies-Bergère with great success. Disguised as a Castillian woman or a lady of the English court, he would flutter about the stage in double-jointed frenzy, 'a genius in his ugliness and the suppleness of his limbs, a terrifying abortion in his supple contortions.'§

Lautrec went to see Little Tich, 'the simulacrum of his own miseries'.

'When smiling at him,' said Natanson, 'it was almost as if Lautrec were smiling at himself in a looking-glass.'

*   *   *

When Count Alphonse heard of his son's drinking, he suggested:

---

* † Thadée Natanson.
‡ Recorded by Thadée Natanson. The scene probably took place in his house.
§ Jean Lorrain.

'He should go to live in England; he will attract less attention in society.' This suggestion was all the more curious since Lautrec hardly drank at all when in London, and his friends were well aware of it.

The idea of a journey to London was worth considering, even as a temporary distraction for Lautrec. Countess Adèle and Joyant, who were constantly trying to find some such counter-interest to drinking, arranged an exhibition of his pictures at the Goupil Gallery in Regent Street, which was a branch of the firm of Boussod et Valadon. So as to give Lautrec plenty to do, he was left to organise the exhibition himself. Joyant was to join him only on the eve of the private view.

The proposal attracted Lautrec and he set about making a selection of his pictures. Before sending them to England, he invited some twenty of his friends to his studio for a pre-view. 'This is how one should show one's work,' he said, 'only to those who may be interested.' On the invitation card—a poodle standing on its hind legs facing a little girl—Lautrec had again made a mistake in writing his address, having put 14 this time as the number of his studio.

Taking with him his 'legendary' travelling bag in khaki cloth—which when packed tight was rather the same shape as its owner—Lautrec left for London. He was bored to death. He did, however, abstain from drinking, partly due to the fact that one evening he saw a drunkard being brutally treated by the police in front of his hotel at Charing Cross. The man, who was wearing a top-hat, had begun quarrelling with the porters after being thrown out of the hotel. Called in to help, the police had siezed the man, picked him up and dropped him on his back on the pavement two or three times, till he fainted, and then carried him away. Lautrec was appalled at the sight of this treatment.

While waiting for Joyant to arrive, he wandered about London like a lost soul. For the first time in his life, he was thrown back on his own company, and he was keenly aware of the situation. In his melancholy, he went to the station every day to meet the trains from the Continent. There he might chance on someone he knew. But Joyant arrived at last.

The exhibition opened on Monday, May 2, 1898. There can be little doubt that Joyant sponsored it mainly as a pretext to distract

Lautrec from his many temptations, for it was a risky venture. The English critics and public had not been prepared for the understanding and appreciation of Lautrec's work. Victorian society in general was utterly unaware of the French artistic movement of these last decades; its approbation was largely limited to the demure affectations of the Pre-Raphaelites, and to the Royal Academy. In the ordinary way, the Goupil Gallery sold Corots, Théodore Rousseaus or the pictures of the minor Dutch masters, such as Mauve or the brothers Maris.* What impression would Lautrec's seventy-eight works create in such an atmosphere?

Moreover, Lautrec was almost unknown in England, though for two consecutive years, 1895 and 1896, he had contributed to an exhibition of posters at the Royal Aquarium. If he had been heard of, it was as a painter of places of 'ill-fame,' which was even more vexatious. When in France, Englishmen might hasten off to the Moulin Rouge, the Jardin de Paris, or other places of licentious amusement, but here, at home, all was respectability. English prudery was bound to find Lautrec's work shocking.

In spite of these unfavourable circumstances, the Prince of Wales had promised to attend the private view. The pictures of the Moulin Rouge, of Jane Avril and of La Goulue would recall many memories to the Prince—'Hullo, Wales, are you paying for the champagne?' Since Royalty was a little late in arriving, Lautrec sank on to a sofa and fell asleep. When he woke up, he was told the Prince of Wales had already passed by and had insisted he should not be awakened. 'A nice chap!' Lautrec remarked, and promptly went to sleep again.

Partly due to stories of the painter's scandalous reputation, crowds flocked to the Goupil Gallery. The eagerness with which the English came to see these evocations of Parisian debauchery was matched only by their readiness to be shocked by them. To appease the public, the managers of the gallery tried to mitigate the effect of Lautrec's pictures by hanging unexceptionable works by the 1830 landscape painters beside them. The press, declaring that his subjects were 'unlikely to

---

* Did Lautrec know that, twenty years earlier, his friend Vincent Van Gogh had worked as an employee in the Goupil Gallery in London and had sold pictures similar to these?

commend themselves to old ladies,' slated the artist: 'He has but one idea in his head, and this is vulgarity'; in short his work was 'revoltingly ugly' and 'really monstrous.'* When the exhibition closed, at the beginning of June, the *Lady's Pictorial* heaved a sigh of satisfaction: 'For which relief much thanks. Again the art of such men as Corot, Daubigny, Swan and Maris hangs here to delight us instead of affright us.'

In earlier days, this reception would no doubt have saddened the painter. Now he said: 'It's of no importance!'

He merely wanted to get back to France as quickly as possible.

Before going on to Paris, he stayed for some time on the coast of Normandy with Dethomas, who had no doubt suggested the halt so as to defer the painter's return to the Avenue Frochot for as long as possible.

Dethomas made a charcoal drawing of him on the beach at Granville. And Lautrec painted a portrait of Bouglé at Arromanches. He started a second, but did not complete it.

   * * *

Despite the excursions, outings and distractions arranged by Lautrec's friends, they had to admit they could not save him.

That Lautrec was conscious of the harm he was inflicting on himself is certain. He seemed to acquiesce in it, accepting the 'shipwreck of his life'† with full knowledge of what he was doing. The combined effects of alcohol, sexual excess and nervous exhaustion accumulating over the past years had clearly sapped his will. And now he appeared to have no wish even to exercise it.

His walk had become more cumbersome and slow; and his speech more disconnected, his words being lisped and mumbled so that they could not always be understood. His pince-nez, remarked Natanson, shone brighter than his eyes.

Trying to limit Lautrec's excesses was a thankless task for his friends. Not only were they subjected to his ill-will, his violent denials and his stubborn temper, but he often succeeded in escaping from them. He

* From articles in the *Art Journal*, the *Daily Chronicle*, the *Lady's Pictorial* and the *Star*.

† Gerstle Mack.

would disappear for a night or sometimes for days on end, going off with strangers about Paris. He was frequently in trouble with the police and would be carried home, unconscious or even resisting, with a black eye or a bloody nose. One day he returned to the Avenue Frochot with a broken collar-bone. He explained that he had 'fallen downstairs from the fourth floor in the middle of the night.'*

From now on 'a collar-bone' took its place in his vocabulary to signify 'a place to which one had better not go.'† These places were, however, legion and Lautrec found them out.

Fortunately summer came, the season when he traditionally went off to 'refit.' Going first to Malromé where he wanted to paint the portrait of a cousin's baby—having previously asked, to its mother's indignation, that its head should be 'cooked in the sun'—and then, in September to Villeneuve-sur-Yonne, to stay with the Natansons.

As usual, a stay in the country had a calming effect on him. He rested, amused himself and entertained his hosts and their guests. They were never to forget the afternoon of violent storm when Lautrec appeared from under the trees through the rain and lightning dressed in a lemon yellow oilskin and a sou'wester which, he claimed, were 'peculiarly sportsman-like.'

Taking charge of the kitchen, Lautrec cooked his favourite dishes. Dressed in yellow trousers and a red shirt, a cloth about his neck, he busied himself inventing menus. Vuillard, who was also staying at Villeneuve, painted him in the act of placing a saucepan on the stove.

On his return to Paris, Lautrec, to thank the Natansons for their hospitality, invited them and a few friends to a dinner which even a devoted gourmet could not help calling 'royal.' At the end of the meal, which was accompanied by the finest wines, Lautrec struggled to his feet and said: 'Follow me'. He took them all to the Dihaus', who were somewhat startled by the invasion, and led them up to Degas' picture *Les Musiciens à l'orchestre*, which had so much delighted his youth. 'This is your dessert!' he said. Lautrec loved painting no less than women. As Vuillard remarked, when Lautrec spoke of painting his voice assumed a grave note.

* * *

* † Joyant.

Winter came, and with it the painter's condition took a more serious turn.

Followed by a bitch, called Pamela, 'with a temper like a bear-cub,' Lautrec ceaselessly roamed about Paris. He looked about him suspiciously. People were out to hurt him and injure him. His allowance had no doubt been reduced, for he never had enough money. On one occasion he arrived at Durand-Ruel's in the Rue Laffitte with a woman in tow. He wanted cash, and held out his hat. 'For Madame, with whom I've spent the night!' Durand-Ruel refused; and Lautrec stood begging in front of the gallery, ranting against the dealer to the gathering crowd.

He began to have delusions that he was being persecuted by flies. Why should they attack him? What did they want with him? He would explode with anger. And his laughter, said Natanson sadly, 'resembled his laughter of the past only like dead friends, or those who visited us in our dreams.'

Lautrec was frightened, too. He went to bed with his 'buttonhook' so that he could defend himself if he were attacked. But his enemies were innumerable. Even microbes were in league against him. His studio was infested by them. They were swarming everywhere. Alarmed, he bought paraffin and sprayed the floor with it.

A keeper was discreetly commissioned to look after the artist. Failing a voyage to Japan, there was talk of a holiday in Italy, but in the meantime a keeper might prevent the worst outbursts.

Lautrec made no difficulties in accepting his keeper: he introduced him to his friends as the police commissioner of his district, with whom he and Pamela went out in the evenings to make police raids on the neighbourhood. Unfortunately the keeper was unable to resist alcohol, and on every 'raid' Lautrec was able to abandon him dead drunk in a bar.

At the beginning of 1899, Jane Avril, in loyalty to the painter to whom she owed, so she said, her fame, commissioned Lautrec to design a new poster. He produced a tortured, perverse composition in which he depicted the dancer with a cobra coiled round her bent body. The poster was not used.

At the same time, during February, he began to make nightmarish and unbalanced lithographs; one was of a dog with spectacles on its nose, a pipe under its tail and spurs on its feet.

Lautrec suffered from hallucinations and exhausted himself struggling against imaginary enemies. He tried to fight a cardboard elephant; a pack of terriers yapped at his heels; and a monstrous, headless animal prowled about the room trying to drive him against the bed and crush him. In a sweat of terror he would hide under the bedclothes.

'This is what's in store for us!' Lautrec had predicted when he was looking one day with Gauzi at a reproduction of André Gill's *Fou*. Ten years had gone by since then. And now Lautrec would shuffle out in red trousers, a blue umbrella in his hand, and a china dog under his arm. Alcohol, syphilis and despair had done their work. The long suicide was nearly over.

*   *   *

Some fifty years before, a nephew of the celebrated Dr Pinel, who had done so much for lunatics, had founded an asylum in an old eighteenth-century house, the Château Saint-James, at 16, Avenue de Madrid, Neuilly.

It was now run by a Dr Semelaigne. A first-class establishment, it took in only a limited number of patients—twenty-five men and thirty women—whose families were in comfortable circumstances. It cost about 500 or 600 francs a month.*

The Château Saint-James stood in some fifteen acres of grounds. There were groves of old trees, gay flower beds, arbours, fountains, rockeries, and statues by Pajou and Lemoine. It had an atmosphere of Fragonard or Watteau, of embarkations for Cythera. The interior arrangements were perfectly in keeping. Everything possible had been done to disguise the melancholy purpose of the building. It was elegant and decorated with taste, and its fine panelling, parquet and carved mirrors combined period distinction with the advantages of modern hygiene. The patients' rooms had every possible comfort. Some were even three-roomed flats with a bathroom and a private garden.

One morning towards the end of February, Lautrec was taken to this establishment.

* About £80 today. The Saint-James Lunatic Asylum ceased to exist in 1921.

His friends had been forced to abandon the idea of a cruise; the painter's symptoms were now too grave. They had to consider the possibility of confining Lautrec somewhere to undergo an enforced cure for alcoholism. Bourges, as a doctor, thought it inevitable in the very near future. But there was a natural reluctance to take this step. Neither Countess Adèle nor Tapié could resign themselves to it, and Joyant was horrified. As for Count Alphonse, on being informed, he declined to take sides in the matter. He let it be understood that if such a decision were made he would not oppose it, but he wished to remain neutral; as far as he was concerned, he considered it 'revolting' that there should be 'this assault on the freedom to drink both by the French people and those of neighbouring countries.'

There had been a good deal of discussion, but no decision had been reached, when a sharp attack of delirium tremens laid Lautrec low in the Rue des Moulins. The need for treatment became imperative. Next morning, doctors and male nurses seized the painter at the door of his studio, hurried him into a cab and took him to Neuilly.

After a few days of dieting and plain water, Lautrec slowly emerged from the fog. He gazed round the room. It was small, heavy with hangings and had a latticed window. There were bars not only at the window but round the hearth. On the table was an oil-lamp. His room led into another, where sat a man of some fifty years of age, with a small moustache, slender hands, hollow temples and bushy eyebrows.

Alternately blind with anger and overcome with anxiety, Lautrec wandered round his cell. What had happened? He could remember nothing.

He had grown thinner. His cheeks were sunken behind his beard. His hands trembled and his dry lips seemed to have grown smaller and become bloodless.

He could not order his thoughts. He was afraid and cried out. The man from next door came in and tried to quiet him. Lost, Lautrec looked at him, and at the barred window behind which the March twilight was fading into night.

Countess Adèle watched sadly over her son as he slowly emerged from the nightmare. He was like a blind man feeling his way. Little by little, the clouds parted until he realised that his room was a lunatic's cell and that the man who talked so gently to him was his keeper. Slowly he returned to a reality which was more odious than all the fantasies of fever.

His mental reactions were shocked into activity, though they were still somewhat disconnected. At times, he still gave way to fury and shouted at the top of his voice, but he was making an effort to control himself. He was soon considered quiet enough to be allowed to walk in the grounds with his keeper. Lautrec looked at the trees, the statues, the ruins of a temple of Love, the remains of a small canal that led to the Seine, all the delicate graces of the eighteenth century. And he began to take notice of the other patients.

As he gradually recovered his lucidity, he suffered more harshly from his imprisonment. But he kept silence and did not complain; he knew instinctively that he must use cunning. On his bedside table was a bottle of Botot water;* he drank it greedily.

Nevertheless, his health began to improve more rapidly than anyone could have expected. On March 12, Countess Adèle wrote to Joyant: 'He reads and amuses himself by drawing a little.' In Dr Semelaigne's establishment the slightest occupational whims of the patients were encouraged, provided they were harmless. They might tend or devastate their gardens as they pleased; one woman was rearing rabbits in a corner of the grounds; and there were other patients who painted or drew.

By the kitchens, Lautrec found a woodcock's feather (the woodcock, he remarked, had not appeared on the menu) and he made it into a Japanese paint-brush. He drew a seascape in sepia. Then he made portraits of his fellow patients. There was a plan in his mind. By drawing, by showing that he was still a talented artist, he would prove to the authorities that they had no right to keep him shut up among a lot of lunatics. He remembered the book on falconry his father had given him twenty-three years ago with a dedication in which he had praised a free and open-air life. 'Papa,' wrote Lautrec, 'here is your opportunity to do me a good turn. I'm shut up, and everything that is imprisoned dies!'

* A liquid dentifrice with a base of alcohol, made fragrant with aniseed, cloves, cinnamon and peppermint essence.

He resented being likened to the other patients. To him they were 'disgusting.' He did not belong to the same race. How dare they compare him to the old lunatic who stole hats and hid them at the end of the garden where he used them as a latrine? Lautrec suffered not only from his loss of liberty but also from humiliation.

His memory was still clouded; his clearest recollections were of the distant past. But he could reconstruct the circumstances that had led to his confinement, and he fulminated against Tapié and Bourges. He was angry and afraid that they might keep him in the asylum indefinitely—like the mad woman who had been a patient there for forty-seven years. It occurred to him that when the doors of an asylum for rich people had once closed on them, they were likely to re-open reluctantly. Rich patients were good customers, and the fact that they were cured would be admitted only regretfully. What recourse had they against 'family, medical, charitable or interested plots?' Were they going to keep him shut up for ever?

He drew feverishly. If his amnesia had not altogether disappeared, his fingers at least had preserved the memory of forms. These terse drawings, almost bitten into the paper, betray his agitation. But there is an eloquence about them.

In the middle of March, the doctors agreed to allow Lautrec visitors. He at once summoned Joyant and asked him to send as soon as possible 'prepared stones and a box of water-colours with sepia, paint brushes, litho crayons, good quality Chinese ink, and paper. Come quickly and send Albert express.'

Joyant anxiously hurried off to see him. Lautrec's gay and charming letter no doubt reassured him as to the patient's health. Although Lautrec's confinement had seemed both necessary and amply justified, it still caused Joyant a certain disquiet. Was it right to treat 'an artist of such sensibility' as an ordinary invalid? Like Lautrec he too feared the stay in the Avenue de Madrid might become indefinite. 'To be rich and a lunatic,' he thought, 'is very risky.' He felt singularly oppressed when, having crossed the reception rooms, he made his way 'through low doors and by narrow staircases and passages,' pierced by grilles, to the patient's room.

Lautrec welcomed his friend as 'a liberator.' For him, Joyant was a renewal of contact with the outside world.

He was quite calm and talked clearly. He gave Joyant his first sketches and his woodcock-feather brush. 'When I've made a certain number of drawings,' he explained, 'they won't be able to keep me here any longer. I want to get out, they've no right to shut me up.'

The two friends went out into the garden. Lautrec ironically showed Joyant the remains of the old folly. The keeper moved away. The painter turned to Joyant, looked him in the eyes, and said: 'To the rescue!'

*   *   *

Many people were surprised by Lautrec's disappearance from the Paris scene. Some, the better informed, said he was in an asylum run by Dr Blanche. But most people thought this was a joke, probably contrived by Lautrec himself.

Nevertheless, on March 18, *L'Écho de Paris* confirmed the news, although incorrect dates were given and certain facts glossed over. Two days before, it said, Lautrec had been 'taken ill' in an 'establishment near the Opéra'; and he had been removed to an asylum. This fairly discreet news was repeated during subsequent days by the whole press, and the assumption that Lautrec was 'mad' gained immediate credit.

Lautrec's independent behaviour, his frankness of speech and his sallies had unintentionally and unknowingly created many enemies. And they hastened to denigrate him. Lautrec, who had been so 'undisciplined' and so 'given to excesses,' was finished. He would never come out of the asylum alive. Moreover, it was not only recently that he had gone mad; he had been so since his birth. 'It was bound to end thus,' wrote a certain Alexandre Hepp in *Le Journal* of March 20. 'Toulouse-Lautrec was destined for the mad-house. He was shut up yesterday and from now on overt madness officially signs his pictures, drawings and posters, whereas before it was anonymous . . . The influence of his own physical condition certainly had its effect, and in a hundred most curious ways the artist's body seems to have reacted directly, bitterly, physically on his character as if he had no soul to emancipate him . . . To his talent, no one had talent, to his heart, no one had a heart. The world was made up of cretins, wretches and prostitutes; all the men were of Sainte-Anne, Mazas or the Aquarium; as for the women, it was simpler still, for them it was the brothel . . .'

On March 28, Lepelletier in *L'Écho de Paris* was even less restrained, and this was the more shocking coming from a man who was better informed and whose understanding was less elementary:

'By a quirk of character, which seemed like moral castigation, like a visitation of divine wrath upon the seventh generation, this poor man, who was so awkward, ugly and crippled, was an ardent womaniser. He pursued love like a bull in a china shop. He seemed to be expiating, by his unsuccessful pursuits, the too successful debauches of the Counts of Toulouse and compensating, by his continual rebuffs, for their frequent successes in gallantry. He was tortured by the desire to be loved and to inspire passion. He was a hunch-backed Don Juan, pursuing the ideal amid the most tawdry realities. No doubt, he too could produce his list of *mille e tre* lovers, but these thousand and three women's names also appear on the registers that M. Will initials at the Prefecture of Police. This sordid debauchery and those commercial-traveller's expeditions which Toulouse-Lautrec delighted to organise, and in which he involved his friends, together with the irritation aroused by the awareness of his physical deformity and moral decadence, certainly helped to lead him to the mad-house.

'And now, in that strange paradise of human degeneracy, in the curious Valhalla, which is a place of terror only to those unfortunates who are still burdened with sanity, he is as happy as it is possible to be. He rejoices unfettered in what he believes to be his strength, his beauty and his talent. He can paint endless frescoes and unlimited canvases with a bewildering mastery; and, at the same time, he can embrace beautiful bodies, for he is surrounded by lissom, shapely figures, and a ceaseless flood of sensual pleasures fill his being with a continual enjoyment of new sensations. Thanks to his happy lunacy, he sails towards the enchanted isles where he is king, far from the ugliness and sadness of the world. He no longer sells art, he no longer buys love: he is in bliss.'

These articles, with all their errors and inaccuracies, dismayed the painter's friends.

While the artist was busy trying to demonstrate his sanity and the integrity of his talent, these diatribes seemed likely to thwart his efforts by confirming the fact that his proper place was in an asylum. No doubt, people here and there came out in favour of Lautrec. *La Presse* wanted to know whether 'the original artist,' 'the master of the poster,' the 'wonderful lithographer' could really be mad. It was suggested that he had been shut up on 'the advice of someone in his entourage, because he was, so it was said, spending too much money.' What was the truth of the matter? 'An answer should be made at once,' siad *La Presse*, 'so as not to allow these terrible suspicions to remain current any longer.'

But this article, which was wounding for Countess Adèle, was lost among the concert of hostile voices. Joyant decided that some definite action must be taken. He thought of the critic of the *Figaro*, Arsène Alexandre. He got in touch with him and had no difficulty in persuading him to come to the Château Saint-James. All that was required to stop the slanders was for Alexandre to report exactly what he saw.

Lautrec's improvement was now so marked that he had been given the privilege of short walks with his keeper in the neighbourhood of the Château. He welcomed Alexandre and Joyant with delight. 'So you've come to interview me?' he said: he was sure an article in the *Figaro* would support his bid for freedom. He was in very good humour and made jokes. Seeing some bottles of liquid on the table in the reception room where he met Alexandre and Joyant, he laughed: 'Quinine. You shan't have any!' He showed them the garden, the hothouses, the vine arbours, picked violets and told them of his artistic projects.

The next day, March 30, Arsène Alexandre published a long and moving article about his visit under the title *Une Guérison:* 'I was reassured and I hope to reassure,' he wrote . . . 'I saw a lunatic full of wisdom, an alcoholic who does not drink, a lost man who never looked healthier . . . There is such an intense vitality in this supposedly dying man, such an innate strength in this supposedly sickly creature, that those who watched him hurrying to disaster are astonished to see him so splendidly restored to health.'

Alexandre's article was by its very enthusiasm perhaps rather

I

overstating its case. However, the object was attained: the article prevented further slanders. It also had another consequence: twenty-four hours after its publication there was a consultation among the doctors at the Château Saint-James, where they were no doubt beginning to find Lautrec a somewhat embarrassing patient.

For over an hour, two alienists, Doctors Dupré and Séglos, interviewed the painter. They stated in their report that during the whole course of the conversation, Lautrec 'showed no signs of emotional anxiety, excitement, or mental depression. Moreover,' they went on, 'a most searching examination has shown no evidence of the delirious fantasies which we mentioned in our previous report.' Concluding that there was a definite improvement, they finished by declaring:

'There is no doubt that this improvement, which is still recent, cannot be maintained or expected to last unless the convalescent is kept in similar conditions of physical and mental hygiene.

'In consequence, we advise that M. Henri de Toulouse-Lautrec should remain in the establishment where he has recovered his health for some further weeks.

'The precise date of his release can be fixed only by another examination and on the advice of the visiting doctor, Dr Semelaigne. There should be no difficulty about these measures, since the convalescent appears in no way opposed to the idea of prolonging his stay which, moreover, weighs the less heavily on him owing to the fact that Dr Semelaigne has recently authorised experimental outings preparatory to his final release.'

This was true. Now that things had taken a turn for the better, Lautrec felt relieved. His 'captivity' would soon come to an end. He was prepared to wait patiently. His serenity was restored.

*   *   *

One after the other his friends came out to the Avenue de Madrid to visit him: Dethomas, Adolphe Albert and Thadée Natanson. There were a few defections, but Lautrec pretended not to notice.

Despite his emaciation, his pale complexion, his sunken cheeks and his leaden look (Arsène Alexandre had much exaggerated the painter's appearance of good health), Lautrec could still be the exhilarating companion of the past. He laughed and joked and nicknamed the asylum 'Madrid-les-Bains' or 'Saint-James-Plage'. He even joked about his alcoholism: 'To think,' he cried, 'that not one single friend has thought of slipping me some spirits in a flat bottle!' And it was a joke, for he made no attempt to obtain drink during his walks outside the asylum with his keeper. Quite the opposite. He maliciously encouraged his 'guardian angel' to do so instead, and was radiant when he succeeded in bringing him back drunk to the Avenue de Madrid. He described his companions in the asylum and their idiosyncrasies with an equal malice. The mad behaviour of some patient or other would cause him to exclaim, jubilantly: 'What? Splendid, isn't it? Eh? Splendid! But apart from this peculiarity, he's a charming and distinguished fellow. And not at all stupid. Just a little crazy, eh?'

But there were times, too, when he gave way to rancour. Then his laughter froze and he talked bitterly of his fellow patients: 'Their eccentricities,' he said, 'make it quite impossible to forgive the people who've shut me up with them.' He would grow angry and fume about the doctors. 'They think disease and the sick were specially created for their benefit!' He thought morosely of Bourges and Tapié. He would be revenged on them. His voice quivering with resentment, he would mutter: 'I'll pull his whiskers off and wipe myself with them. I'll wipe myself with them, you wait!'

When he and his keeper visited the zoo, they often stood in front of the cages of the ant-eater and the armadillo. Lautrec felt compassion towards them, for they would never again know freedom.

Spurred on by the desire to escape his prison as soon as possible, Lautrec worked ceaselessly. In his cell, which had become a studio, he was accumulating drawings, water-colours, paintings and lithographs. He painted a portrait of his keeper, its orange and blue-grey tones conveying a sense of poignant sadness. He drew the head of an old man in pastel. He was a patient and his face has a peculiar gentleness and resignation. It is clear that great sympathy and understanding went to the making of this work.

But his actual surroundings interested Lautrec much less than the ghosts of the past, which led him back to what had been and helped him to forget his present situation. Lautrec drew the circus he had known so well in the days when Princeteau had taken him to Fernando's.

With a superhuman effort, he unearthed from the depths of his memory the recollection of these scenes down to the smallest detail, recapturing with incredible precision the tumbling clowns, lion-tamers, tight-rope dancers, acrobats and circus-riders. And it was not only once or twice that Lautrec accomplished this remarkable feat of memory. He produced thirty-nine drawings in colour of the circus one after the other.*

In each of these works, almost without exception, Lautrec depicted his performers against a background of empty tiers. The clowns, the horses and the monkey-showmen seem to be moving out of time, out of life. The oddity of the empty tiers, which was no doubt involuntary, creates a sensation of peculiar uneasiness. When Lautrec showed these drawings to Thadée Natanson, Natanson could do nothing but talk and go on talking, for fear that Lautrec should realise how these pictures of a dead world distressed him. 'Shall we ever see the old Lautrec again?' Natanson wondered.†

It was a melancholy question, for though it would have been absurd to search for traces of delirium in these drawings, the free and aggressive touch of the past was absent. Some faults in proportion and a certain awkwardness in composition do not matter. The painful characteristic of these drawings is that they smell of the lamp. They fail to take wing.

Shaken as he was by the weeks he had spent in the intolerable atmosphere of the asylum Lautrec could never quite recover his old self.

Misia came to see him. For Lautrec, she was 'the swallow,' 'the dove of the ark,' the herald of the liberty for which he sighed. Had he not

---

* Of these drawings (*Le Cirque*), twenty-two were published in an album by Manzi-Joyant in 1905. The other seventeen were published in 1931 by the Librairie de France. The Éditons du Livre reproduced the whole collection in 1952.

† In order to explain the curious persistence of this theme of empty tiers, it has been suggested that Lautrec went with his keeper to rehearsals at the Molier Circus in the Rue Benouville, which was not far from the Château Saint-James. There is no foundation for this suggestion. The Molier Circus, whose producer was travelling abroad, gave no performances in Paris during the year 1899.

earned his freedom sufficiently with the fifty works he had completed since he had recovered consciousness? He implored his mother to intervene with the doctors. Weak, as always, where her son was concerned, Countess Adèle, who very likely reproached herself with having caused him such suffering, yielded at last.

At her request, Doctors Dupré, Séglos and Semelaigne met on May 17. Though they still diagnosed 'a slight trembling' and 'some uncertainty of memory,' they authorised his discharge from the Château Saint-James. They added, however, that 'owing to his amnesia, the instability of his character and lack of will-power, it is essential that M. Henri de Toulouse-Lautrec should be subject in his life outside these premises to material and moral conditions of continual supervision so that he may not have an opportunity of relapsing into alcoholic habits and so pave the way to a relapse of a more serious nature than his previous symptoms.'

Two or three days later, Lautrec left the asylum.

CHAPTER TWO

The Bear-Leader

'Alas! Poor Yorick. I knew him, Horatio; a fellow of
infinite jest, of most excellent fancy . . .'

SHAKESPEARE: *Hamlet*

'My bear-leader, a ruined man of the world . . .' Lautrec would
whisper to his friends when he had introduced Monsieur Viaud, the
companion in whose charge Countess Adèle had placed him.

Paul Viaud was a distant relation of Lautrec, an affable Bordelais and
a man of great tact. He was very well suited to his delicate task.
Available because of his reverses of fortune and because he had no
family ties or business interests, he was able to devote himself to
Lautrec. The employment was, in fact, a God-send to him, and he
accepted it with a great deal of goodwill. He liked and understood
Lautrec, and his discretion and equable temper enabled him to
approach his duties with a light hand and even make the artist forget
that he was being supervised. And, finally, he had one capital virtue:
because of a weakness of the stomach he was strictly teetotal.

Lautrec had made no protest against supervision. He looked back in
horror at the time he had spent in the Avenue de Madrid. He was
deeply afraid that he might one day suffer a similar obliteration. This
time he had succeeded in emerging, pencil in hand, from under a cloud
of madness. But could he hope to do so a second time? During these
first days of splendid freedom, his one desire was to get well quickly.
If Viaud did his best to maintain an illusion of independence, Lautrec,
on his side, played up to him and accepted the charade. But he did
more than merely tolerate Viaud's supervision. Even left to himself, he
would have abstained from drinking. To be healthy in body, alert and
clear in mind and precise in memory, these were his sole aims at the
moment. Everything was at present subordinate to his will to live.

Lautrec stayed only a short time in Paris. After a dinner party at the

Dihaus'—where he had the great joy of sitting next to Degas ('You enabled me to recover my son,' Countess Adèle said to Mlle Dihau next day)—and a party in the studio in the Avenue Frochot for his closest friends, who were a little 'embarrassed,' he left with his 'bear-leader' for Le Crotoy.

He was invigorated by the sea air, and went sailing and fishing. At the beginning of July, he went on to Le Havre, to take ship for Bordeaux.

The year before, he had on two or three occasions visited Le Star*, one of the 'boîtes' for English sailors near the harbour.

And now he went back there, not to drink but to recapture the atmosphere, which held so much nostalgia for him. At the back of the hall of Le Star was a stage, hung with purple curtains covered with gold lyres, on which the singers performed. Dockers and their girls mingled with the sailors, who made up most of the audience. From time to time, amid the smoke of foreign tobacco and the smell of gin and whisky, rollicking old English songs were sung in chorus.

Lautrec at once started to draw. There was plenty of time, he could go to Arcachon later. Attracted by the barmaid, Dolly, who had a charming, dimpled face and fair curls, he asked Joyant to send him painting materials as quickly as possible; he felt a need to put his creative powers to the test. Was he still Lautrec? In spite of the phrase: 'I've bought my freedom with my drawings', which he proudly repeated on every possible occasion, he was not altogether reassured.

As soon as he received the materials from Joyant, Lautrec made a drawing of Dolly in red chalk, followed by a painting in oils on a limewood panel, a wood he had used from time to time for his portraits during the last two or three years. Before his illness, he had sometimes been seen scraping and polishing wooden panels in his studio.

He painted 'Miss Dolly' in a dark blue blouse with a pink collar. It is a fine and lively painting, though it bears the imprint of his anxieties. There is a freshness about the English girl and her laughing face that must have seemed to Lautrec the face of hope itself.

Sending his work to Joyant, Lautrec asked his friend to inform 'the

* Le Star was in the Rue du Général-Faidherbe. It closed in 1940.

Administration.' For, on his discharge from the asylum, the painter had not only been provided with a bear-leader, but his finances had been placed under control so as to put his affairs in order and 'moderate his spending.'* From now on, the family steward was to pay a fixed allowance for Lautrec to a solicitor. Into another account, held by the same solicitor, were paid the proceeds of sales of his pictures by Joyant or others on the painter's behalf.† This was a secret account 'so that the steward and the family should not be less generous and cut down the monthly allowance.'‡ Joyant had the decisive say in this 'administration' and to some extent acted as Lautrec's guardian. 'I hope that my guardian will be pleased with his ward,' Lautrec wrote when sending him the portrait of the barmaid. Lautrec himself was undoubtedly pleased with it.

He was staying at the Hôtel de l'Amirauté and was in no hurry to leave Le Havre. There he had met Lucien Guitry and Marthe Brandès. With them he went to Granville, then returned to Le Star, where he had found further subjects for two or three lithographs. Except for alcohol, he had almost entirely returned to his former way of life.

In the second half of July, Lautrec at last decided to take ship for Bordeaux. As soon as he arrived in the south-west, he went to Taussat to stay with one of his local friends, M. Fabre, at the Villa Bagatelle.

Taussat had never been a very productive place for Lautrec; and this year it quickly doused the creative spark that had flamed for a while in Le Havre. He painted little or nothing during this summer. He fished and swam and had the use of an old whale-boat belonging to the Customs office, which he sailed every day with a sailor by the name of Zakarie. When he returned to Paris in the autumn, Lautrec seemed in perfect health both physically and mentally.

---

* Joyant.

† Lautrec's works already had considerable market value. On April 29, one of his pictures (*Jeune Femme Assise*) had realised 1,400 francs (about £240 today), at an auction. Lautrec's pictures were in the hands of a number of dealers, the Bernheim Gallery for instance. It must, however, be added that they were often hidden in the cellar, more or less lost among numbers of other works. 'Excellent, they're maturing!' said the painter.

‡ Joyant.

But was this in fact true? To his more perceptive friends, including Joyant, Lautrec seemed different. 'In this human mechanism,' there was, they thought, something 'broken.' Lautrec's curiosity was destroyed. He could laugh and joke; but it was no longer with the laughter and the vitality of the past. It was as if he were forcing himself to resemble the old Lautrec.

He went daily to the Bois in Calmèse's governess-cart, with Philibert between the shafts. But he took no interest in new sights, clinging merely to his old passions. Most of the works he produced during this winter of 1899 to 1900—for he had gone back to his palette and lithographic crayon—were of horses, jockeys and women on horseback. Besides the proprietor of the livery stable and the little pony, he made lithographs of the racecourse: *Le Jockey ou Chevaux de course, Le Paddock, Jockey se rendant au poteau, L'Entraineur et son Jockey, L'Amazone et le Chien*. He also painted a canvas called *Aux Courses*. As Joyant said, he was like a hunted roe-deer returning to his original cover. And yet, with what chagrin Lautrec must have looked at these jockeys and horses. A doctor had advised him to exercise on a wooden horse in his room.

Returning to the more immediate past, Lautrec painted a fierce portrait of Lucy Jourdan, a regular customer of La Souris, supping in the Rat-Mort restaurant. Shortly before his confinement in the asylum, Lautrec's work had been showing a certain evolution in technique. This evolution had now become more marked. His art, from the very first manifestations of his mastery, had been dominated by line. And as his talent gained strength, so his line had become increasingly forceful. But contrary to his previous method, he was now abandoning line for tones and colour values. Lautrec's intelligence as a painter was so developed and his eye so sensitive, that he at once obtained remarkable results with his new technique. He translated the effects of light in his portrait of Lucy Jourdan with extraordinary mastery, and at the same time succeeded in rendering with great force the psychological character of his sitter. His colour acquired warmth, resonance and subtlety.

But why had this fundamental change in technique taken place? It is inconceivable that Lautrec was unaware that he was stripping his work of its characteristic originality. Was he, in fact, altering his technique by an effort of will? It would seem that line as such was now escaping him; he could no longer handle it with the old vibrant intensity and sober explicitness. By resorting to tonal values he could perhaps achieve by other means what he was in process of losing, and attempt to disguise a frustration which he knew to be irremediable.

The only satisfaction Lautrec had achieved from his life had been derived from his art. In his worst moments of depression, it had sufficed to take a pencil or brush in his hand for him to recover his happiness. Without art, his life would have been an appalling void. Lautrec did not reveal his secret thoughts but one may well ask whether he was not haunted during these winter days by tragic and insistent questions. He was thirty-five. Was his one support to be taken from him? Could the journalists who had written about him during his stay in the asylum have been right? Had the crisis in February 1889 put an end to his career? Was he to do no more than merely survive?

For five or six months, first under treatment in the asylum and then in his delight at having escaped from it, he had resisted the temptation of alcohol. But that was over now. Lautrec had begun to drink again.

What could Viaud do? Remonstrance was of little use. In was difficult for him to assume an attitude of severity. Without the painter's co-operation he was bound to fail in his task. To put his foot down would have caused a rupture which no one could have remedied. Forced to give lee-way, Viaud had been obliged to let Lautrec order a drink here and there, at Weber's for instance. Soon Lautrec was drinking without restraint.

In so far as he could, Viaud tried to prevent excesses. Fortunately, Lautrec on his side seemed to wish to prolong the *modus vivendi* which had been established between them. He even hid himself to drink; and Viaud was far from knowing everything that went on. He had of course noticed the walking-stick with a silver knob which Lautrec had recently bought from an Italian antique-dealer. But there was one thing about it he did not know: it was hollow and concealed a long glass container which could hold about half a litre. And in the knob there was a little cup. Every morning, while he was dressing, Lautrec filled his 'walking-stick flask' with port, rum or brandy, his provision of alcohol for the day.

Lautrec's friends, those who did not heedlessly and inconsiderately encourage his drinking, were desperately concerned. They tried to frighten him with the inevitable consequences of a relapse. They painted the results of his dissipation in sombre colours. Did he want to go back to Madrid-les-Bains? Why could he not be more sensible? But Lautrec was in no mood to listen to reason. The deep fear within him was not of a kind, suggested Arsène Alexandre, to 'prevent him, but on the contrary to hasten him towards his end by means whose effectiveness had been only too well established.' Suicide, madness, and an early death? So be it. 'Don't talk to me of vines and things,' Lautrec said, 'unless they're in a glass.' As soon as Viaud's back was turned, he 'filled himself up with juice.'

He became aggressive again. When a society woman simperingly complimented him on his work: 'All right! All right! Don't make so much fuss!' he replied rudely.

One night, at Weber's, someone told the story of Count Alphonse's latest extravagance. Having returned to Paris, the Templar—he was living near the Trocadéro, in a ground floor flat in the Rue Boissière—was amusing everyone by 'behaving like an old trapper.'* He spent his time searching Paris for an otter to tame, or for a Kirghiz horse-switch. One afternoon, strolling down the boulevards with Count d'Avaray, he saw a working woman gazing enviously at a ring in a jeweller's shop. Taking her by the arm, he led her into the shop, bought the ring for 5,000 francs† and gave it to her. 'But, Monsieur, I don't know you!' she cried, utterly bewildered. 'Nor I you, Madame,' he replied, 'but it shan't be said that such a pretty woman desired a jewel in vain!' Raising his hat, he took his leave and rejoined his dumbfounded companion.

'And they accuse me of extravagance!' exclaimed Lautrec. Upon which, a young man with a pale face, 'doe's eyes' and as 'covered with wool as a Chinese bibelot,'‡ replied in a hesitating, insinuating voice,

---

* Joyant.
† Approximately £800 today.
‡ Léon Daudet.

that 'such gestures were not stupid, that they even had a certain useful-
ness for they asserted caste.' His name was Marcel Proust. Without
even acknowledging his presence, Lautrec muttered in an aside that
this was just middle-class stupidity, which was always prepared to
'admire an absurd gesture or a sunset.'

Joyant, thinking it might please Lautrec, tried to obtain the Legion
of Honour for him; he introduced him to a minister who admired his
pictures, but the painter interrupted His Excellency by saying: 'Have
you considered, Monsieur le Ministre, how odd the red ribbon will
look when I go to paint a brothel?' For Lautrec had, of course, returned
to the Rue des Moulins.

How could the painter's interest be aroused, how could he be
brought back to a more sensible way of life and his will to live be
restored? Joyant tried again, but the results were not very happy. He
obtained commissions for Lautrec to paint portraits of fashionable
women. But it was no greater pleasure to Lautrec than it was to his
sitters. After two or three sittings they refused to go on, horrified by
the deformed dwarf who 'mercilessly took them to pieces.' Joyant
took him to see mannequins displaying dresses at the big couturiers;
but they made no appeal to Lautrec. Their sophisticated beauty and
formal attitudes utterly bored him.

Nevertheless, he continued to work intermittently. In January,
probably commissioned by the Natansons, he designed a poster for
La Gitane, a play by Jean Richepin, which opened on the 22nd of that
month at the Théâtre Antoine. In it appeared Marthe Mellot, Alfred
Natanson's wife. Lautrec took little interest in the play itself. He
spent the first night drinking at the theatre bar. Though he had
not listened to a single scene of *La Gitane*, it did not prevent his
proclaiming that the play had had 'an enormous success,' an 'un-
precedented success.' 'A success! It was a complete failure. There was
even booing,' someone said. 'Quite possibly,' replied Lautrec, 'but they
were just spiteful people!'

He painted an occasional portrait: one in luminous colours of Mlle
Margouin, the mistress of a friend and a milliner by trade, a pretty
blonde, with 'a charming face like that of an awakened squirrel'.* She

* Leclercq.

was rather child-like and he enjoyed behaving like a child too. He
called her 'the Croquesi-Margouin.' From a brief stay at Villeneuve,
he brought back a portrait of Coolus. Going into Coolus' room one
day, he swept away the pages of a play on which the writer was
engaged and said: 'You've worked enough! I need you.' He led
'Colette' to his easel and said: 'Sit down there, I'm going to paint your
portrait in the manner of El Greco!' It was, of course, merely a joke;
there is nothing of El Greco in the portrait.

These works did not come easily. When, in the spring, Joyant took
Lautrec once again to the Somme estuary, Lautrec decided to paint
his friend, posing with a shotgun and wearing his yellow oilskins and
a sou'wester. But he encountered great difficulties. Nearly every
morning he unhappily obliterated what he had painted the day before.
He struggled with the portrait which he could not finish and exhausted
himself and his subject with innumerable sittings.*

At the same time, he was busy illustrating a couple of Dihau's
songs: *Tes Yeux* and *Au Jardin de mon Coeur*. His design for the second
song depicted a man in an attitude of supplication at the feet of a cruel
woman. The song was very 'sniveldrop' according to Lautrec; and
the theme very 'sniveldrop' too.

In mid-April, the Universal Exhibition of 1900 opened. Lautrec—
who was a member of the board of selectors for posters—visited it in
a bath-chair. The explorers whom he met at Weber's, the 'Africans,'
welcomed him. But the Negroes, the Japanese dances and the
elephants from the Congo, which in the old days he would have
greeted with enthusiasm, aroused no response now. Even the Japanese
Pavilion, which he had hoped to enjoy, left him indifferent.

In May, cutting short his stay in Paris, he went to Le Crotoy. Before
leaving he gave his hollow stick to a friend. Viaud had discovered the
trick.†

                              *   *   *

This time the Channel coast did not restore Lautrec's desire to work.
Lucien Guitry, whom he met at Honfleur, suggested he should

---

* 'Not less than seventy-five,' wrote Joyant, who remembered it as a 'torture'.
† The friend who was given the stick, Curnonsky, later gave it to the museum
at Albi, where it is at present.

decorate the programme of *L'Assommoir*, which was to be revived in November at the Théâtre de la Renaissance. Lautrec did no more than make a sketch for it.

Everything was going wrong. At Le Havre, the police were keeping Le Star and the other similar establishments under surveillance. 'No more barmaids!' Besides, he was short of money. 'H.L. and Co. are most *Limited*!' he wrote to Joyant. The family steward, arguing that the vines had been ravaged by storms and that the wine could be sold only at a loss, was trying to reduce the painter's allowance. But to this Lautrec would not agree. He was furious. 'An unhealthy exasperation, certainly,' said Joyant, and aggravated 'by family misunderstandings,' but none the less justified.

Now Lautrec became belligerent. He wanted his money. It became an obsession. There was a good deal of wrangling and Joyant intervened, trying, though it was by no means easy, to 'serve as a buffer.' Lautrec, cut to the quick, became as pig-headed as an angry child. He wanted the money, not so much to have it or spend it, as to proclaim 'his right to freedom,' his right to use and abuse his days as he pleased. With a 'stubborn anxiety to show that he still existed,' he shook off Viaud's tutelage and drank openly, perhaps even more than he wanted to.

It was in this frame of mind that, on June 30, Lautrec took ship at Le Havre for Bordeaux. At Taussat he grew calmer. He stayed there till the end of September and then went to spend part of the autumn at Malromé.

It was a fine autumn that year. Under the yellowing trees in the park, Lautrec crouched by the lake and amused a group of children by rolling iridescent drops of water about on the leaves of water-lilies. The children were enchanted by the play of colour.*

Taussat had 'refitted' Lautrec once again. 'Shout as loud as you can,' he told the children, delighted to 'make the grown-ups jump' and in particular the governess, who 'frowned with a disapproving air' at the din.† Once more he felt the need to draw and paint. In the Château

*Recorded by Mary Tapié de Céleyran.
† Mary Tapié de Céleyran.

dining-room, above the chimney-piece, he began a mural decoration. It was a portrait of Viaud dressed as an admiral. He clothed his 'bear-leader' in a scarlet coat, standing at a ship's rail; on his head was a tie-wig and on his hand a gauntlet.

The painting made little progress. Lautrec was working more and more slowly. When he left Malromé, it was still unfinished. But the desire to work was coming alive in him again.

As soon as he reached Bordeaux, which he had chosen as his winter residence instead of Paris, he set about looking for a studio. In the meantime, he found temporary accomodation with Viaud at 66, Rue de Caudéran. He eventually found a studio in the Rue de la Porte-Dijeaux, where the art dealer Imberti, of the Cours de l'Intendance, kept his stock. It was a big room, but not very well lit since the light came only from a small skylight.

Lautrec began working with an intensity comparable to the past. 'I'm working very hard,' he wrote to Joyant on December 6. *La Belle Hélène*, at the Grand-Théâtre, 'delighted' him. 'I've already captured it,' he said; and then added: 'Hélène is played by a fat whore called Cocyte.'

A few days later, he went to the same theatre with the editor of *La Petite Gironde* to see Isidore de Lara's opera, *Messaline*. 'Splendid! Splendid!' he kept saying at the top of his voice. There were protests from the audience around him, but he paid no attention to them. 'She's divine!' he cried pointing to the principal singer, Mlle Ganne. Then, suddenly, without a word to his companion, he got to his feet, jostled his way past his neighbours and went out. For two days, he shut himself up in his studio, excitedly making sketches of what he had seen.*

Though he was painting slowly and painfully, and with many corrections, he produced no less than six pictures inspired by *Messaline* during these last days of 1900 and the first weeks of 1901. He made portraits of the old violinist, Dancla, who was still giving recitals at the age of eighty-three; of M. Fabre, of Taussat; and of a certain Mme Marthe. But his style was growing clumsy and the results were more frequently mediocre. To what extent was Lautrec aware of this? When

* Recorded by Albert Rèche.

he sent his pictures of *Messaline* to Joyant, he said: 'I am very satisfied: I think you will be even more so.'*

His physical health was no better. He was hardly eating, and growing thinner and weaker, but this did not prevent him drinking and frequenting brothels. 'Send me as soon as possible . . . the cash I need to go about,' he wrote to Joyant. The financial problem had still not been settled, and Joyant found it impossible to unravel an 'imbroglio in which the actors are all more or less intractable and unable to understand each other.' The thought of being short of money was intolerable to Lautrec. In the past he had never much bothered about the commercial value of his work, but now it became a cause of anxiety. 'I see in *The New York Herald* that pictures of mine have been sold in a sale organised by Mancini. Will you be kind enough to look about the prices and write me about?' [*sic*, in English]. He had taken part in an exhibition of modern art organised by Imberti, but had sold nothing, although, as he said, the press had been 'very polite about my daubs.' He felt that everyone was persecuting him. Almost at the end of his tether, he stubbornly continued to pursue his pleasures and his work, as if he needed to prove not only to others but also to himself that his vitality at least was not impaired.

This feverish pace could not last long. At the end of March, he had a relapse. Lautrec found that his legs would no longer support him.

It was a brief attack and not a very serious one: and after being given electrical treatment and dosed with *nux vomica*, he recovered fairly rapidly. 'Both Bacchus and Venus are barred,' he wrote to Joyant on April 2. 'I'm painting and even sculpting. When I get bored, I write poetry.'†

Guibert (he drew him running after a Bordelaise on the harbour quay) and then Dethomas came to visit him, as well as his old

---

* 'I am very satisfied': some critics have enlarged on this opinion, seeing in Lautrec's change of style a widening of his talent. It is difficult to subscribe to this judgment. The final period of Lautrec's life was a decline, and, in agreement with the remarks of Douglas Cooper, one can look on most of the works he made at this period only as a tragic sequel to the extraordinary flowering of the previous years. There is a temptation to admire everything by an artist one loves; but it is often hazardous.

† Nothing further is known of Lautrec's sculpture and poetry.

master Princeteau. But Lautrec wanted to get back to Paris as soon as possible.

Illness had twice laid him low. The second crisis, though not in itself serious, was nevertheless a warning. Lautrec knew that the third could be fatal. He wanted to see Paris again before he died.

* * *

He reached the Avenue Frochot on April 15.

His physical appearance horrified his friends. 'Look what's happened to him!' they exclaimed in distress. Lautrec was hardly a shadow of his former self. He could walk only with difficulty and his clothes hung loosely on him.

On April 25, he was pleased to learn that some of his paintings, auctioned at the Hôtel Drouot in the Depeaux sale, had achieved high prices: one, *La Toilette*, had found a buyer at 4,000 francs.* He took up his brushes and, as at Bordeaux, went desperately to work on new paintings—scenes from the Bois de Boulogne, a portrait of the poet André Rivoire and another of the architect, Louis-Octave Raquin, about which Tristan Bernard wrote some verses:

> *Le timide Octave Raquin*
> *N'a pas l'allure triomphale,*
> *Ressemblerait à Charles Quint*
> *S'il était moins hydrocéphale.*

Tapié de Céleyran had taken his degree as a doctor of medicine in 1899 with the thesis *Sur un Cas d'Élytrocèle postérieure*, dedicated to the memory of Péan the surgeon (who had died after a short illness the previous year). Lautrec reconstructed the scene of the thesis being argued in a canvas in which he painted his cousin face to face with their common friend, Professor Wurtz, a member of the examining board.

It is an academically dull canvas such as Cormon would have appreciated. Lautrec's work had reached its conclusion. His hand had lost its genius. And with it Lautrec had lost his reason for living.

---

* About £600 today. His three other paintings in the sale went for 3,000 francs (*En Meublé*), 2,100 francs (*La Pierreuse*) and 1,860 francs (*Gens chic*).

From the disorder of his studio, Lautrec brought out all the canvases, boards and panels he had accumulated during the creative years. If he had wanted to see Paris again before dying, it was perhaps above all to take a last look at his work and give it a final touch.

Since he had lived in this studio, he had accumulated an enormous number of unfinished sketches, some of which had been lying there for years. One by one, he went over his pictures, divided them into two lots, signing those that seemed good to him and putting the others aside.

On July 15, when he left Paris, Lautrec closed the door on a studio in perfect order. It already had the cold look of a museum.*

Tapié de Céleyran, Joyant and various other friends accompanied the painter and his 'bear-leader' to the Gare d'Orléans. They knew he had not long to live. Until the last moment, Lautrec was joking and trying to d becole his friends about his health. He even talked about coming 'ly ve oon. But the moment of truth had come. Saying good-bye to Renée Vert, he said: 'We can embrace, for you won't see me again.'

And to diminish the effect of this admission, he laughingly raised his finger, and added: 'When I'm dead, I shall have a nose like Cyrano!'

---

* The works left in his studio, together with a few gifts and acquisitions, went to form the very important basis of the museum at Albi. For the years 1899, 1900 and 1901, Joyant catalogues respectively fifteen, twenty-one and ten paintings.

CHAPTER THREE

The Flies

'Everyone is born a king, and most people die in exile.'
OSCAR WILDE: *A Woman of No Importance*

THE sands were burning hot and the air heady with the scent of the pines. But this time Taussat did not revive Lautrec. Amid the heat and thunderstorms of summer, his exhaustion was increasingly apparent. He was becoming weaker every day and was evidently failing. His arms and legs were emaciated and he had a pain in his chest. The doctors said he was consumptive.

One night in the middle of August, he collapsed with some attack of paralysis.

*   *   *

Viaud sent a telegram to Countess Adèle, who came at once and took Lautrec back to the Château de Malromé. This was his wish. They arrived there on August 20.

At Malromé, Lautrec emerged from his torpor and seemed to revive a little. 'I've eaten, eh?' he said, having forced himself to swallow a few mouthfuls. 'I've eaten, eh?' he insisted.

In the château dining-room, above the chimney-piece, Viaud's portrait as an admiral was still unfinished. With extraordinary strength of mind Lautrec hoisted himself on to a step-ladder and started to paint. But he was too weak to go on for long at a time. The sweat poured off him and his legs gave way. He had to get off the step-ladder and draw breath between every few strokes of the brush. Finally he gave up the attempt because the brush kept falling from his hand.

The paralysis gradually spread through his body. He could neither walk nor eat. He was taken out in a carriage into the park. At meals, he was brought to the table in a wheel-chair. The portrait of his 'bear-leader' was opposite him on the wall. He would never finish it. His hands might have been anyone's hands now.

His mother wanted him to see a priest. Why not? The sorry life that had been allotted him was almost over. He would never scandalise anyone again. He had run a wild course, and he could still smell the scent of the free and dangerous life he had lived. But now he was exhausted. He had returned to the bosom of his family.

He dreamed of Le Bosc, its tiled roofs and ivy-covered tower, the fields in which the cow-bells rang; and the high woods beyond in which the 'Black Prince' used to ride.

'Look after yourself, Monsieur Henri, and keep your courage up. See you again soon!' the priest said. 'Yes, and next time,' replied Lautrec with irony, 'you'll come back with your little candles and your hand-bell . . .'

The grapes were ripening on the sun-warmed vines, but Lautrec could no longer leave his room.

He had become almost completely deaf. He no longer laughed, and spoke only very little. He was scarcely aware of what went on round him.

His body took up very little room in the bed under the single sheet that was his only covering because of the heat; he lay with his eyes fixed on the ceiling.

He was nearly thirty-seven, the age at which his friend Vincent had died. The age at which Raphael and Watteau had died. Perhaps he thought of La Goulue and Valentin le Désossé, of Rosa la Rouge, of Bruant roaring out his insults, and of the procession of women in his life, unchaste and consoling, or inaccessible and crucifying. Of Elsa la Viennoise, of Rolande of the Rue des Moulins, of Mireille of the Rue d'Amboise, of Valadon and of Marie Charlet . . . 'And when night begins to fall I hope Jeanne d'Armagnac will come to my bedside. She does sometimes, and cheers me up and plays with me, and I listen to her talk, without daring to look at her. She is so tall and beautiful! And I am neither tall nor beautiful . . .' Everything had to be paid for in this world. Genius, like the rest.

Lautrec was delirious; his eyes wide open. Outside, the oppressive heat of early September lay over Malromé. The air was thick, almost syrupy. The shutters of the two windows in the room had been half closed so that shadow might give a semblance of freshness. Flies buzzed and stung him. Now and then he tried to raise himself to brush them away, but he could no longer do even that. The sheet seemed to crush his limbs as if it were of lead. He gasped for breath. 'Mama!' he called. 'Mama, I'm thirsty.'

*   *   *

His mother knelt at the foot of the bed and prayed; beside her a nun was telling her beads.

They tried to keep up his strength with port and spirits. He was no longer delirious. The Curé of Malromé had given him the last sacraments; and, a little while before, when his father, who had arrived from Paris by the evening train, had come into the room, Lautrec had looked at him for a moment and said: 'I knew you'd be in at the death, Papa.'

There were other relations there too: Tapié, Louis Pascal and his mother. No one spoke. Old Adeline moved silently about. Lautrec's breathing was becoming increasingly difficult. From time to time, Countess Adèle rose to her feet and put her hand on her son's damp forehead. With an effort, he leaned towards her, and said: 'Mama . . . You! No one but you!' And in a whisper: 'Dying's damned hard!'

The heat was oppressive and the flies buzzed incessantly.

Count Alphonse, looking for something useful to do, suggested he should cut off his son's beard. It was an Arab custom. Prevented from doing so, he knelt by the bed, pulled the elastic from his boots and flicked carefully at the flies on the sheet.

When Tapié bent over his cousin in the darkened room and saw what was going on, Lautrec looked up at him and said: 'The old fool!'

These were the last words he uttered.

As night fell there was a low murmur of thunder in the distance. Countess Adèle and the nun continued to pray. Lautrec's end seemed interminably prolonged. It was a quarter past two in the morning when he died.

A little later, when the family were beginning the vigil, the storm broke over Malromé. The rain fell in torrents. Lightning split the sky. And then, between two flashes, shots were heard in the night answering the thunder. Count Alphonse was shooting owls from one of the château towers.

EPILOGUE

LAUTREC was buried in the cemetery of Saint-André-du-Bois, near Malromé. (Later on, fearing the cemetery was to be abandoned, Countess Adèle transferred her son's remains to Verdelais nearby.)

Count Alphonse was conspicuous at the funeral for his eccentricity. Instead of following in the procession, he took his place on the box of the hearse 'to see how the coachman drove and whether his son Henri was being taken to his last resting-place in a manner proper to a gentleman'.* Whipping up the horse, which was going too slowly for him, he increased the pace to such an extent that the mourners who were walking behind had to run through the muddy lanes to keep up.†

* * *

The news of the painter's death was received in a variety of ways. His enemies once again took the opportunity to attack him. 'It is fortunate for humanity that there are few artists of his sort,' wrote Jules Roques in *Le Courrier français*. 'Lautrec's talent, for it would be absurd to deny him one, was an immoral talent of pernicious and unfortunate influence.' As for Lepelletier, he renewed his attack of 1899 in *L'Écho de Paris*: 'Among the painters of our period, Lautrec will certainly leave the trace of his curious and immoral talent, which was that of a deformed man, who saw ugliness in everything about him and exaggerated that ugliness, while recording all the blemishes, perversities and realities of life . . .'

And, indeed, these opinions were similar to those held by Count Alphonse himself. Joyant, who defended his friend's work and devoted himself to that task until his death, received on several occasions

* Recorded by Mary Tapié de Céleyran.
† Recorded by Albert Rèche.

letters from Count Alphonse expressing his contempt for his son's
work with remarkable heartlessness:

'I do not propose to become converted and praise up to the skies,
now that he is dead, what I could not understand when he was alive,
except to say that they are daring and hazardous studio studies.'
(October 22, 1901).

'Though in my opinion [his works] have been for the most part
rather too neglected . . . merely because the artist is dead and
was my son, I cannot go into ecstasies about what I consider to
be no more than rough-hewn works, the result of his temperamental
audacity . . .' (February 4, 1902).

And when, after an exhibition of Lautrec's works at Toulouse (1907),
a committee was formed to erect a statue to the painter, Count
Alphonse wrote to the committee, of which Arsène Alexandre had
become President (1909), that 'his son had no talent and that he would
oppose the proposal to the utmost of his power.'* Similarly, in 1912,
having heard that Gustave Coquiot was writing a book about Lautrec,
he threatened to 'chastise' him in single combat. 'There was considerable difficulty,' recorded Coquiot, 'in preventing his riding post-haste
to me in Paris.'

But before Count Alphonse died in Albi, in December 1912, he
wrote to Joyant: 'You believed in his work more than I did and you
were right.'

Joyant, to whom Countess Adèle had given complete freedom of
action, wanted to give a worthy setting to the works Lautrec had left
at his death. It so happened that, due to the separation of Church and
State, the Bishop's Palace at Albi, the Palais de la Berbie, had become
the property of the district of Tarn which, in 1907, had handed it over
to the town of Albi on condition that it became a museum.

Joyant started negotiations to have part of this museum in Lautrec's
birth-place devoted to his work. In July 1922, when the organisation
of the Palais de la Berbie was under way, Joyant's plans succeeded.
On the 30th, Léon Bérard, Minister of Public Education and Fine
Arts, opened the Musée de Toulouse-Lautrec in the Palais de la Berbie.
On the following day, a deed was drawn up making the agreement

* Recorded by L. Charles-Bellet.

legal and the town of Albi became the owners in perpetuity of Lautrec's works given by Countess Adèle. A year later, the museum was endowed by the corporation.

To the works left in the painter's studio were added gifts from Joyant, Gabriel Tapié de Céleyran, Romain Coolus, and from Colonel Wurtz. Since then, the gallery has acquired further paintings. At the present time, its catalogue lists 215 paintings and pastels, 140 drawings, 103 lithographs, 25 posters and 8 dry-points. The museum also owns 17 lithographic stones, 7 zinc plates and one piece of ceramic, as well as a number of portraits of Lautrec by his uncle, Charles de Toulouse-Lautrec, and his friends Anquetin, Adolphe Albert, Vuillard, Dethomas, Manzi and others.

In 1926 and 1927, Joyant completed the task of establishing Lautrec's fame with the publication of a two-volume catalogue of his works. This loyal friend died in 1930, the same year as Countess Adèle and Gabriel Tapié de Céleyran.

*   *   *

The opening of the Musée de Toulouse-Lautrec in the Palais de la Berbie put an end to the official hostility from which the painter's work had suffered for many long years.

In 1902, on behalf of Countess Adèle, Joyant had suggested to the keeper of the Musée du Luxembourg, Léonce Bénédite, that he should select any pictures he wished from the painter's studio. After much hesitation, Bénédite accepted a single work, *La Femme au boa*, which was rather furtively hung in the Salle Caillebotte in 1903. It was transferred to the Louvre in 1947.

In the meantime, the Société des Amis du Luxembourg had offered the museum, in 1905, the *Portrait de Monsieur Delaporte au Jardin de Paris*. It was accepted by the advisory committee to the National Museums, but refused by the superior Council of Museums on the vehement protest of the chairman —Lautrec's old master, Bonnat.

Bonnat (who died in 1922) never changed his opinion. When Paul Leclercq gave the portrait of himself by Lautrec to the Louvre in 1920, Bonnat said: 'You're making a pretty Louvre for us!'

By now, however, besides *La Femme au boa*, there were two other

Lautrecs in the collections of the national museums: in 1914, *La Clownesse Cha-U-Kao* and *La Toilette* had gone respectively to the Louvre as a gift from Isaac de Camondo and to the Luxembourg by the legacy of Pierre Goujon.

Moreover, in 1902, the Bibliothèque Nationale had accepted from Countess Adèle the gift of a collection of engravings: 371 original lithographs, first states, successive printings, complete sequences.*

* * *

During these years, Lautrec's work continued to gain in prestige and to extend its influence. During his short lifetime he had made nearly 600 paintings, approximately 330 lithographs, 31 posters, 9 dry-points and 3 monotypes as well as thousands of drawings and sketches, and it was not long before he was assessed as one of the most important artists of the modern period. Many painters have been influenced by Lautrec, notably Picasso, who in his early days derived considerable inspiration from his work.

Also, the auction prices of Lautrec's pictures were steadily increasing. Barely five years after the painter's death, in 1906, his *Intérieur de Cabaret* found a buyer at 7,000 gold francs. In 1914, *Dans le Lit* went for 15,000 gold francs (£2,000 or more today).

* * *

After Lautrec's death, his circle of friends rapidly broke up. Gabriel. Tapié de Céleyran, who did not much care for the excitements of the capital, went back to Albi. Joyant and Manzi started an art gallery in the Rue de la Ville-l'Évêque; between 1910 and 1913 they published a review, *Les Arts*. Viaud took to fashion designing: he succeeded in restoring his fortunes with the leg-of-mutton sleeve, which became very popular in America.

The artists and writers who were grouped round *La Revue blanche* also dispersed and the Natansons published the last issue of the magazine on April 15, 1903. Most of their contributors, both painters and writers, had brilliant careers.

During its eleven and a half years of existence, *La Revue blanche* played a very important part in the literary and, in particular, the

---

* Catalogue of gifts to the Cabinet des Estampes.

artistic history of the period. As Thadée Natanson wrote, 'the painters who were usually called "les Nabis" might well have been called "the painters of *La Revue blanche*".'

When the review ceased publication, Félix Fénéon, as anxious for obscurity as ever, went to the *Matin*, where he had the curious job of producing 'News in three lines'. Then, in 1906, he went to the Bernheim Gallery. This appointment, though deliberately kept secret, was nevertheless of great importance in many ways.

As for Thadée Natanson, a great personal sorrow was in store for him: Misia left him to marry, in 1902, Alfred Edwards, the editor of the *Matin*. He spent the last years of his life writing his reminiscences of the painters he had known, in particular of Lautrec and Bonnard.

Cormon's pupils had varied fates. Some went into professions that bore no relation to painting: Charles-Édouard Lucas became a business man. Some adopted semi-artistic careers: Henri Rachou became keeper of the museum at Toulouse. Others, however, remained faithful to their first vocation, though they only partially realised their ambitions: Anquetin, whom everyone, including himself, thought destined for fame, died unknown in 1932. Émile Bernard also failed to fulfil expectations. In 1893, he travelled to the eastern Mediterranean and Egypt, where he lived for many years. He returned to Europe in 1904. Deliberately turning his back on the enthusiasms of his youth, he became the theoretician of neo-classicism and founded a review, *La Rénovation esthétique*. Together with his friend Anquetin, he fought for his ideas, but they never made the mark he expected. The important part he had played in the evolution of modern painting in 1893 was forgotten: an injustice which is beginning to be repaired today.

During the course of this book, I have already referred to the fate of La Goulue and some of the other dancers of the Moulin Rouge. But of most of them all traces have been lost. Valentin le Désossé, as one might expect, ended his life in comfortable circumstances. He died in 1907 at the house of his solicitor brother.

Bruant, who had retired to Courtenay, was a candidate at Belleville for the parliamentary elections of 1898. Disdaining political speeches, he campaigned with song. The electors applauded him but failed to vote for him. The 'popular singer' spent his retirement in writing novels for serialisation, a melodrama and a dictionary of slang. In the autumn of 1924, impoverished as a result of the First World War, he gave recitals at *L'Empire* in the Avenue de Wagram. He had a triumphant success. But he was then seventy-three and the effort was too much for him. Returning to Courtenay, he died a few weeks later, in February 1925.

Jane Avril ceased dancing in 1905. She married the designer Maurice Biais, soon became a widow, and spent the rest of her life in melancholy retirement. 'Alone? Am I not always alone? My dreams were so unrealistic! . . . I have fluttered through my time without ever revealing my inner self.' Poverty saddened her last years. She died in 1943 in a home for old people at Jouy-en-Josas.

Yvette Guilbert changed her act completely in 1900. From then on she sang old French songs and sentimental ballads, which brought her new fame. A great star, she went on singing well into old age.

It has been impossible to discover how Lautrec's 'little friends' in the Rue d'Amboise and the Rue des Moulins ended their lives. Nevertheless, there is a footnote. After the sale of the furniture from the Rue des Moulins, in 1946, a Parisian second-hand dealer put on display one of the lots he had bought: an elaborately decorated copper bath. One day, two very old ladies stopped in front of his shop-window and gazed at the bath for a long time. They even went into the shop to get a closer look at it. The dealer asked them if they wanted to buy it and. they replied: 'Oh, no! We're merely looking . . . It brings back so many memories!'

They were two old prostitutes from the brothel. Perhaps, locked in their hearts, they still preserved the memory of a little crippled man of genius who had loved them better than anyone else.

BIBLIOGRAPHY

LAUTREC's writings consist only of a certain number of letters, of which there have been no complete edition. Most of those of which we have knowledge were published by Maurice Joyant in his *Henri de Toulouse-Lautrec*. His youthful letters have been quoted at some length by Mary Tapié de Céleyran in *Notre Oncle Lautrec*. A sort of letter-diary, *Cahier de Zig-Zags*, which dates from 1881, was published in *L'Amour de l'Art* in April, 1931. The letters to Étienne Devismes were published in facsimile in Devismes' *Cocotte*, with illustrations by Toulouse-Lautrec (Éditions du Chêne, Paris, 1953). There are various letters quoted in a number of works: a letter from Lautrec to his mother in *Toulouse-Lautrec en Belgique* by M. G. Dortu, Madeleine Grillaert and Jean Adhémar; a letter to Bruant in *Aristide Bruant* by Jeanne Landre; and another to Robert de Montcabrier in *Le Musée d'Albi* by L. Charles-Bellet, etc.

*　　*　　*

Although the artist's own writings are few, fortunately the recollections of his contemporaries are many, concerning not only Lautrec himself but also the circle in which he moved. The most important of all these is the work of the painter's loyal friend, Maurice Joyant: *Henri de Toulouse-Lautrec* (2 Vols. Floury, Paris, 1926–1927). Of the rest, the most important are:

ALEXANDRE (Arsène): *Toulouse-Lautrec* (special number of *Figaro illustré*, April 1902). *Offrande pour un Monument* (in *Comoedia*, August 7, 1909).

ASTRE (Achille): *Henri de Toulouse-Lautrec* (Éd. Nilsson Paris 1938).

AVRIL (Jane): *Mes Mémoires* (in *Paris-Midi*, August 7–26, 1933).

B . . . (H.): *A travers les cafés-concerts:* I. *Yvette Guilbert* . . . , III. *Edmée Lescot* . . . , VII. *Polaire* . . . (in *Fin de Siècle*, February 9, February 16, March 5, 1896).

BARAGNON (L.-N.): *Toulouse-Lautrec chez Péan* (in *La Chronique médicale*, February 15, 1902).

BERNARD (Émile): *Les Ateliers* (in *Mercure de France*, February 1895). *Notes sur l'École dite de 'Pont-Aven'* (in *Mercure de France*, December, 1903) *Des Relations d'Émile Bernard avec Toulouse-Lautrec* (in *Art-Documents*, Geneva, March 1952). *L'Aventure de ma Vie* (unpublished manuscript).

BERNARD (Jean-Jacques): *Mon Père Tristan Bernard* (Albin Michel, Paris, 1955).

BERNARD (Tristan): *Toulouse-Lautrec sportsman* (in *L'Amour de l'Art*, April 1931). Preface to the *Catalogue de l'Exposition Henri de Toulouse-Lautrec* (April 9 to May 17, 1931) (Musée des Arts décoratifs, Paris, 1931).

BERTIE-MARRIOTT (C.): *Gloires parisiennes. Mes Entretiens*, 3ᵉ série (L. Sauvaitre, Paris, 1888).

BLANCHE (Jacques-Émile): *Propos de Peintre. Dates* (Émile-Paul, Paris, 1921). *Sur Henri de Toulouse-Lautrec* (in *L'Art vivant*, June 1931).

BONMARIAGE (Sylvain): *Henri de Toulouse-Lautrec pile et face* (in *Maintenant*, No. 6, July 1947). *Henri de Toulouse-Lautrec tel qu'il fut* (unpublished manuscript).

BOIS (Jules): *Dufour, chef d'orchestre à l'Élysée-Montmartre* (in *Le Courrier français*, January 4, 1891).

BRUANT (Aristide): *Dans la Rue* (Eugène Rey, Paris, 1924.) *Cabaret des Décadents* (in *Le Courrier français*, January 20, 1895).

COOLUS (Romain): *Souvenirs sur Toulouse-Lautrec* (in *L'Amour de l'Art*, April 1931).

COQUIOT (Gustave): *Henri de Toulouse-Lautrec* (Auguste Blaizot, Paris, 1913). *Lautrec ou Quinze Ans de Mœurs parisiennes (1885–1900)* (Ollendorff, Paris, 1921). *Les Indépendants (1884–1920)* (Ollendorff, Paris, 1921). *Des Peintres maudits* (Delpeuch, Paris, 1924).

CRAUZAT (E. de): *La Loïe Fuller* (in *L'Estampe et l'Affiche*, December 15, 1897).

CURNONSKY: Preface to the Album of Toulouse-Lautrec *Submersion* (Arts et Métiers Graphiques, Paris, 1938).

DAUDET (Léon): *Salons et Journaux* (Grasset, Paris, 1932).

DAURELLE (Jacques): *Un Poète anglais à Paris: Oscar Wilde* (in *L'Écho de Paris*, December 6, 1891). *Chez les jeunes Peintres*, interviews with Anquetin, Toulouse-Lautrec, Émile Bernard, Maurice Denis, Bonnard (in *L'Écho de Paris*, December 28, 1891).

DAVIS (Richard Harding): *About Paris* (Harper, New York, 1895).

DELORME, POZZI, etc: *A la Mémoire du docteur Péan* (Imprimerie Levé, Paris, 1898).

DONNAY (Maurice): *Des Souvenirs . . .* (Fayard, Paris, 1933).

DONOS (Charles): *De Toulouse-Lautrec* (in *Les Hommes d'Aujourd'hui*, Volume IX, No. 460).

Elysée-Montmarte (*L'*) (in *Le Courrier français*, June 20, 1886).

FAURE (Jean-Louis): *En marge de la Chirurgie*, Volume IV, (Jean Crès, Paris, 1935).

FRICHET (Henry): *Le Cirque et les Forains* (Alfred Mame, Tours, 1898).

FULLER (Loïe): *Quinze Ans de ma Vie* (Juven, Paris, 1908).

GAUZI (François): *Lautrec et son Temps* (David Perret, Paris, 1954). English edition: *My Friend Toulouse-Lautrec* (Spearman, London, 1957).

GEFFROY (Gustave): *Henri de Toulouse-Lautrec* (in *Gazette des Beaux-Arts*, August 1914). *L'Oeuvre de Toulouse-Lautrec. L'Historien du Plaisir de Paris* (in *Les Annales politiques et littéraires*, August 13, 1922).

GEORGES-MICHEL (Georges): *De Renoir à Picasso. Les Peintres que j'ai connus* (Arthème Fayard, Paris, 1954).

GRAND-CARTERET (John): *Raphaël et Gambrinus ou l'Art dans la Brasserie* (Louis Westhausser, Paris, 1886).

Guide des Plaisirs à Paris (Éd. Photographique, Paris, 1900).

GUILBERT (Yvette): *La Chanson de ma Vie* (Grasset, Paris, 1927). *Yvette Guilbert nous parle de Toulouse-Lautrec*, interview reported by Pierre Lazareff (in *L'Art vivant*, April 1931).

HARTRICK (A. S.): *A Painter's Pilgrimage through Fifty Years* (University Press, Cambridge, 1939).

JEANÈS (J. E. S.): *D'après nature* (Granvelle, Besançon, 1946).

K

Jourdain (Francis): *Renoir. Le Moulin de la Galette* (Braun, Paris, 1947). *Lautrec* (Braun, Paris, 1951). *Né en 1876* (Les Éditions du Pavillon, Paris, 1951). *Toulouse-Lautrec*, and *Lautrec, peintre-graveur*, by Jean Adhémar and *Répertoire Lautrec*, by the same (Tisné, Paris, 1952). *J'ai connu Lautrec, Cézanne, Monet . . .* , reported by Henri Perruchot (in *L'Oeil*, September 1956). *Mon Ami Émile Bernard* (unpublished manuscript in the collection of Michel-Ange Bernard).

Joyant (Maurice): *Toulouse-Lautrec* (in *L'Art et les Artistes*, February, 1927). *La Cuisine de monsieur Momo, Célibataire* (Éd. Pellet, Paris, 1930).

Kolb (Jean): *La Goulue est morte misérablement à l'hôpital* (in *Paris-Soir*, January 31, 1929).

Lazareff (Pierre): *La triste fin de La Goulue qui fut la Reine de Paris* (in *Paris-Midi*, January 31, 1929).

Leclercq (Paul): *Autour de Toulouse-Lautrec* (Cailler, Geneva, 1954). *Henri de Toulouse-Lautrec* (Verlags Der Arche, Zurich).

L'Hers (Jean de): *La Vie et l'Oeuvre d'Henri de Toulouse-Lautrec* (in *L'Express du Midi*, June 6, 1914).

Lugné-Poe: *Sous les Étoiles* (Gallimard, Paris, 1933).

M . . . (G.): *Les Toulouse-Lautrec du Docteur* (in *L'Éclair*, June 18, 1914).

Maindrow (Ernest): *Les Affiches illustrées (1886-1895)* (G. Boudet, Paris, 1896).

Maurin (Charles): *Lettres inédites* (private collection).

Mellerio (André): *La Lithographie originale en couleurs* (L'Estampe et l'Affiche, Paris, 1898).

Mézières, Caron, Brochin, etc: *Inauguration du Monument Péan (December 16, 1909)* (Imprimerie Levé, Paris, 1910).

Molier (E.): *Cirque Molier (1880-1904)* (Paul Dupont, Paris, 1905).

Montorgueil (Georges): *Le Café-Concert* (Éd. de 'L'Estampe originale', Paris, 1893). *Paris dansant* (Théophile Belin, Paris, 1898). *La Vie à Montmartre* (G. Boudet, Paris, 1899).

Mourey (Gabriel): *Les Directeurs de Cafés-concerts. M. Pierre Ducarre* (in *Le Courrier français*, June 7, 1891).

NATANSON (Thadée): *Peints à leur tour* (Albin Michel, Paris, 1948). *Un Henri de Toulouse-Lautrec* (Cailler, Geneva, 1951).

NOVOTNY (Fritz): *Drawings of Yvette Guilbert by Toulouse-Lautrec* (in *The Burlington Magazine*, London, June 1949).

PÉAN (Jules-Émile): *Comment on devient un grand chirurgien* (in *La Chronique médicale*, February 15, 1902).

POITOU (René): *Le Père 'la Pudeur'* (in *Le Courrier français*, August 9, 1891).

RENARD (Jules): *Journal* (Gallimard, Paris, 1935).

RIVOIRE (André): *Henri de Toulouse-Lautrec* (in *La Revue de l'Art ancien et moderne*, December 1901 and April 1902).

ROTHENSTEIN (William): *Men and Memories* (Faber and Faber, London, 1931).

SARRAZIN (Jehan): *Souvenirs de Montmartre et du Quartier latin* (Jehan Sarrazin, edit., Paris, 1895).

SERT (Misia): *Misia* (Gallimard, Paris, 1952).

SMITH (F. Berkeley): *How Paris amuses itself* (Funk and Wagnalls Company, New York-London, 1903).

SOUDAY (Paul): *Le Chat Noir raconté par M. Rodolphe Salis* (in *Le Temps*, January 15, 1896).

SYMONS (Arthur): *Notes on Toulouse-Lautrec and his lithographs* (in *The Print Collector's Quarterly*, December 1922). *Parisian Nights* (The Beaumont Press, London, 1926). *From Toulouse-Lautrec to Rodin* (The Bodley Head, London, 1929).

TAPIÉ DE CÉLEYRAN (Gabriel): *Henri de Toulouse-Lautrec et ses relations médicales* (in *La Chronique médicale*, December 1, 1922). Preface to *Cocotte*, by Henri de Toulouse-Lautrec and Étienne Devismes (Éd. du Chêne, Paris, 1953).

TAPIÉ DE CÉLEYRAN (Mary): *Toulouse-Lautrec en Rouergue* (in *Revue du Rouergue*, October-December 1952). *Notre Oncle Lautrec* (Cailler, Geneva, 1956).

TOUSSAINT (Franz): *Sentiments distingués* (Laffont, Paris, 1945).

VALENTIN LE DÉSOSSÉ: *Valentin le Désossé raconte sa Vie* (in *Les Lettres françaises*, March 15, 1956).

VUILLARD: *Lautrec raconté par Vuillard*, reported by Germain Bazin (in *L'Amour de l'Art*, April 1931).

WEINDEL (Henri de): *Valentin le Grand* (in *Fin de Siècle*, February 18, 1893).

WILLETTE (A.): *Feu Pierrot* (Floury, Paris, 1919).

To the unpublished manuscripts of Émile Bernard, Sylvain Bonmariage, Francis Jourdain and Charles Maurin mentioned above, must be added information, written, oral, or in the form of documents or photographs, made available by MM. Jean Adhémar, Georges Beaute, Michel-Ange Bernard, Sylvain Bonmariage, Dr R. Chantemesse, Dr Louis Chouquet, MM. André Devèche and André Dignimont, Mme Marcelle Duchemin, M. and Mme Maurice Exsteens, Mme du Ferron-Anquetin, MM. Edmond Heuze, Francis Jourdain, Édouard Julien, Louis Lacroix, Charles Laurent and R. G. Michel, Professor Henri Mondor, MM. Pierre Paret, Émile Pottier, Romi and Séré de Rivière, Dr Semelaigne (junior), Mlle Mary Tapié de Céleyran and Mme Tulard. I have also been permitted to examine twenty photographs of erotic Japanese prints which once belonged to Lautrec in the reserved section of the Cabinet des Estampes in Paris.

In addition to the articles mentioned in the text or referred to in the bibliography, I have derived useful information from the following publications:

Annuaire des Artistes; L'Aurore; Le Courrier français; L'Écho de Paris; Figaro illustré; Fin de Siècle; Gil Blas; L'Illustration; Le Journal; La Justice; Le Matin; Le Mirliton; Le Monde moderne; La Plume; La Presse; Le Rapide; La Revue blanche; La Revue encyclopédique; Le Rire; Le Temps; Le Triboulet; La Vie parisienne, etc.

I have also examined with advantage the collection of press-cuttings assembled by Bernard Prost, now in the Cabinet des Estampes in Paris.

Finally, some information has been gathered, with due precaution, from the fiction of the period. In 1899, Lautrec was the hero of a novel by Hugues Rebell: *La Câlineuse*. Both Zola and Courteline used Bruant for one of their characters: the first in *Paris* and the second in *Messieurs les Ronds de Cuir*. Bruant also appears in the play by Catulle

Mendès and Courteline entitled *Les Joyeuses Commères de Paris.* Le
Goffic put Le Star at Le Havre into his novel *La Payse.*

*   *   *

Lautrec's work has been catalogued chronologically in Maurice
Joyant's two volume work (Vol. I: paintings; Vol. II: drawings,
engravings and posters). And Loÿs Delteil has catalogued the engravings in Vols. X and XI of his important work *Le Peintre Graveur
illustré* (published by the author, Paris, 1920). Édouard Julien has also
listed the important collection in the Musée d'Albi in his work
Toulouse-Lautrec au Musée d'Albi (Palais de la Berbie, Albi, 1952).

Much has been written about Lautrec, his friends, relations and the
various circles in which he lived. The reader will find below the list of
the principal works which, together with those already mentioned,
form the essential basis of my sources:

ABENSOUR (Léon): *Aristide Bruant* (in *Le Larousse mensuel,* July 1925).

ADHÉMAR (Jean): *Lautrec et son Photographe habituel* (in *Æsculape,*
December 1951). *Lautrec peintre-graveur* and *Répertoire Lautrec* in
Francis Jourdain's: *Toulouse-Lautrec,* (Tisné, Paris, 1952). *'Elles' par
Toulouse-Lautrec,* preface by Jean Vallery-Radot (Éditions du
Livre, Monte-Carlo, 1952). See DORTU and *Oeuvre graphique . . .*

APOLLONIO (Umbro): *Toulouse-Lautrec et l'Italie* in *Toulouse-Lautrec,
l'Oeuvre graphique* (Collection Charell, 1952).

AROUT (Georges): *Toulouse-Lautrec* (Nathan, Paris, 1954).

AURIANT: *Souvenirs sur Émile Bernard* (in *Maintenant,* No. 7, 1947).
Henri de Toulouse-Lautrec (in *Quo Vadis,* October-December 1951).

BEACHBOARD (Robert): *La Trinité maudite (Valadon, Utter, Utrillo)*
(Amiot-Dumont, Paris, 1952).

BÉNÉZIT, (Emmanuel): *Dictionnaire des Peintres, Sculpteurs, Dessinateurs
et Graveurs* (8 vols., Gründ, Paris, 1948–1955).

BERCY (Anne de) and ZIWÈS (Armand): *A Montmartre . . . le soir* (Grasset, Paris, 1951).

BRIN (Irène): *Images de Lautrec* (Carlo Bestetti, Rome, 1947).

CANYAMERES (Ferran): *L'Homme de la Belle Époque (Moulin-Rouge, la
Vie de son Fondateur).* (Les Éditions Universelles, Paris, 1946).

CARCO (Francis): *La Belle Époque au temps de Bruant* (Gallimard, Paris, 1954).

CASSOU (Jean): *Toulouse-Lautrec* (in *L'Art et les Artistes*, April 1938).

CHARLES-BELLET (L.): *De la Foire au Musée* (in *L'Archer*, April 1931). *Le Musée d'Albi* (Syndicat d'Initiative, Albi, 1951). See *Inauguration* . . .

COOPER (Douglas): *Toulouse-Lautrec* (Nouvelles Éditions Françaises, Paris, 1955). *Henri de Toulouse-Lautrec* (Thames and Hudson, London, 1954; new edn. 1956).

DELANNOY (Jean): *Valentin le Désossé témoin de la 'Belle Époque'* (in *Miroir de l'Histoire*, February 1956).

DELAROCHE-VERNET HENRAUX (Marie): *Henri de Toulouse-Lautrec dessinateur* (Quatre Chemins-Éditart, Paris, 1948).

DEVERIN (Édouard): *Fénéon l'énigmatique* (in *Mercure de France*, February 15, 1934).

DEVOISINS (L.): *Toulouse-Lautrec* (Imprimerie coopérative du Sud-Ouest, Albi).

DORIVAL (Bernard): *Les Étapes de la Peinture française contemporaine*, Vol. I: *De l'Impressionisme au Fauvisme* (Gallimard, Paris, 1943).

DORTU (M.-G.): *L'Étrange Toulouse-Lautrec* (in *Art et Style*, May 1951). *Toulouse-Lautrec* (Les Éditions du Chêne, Paris, 1952). *Toulouse-Lautrec. Album de Marine* (Berggruen et Cie, Paris, 1953).

DORTU (M.-G.), GRILLAERT (Madeleine), ADHÉMAR (Jean): *Toulouse-Lautrec en Belgique* (Quatre Chemins-Éditart, Paris, 1955).

DUBARRY (J.-J.): *La Maladie de Toulouse-Lautrec* (in *La Presse médicale*, No. 32, 1956).

DUMONT (Henri): *Lautrec* (Éd. Hypérion, Paris, 1950).

DURET (Théodore): *Lautrec* (Bernheim-Jeune, Paris, 1920).

DUTHUIT (Georges): *Deux Lautrec mutilés* (in *L'Amour de l'Art*, November 1926).

ESSWEIN (H.) and HYMEL (A. W.) *Henri de Toulouse-Lautrec* (Piper Verlag, Munich, 1905) Vol. III of *Modernen Illustratoren* (Piper Verlag, Munich, 1912).

EUGNY (Anne d'): *Toulouse-Lautrec et ses Modèles* (in *L'Amour de l'Art*, No. VII, 1946).

FELS (Florent): *Utrillo* (Librairie de France, Paris, 1930).

FLORISOONE (Michel): *Lautrec hors du temps*, in *Catalogue de l'Exposition Toulouse-Lautrec en l'honneur du cinquantième anniversaire de sa mort* (Orangerie des Tuileries, Paris, 1951). *Connaissance de Lautrec* (in *Art et Style*, May 1951).

FOCILLON (Henri): *Lautrec* (in *Gazette des Beaux-Arts*, June 1931).

FOSCA (François): *Henri de Toulouse-Lautrec* (Librairie de France, Paris, 1928).

GAUDION (Georges): *Notes sur l'art de Henri de Toulouse-Lautrec* (in *L'Archer*, April 1931).

GRILLAERT (Madeleine): *Trois Aspects de Toulouse-Lautrec* (Unpublished manuscript. Cabinet des Estampes, Paris). See DORTU.

GUÉRIN (Marcel): *Toulouse-Lautrec. Lithographies* (Gründ, Paris, 1948).

Henri de Toulouse-Lautrec, a film in black and white. Produced by Pantheon Productions (France). Directed by Robert Hessens.[n.d.]

Henri de Toulouse-Lautrec: One Hundred and Ten Unpublished Drawings (Boston Book and Art Shop, Boston, Mass; and Faber and Faber, London, 1955).

HANSON (L. and H.): *The Tragic Life of Toulouse-Lautrec* (Secker and Warburg, London, 1956).

HUYGHE (René): *Aspects de Toulouse-Lautrec* (in *L'Amour de l'Art*, April 1931).

Inauguration de l'installation du musée d'Albi et de la galerie Henri de Toulouse-Lautrec au palais de la Berbie, 30 juillet 1922. Discours de MM. Charles-Bellet, Maurice Joyant et Léon Bérard, ministre de l'Instruction publique et des Beaux-Arts (Musée d'Albi, Albi, 1922).

JEDLICKA (Gotthard): *L'Écriture de Lautrec* (in *Formes*, March 1931). *Henri de Toulouse-Lautrec* (Eugen Rentsch, Erlenbach-Zurich, 1943).

JULIEN (Édouard): *Dessins de Lautrec* (Les Documents d'Art, Monaco, 1942). *Les Affiches de Toulouse-Lautrec* (Éd. du Livre, Monte-Carlo, 1950). *Lautrec. Dessins* (Braun, Paris, 1951). *Toulouse-Lautrec vu par ses Contemporains* (in *Art et Style*, May 1951). *Toulouse-Lautrec. Au Cirque* (Éd. du Livre, Monte-Carlo, 1952). *Pour connaître*

Toulouse-Lautrec (Imprimerie Coopérative du Sud-Ouest, Albi, 1954). *Lautrec* (The Uffici Press, Milan, n.d.). *Toulouse-Lautrec: Moulin Rouge* (Methuen, London, 1958).

LAMY (Maurice): *L'Infirmité de Toulouse-Lautrec*, with a reply from G. Séjournet (in *La Presse médicale*, February 8, 1956).

LANDRE (Jeanne): *Aristide Bruant* (La Nouvelle Société d'Édition, Paris, 1930).

LANDOLT (Hanspeter): *Henri de Toulouse-Lautrec. Drawings and Sketches in Colour* (Macmillan, New York, 1955).

LAPPARENT (Paul de): *Toulouse-Lautrec* (Rieder, Paris, 1927).

LAPRADE (Jacques de): *Lautrec* (Aimery Somogy, Paris, 1954, and Heineman, London, 1954).

LASSAIGNE (Jacques): *Toulouse-Lautrec* (Hypérion, Paris, 1939). *Lautrec* (Skira, Geneva, 1953).

LA TOURETTE (Gilles de): *Lautrec* (Skira, Paris, 1938).

LEMONNIER (Léon): *Oscar Wilde* (Didier, Paris, 1938).

LÉVY (Gaston): *Réflexions sur la Maladie de Toulouse-Lautrec* (in *La Semaine des Hôpitaux de Paris*, July 10, 1957). Fifty years after his death a diagnosis was made of Toulouse-Lautrec's physical condition (in *Arts*, July 24, 1957).

MAC ORLAN (Pierre): *Lautrec, peintre de la Lumière froide* (Floury, Paris, 1934).

MACK (Gerstle): *Toulouse-Lautrec* (Alfred A. Knopf, New York, 1938).

MARTRINCHARD (Robert): *Princeteau, professeur et ami de Toulouse-Lautrec, sa Vie, son Oeuvre* (Bordeaux, 1956).

MAUS (Madeleine-Octave): *Trente Années de Lutte pour l'Art (1884–1914)* (L'Oiseau Bleu, Brussels, 1926).

MAXENCE (Edgar): *Notice sur la Vie et les Travaux de M. Fernand Cormon* (Institut de France, Typographie de Firmin-Didot, Paris, 1925).

MOULY (Charles): *Au Château du Bosc en Rouergue* (in *La Dépêche du Midi*, January 25, 1954).

NEPVEU-DEGAS (Jean): *Toulouse-Lautrec et le Théâtre* (in *Revue de la Société d'Histoire du Théâtre*, No. III, 1951).

NICOLSON (Benedict): *Notes on Henri de Toulouse-Lautrec* (in *The Burlington Magazine*, September 1951).

Oeuvre graphique de Toulouse-Lautrec. Exhibition in the Bibliothèque nationale. Preface by Julien Cain. *Les Lithographies de Toulouse-Lautrec, Peintre de la Vie*, by Jean Vallery-Radot. Catalogue by Jean Adhémar (Les Presses artistiques, Paris, 1951).

PAULHAN (Jean): *F. F. ou le Critique* (Gallimard, Paris, 1945).

PÉRUSSAUX (Charles): *Suivre Lautrec pas à pas dans la Création d'une Lithographie* (in *Les Lettres françaises*, February 17, 1955). *L'Enfance de Lautrec faillit ressembler aux romans de la comtesse de Ségur* (in *Les Lettres françaises*, April 7, 1955). *Au Cirque avec Henri de Toulouse-Lautrec* (in *Les Lettres françaises*, December 8, 1955).

PIGASSE (Jules): *Toulouse-Lautrec* (Imprimerie Coopérative du Sud-Ouest, Albi, 1907).

RÈCHE (Albert): *Sur la Tombe de Toulouse-Lautrec* (in *Le Figaro Littéraire*, July 14, 1951).

REWALD (John): *Félix Fénéon* (in *Gazette des Beaux-Arts*, July-August 1947 and February 1948). *Post-Impressionism: From Van Gogh to Gauguin* (The Museum of Modern Art, New York, 1956).

ROGER-MARX (Claude): *Les Dessins de Maxime Dethomas* (in *Comoedia illustré*, October 5, 1912). *Toulouse-Lautrec graveur* (in *L'Amour de l'Art*, April 1931). *Les Lithographies de Toulouse-Lautrec* (Hazan, Paris, 1948). *Yvette Guilbert vue par Toulouse-Lautrec* (Au Pont des Arts, Paris, 1950). *Les Lithographies de Toulouse-Lautrec* in *Toulouse-Lautrec, l'Oeuvre graphique* (Collection Charell, 1952). *Toulouse-Lautrec, le plus grand Nain du Monde* (in *La Revue de Paris*, April 1954). *Toulouse-Lautrec* (Éditions universitaires, Paris, 1957).

ROMI: *Petite Histoire des Cafés-concerts parisiens* (Jean Chitry et Cie, Paris, 1950). *Maisons closes. L'Histoire, l'Art, la Littérature, les Moeurs* (Published by the author, Paris, 1952).

ROTZLER (Willy): *Affiches de Henri de Toulouse-Lautrec* (Éd. Holbein, Bâle, and Éd. du Chêne, Paris, 1946).

ROUCHON (Ulysse): *Charles Maurin* (Le Puy-en-Velay, 1922).

SALOMON (Jacques): *Vuillard* (Albin Michel, Paris, 1945).

298   *Bibliography*

SCHAUB-KOCH (Émile): *Psychanalyse d'un Peintre moderne* (*Henri de Toulouse-Lautrec*) (L'Édition littéraire internationale, Paris, 1935).

SCHNIEWIND (Carl O.): *Toulouse-Lautrec* (The Art Institute of Chicago, Chicago, 1949). Introduction to *A Sketchbook by Toulouse-Lautrec owned by the Art Institute of Chicago* (Curt Valentin, New York, 1952).

SÉJOURNET (G.): *La Maladie de Toulouse-Lautrec* (in *La Presse médicale*, December 25, 1955). See LAMY.

TABARANT (A.): *La Fin douloureuse de celle qui fut Olympia* (in *L'Oeuvre*, July 10, 1932).

THOMAS (Louis): *Henri de Toulouse-Lautrec* (in *La Nouvelle Revue*, July 1, 1913).

Toulouse-Lautrec au Château du Bosc (in *Vogue*, September 1954).

VAILLANT (Annette): *Livret de Famille* (in *L'Oeil*, December 1956).

VALLERY-RADOT (Jean): See ADHÉMAR and *Oeuvre graphique* . . .

VALLERY-RADOT (Pierre): *Toulouse-Lautrec. Aspect médical de son Oeuvre* (in *Histoire de la Médecine*, July 1951). *La Médecine et les Médecins dans l'Oeuvre de Toulouse-Lautrec* (in *La Presse médicale*, July 14, 1951).

VAUXCELLES (Louis): *Deux mots de Lautrec* (in *L'Amour de l'Art*, September 1922).

VENTURI (Lionello): *De Manet à Lautrec* (Albin Michel, Paris, 1953). .

WARNOD (André): *Bals, Cafés et Cabarets* (Figuière, Paris, 1913). *Les Bals de Paris* (Crès, Paris, 1922). *Les Décorations de Toulouse-Lautrec* (in *Comoedia*, December 11, 1923). *Les Peintres de Montmartre* (La Renaissance du Livre, Paris, 1928).

WILENSKI (R. A.): *Toulouse-Lautrec* (Faber, London, 1955).

YAKI (Paul): *Le Montmartre de nos vingt Ans* (Tallandier, Paris, 1949).

ZÉVAÈS (Alexandre): *Aristide Bruant* (Éd. de la Nouvelle Revue critique, Paris, 1943).

ZIWÈS (Armand): See BERCY.

CHRONOLOGY

1807 Birth of Léonce Tapié de Céleyran, the painter's maternal grandfather.

1812 Birth of Raymond Casimir de Toulouse-Lautrec, the painter's paternal grandfather.

1813 Birth of Gabrielle d'Imbert du Bosc, the painter's paternal grandmother.

1815 Birth of Louise d'Imbert du Bosc, the painter's maternal grandmother.

1824 *The triumph of the Romantic Movement in the Salon (Delacroix' Massacres de Scio).*

1825 *Birth of Désiré Dihau.*

1829 *Birth of John Lewis Brown.*

1830 *Birth of Péan.*

1833 *Birth of Bonnat.*

1834 *Births of Degas and Whistler.*

1836 *Birth of Jules Chéret.*

1837 Raymond Casimir de Toulouse-Lautrec married Gabrielle d'Imbert du Bosc.

1838 August 10, birth of Alphonse de Toulouse-Lautrec, father of the painter, at Albi.

1839 *Birth of Joseph Oller.*

1840 Léonce Tapié de Céleyran married Louise d'Imbert du Bosc.

1841 November 23, birth at Narbonne of Adèle Tapié de Céleyran, the painter's mother.

1843 *Birth of Princeteau.*

1845 *Birth of Cormon.*

1847 Death of Léonce Tapié de Céleyran.

1851 *Births of Bruant and Salis.*

1852 *Birth of Forain.*

1853 *Birth of Vincent Van Gogh.*

1855 *Birth of Adolphe Albert.*

1856 *Births of Henri Rachou, Charles Maurin and Renée Vert.*

1857 *Births of Willette and Théo Van Gogh.*

1859 *Birth of Seurat.*

1861 *Births of Louis Anquetin, René Grenier and Félix Fénéon.*

1862 *Birth of François Gauzi. First known drawings by Van Gogh.*

1863 May 9, marriage of Alphonse de Toulouse-Lautrec to Adèle
      Tapié de Céleyran.
      Salon des Refusés (Le Déjeuner sur l'Herbe *by Manet*).
      Death of Delacroix.

1864 November 24, birth of Henri-Marie-Raymond de Toulouse-
      Lautrec Montfa, at Albi, in the Hôtel du Bosc, 14, Rue de
      l'École-Mage (today, Rue Henri-de-Toulouse-Lautrec).

1865 *Manet painted* Olympia. *Births of Suzanne Valadon and Félix
      Vallotton.*

1866 *Births of Tristan Bernard and Henry de Groux.*

1867 August 28, birth of Richard de Toulouse-Lautrec, the painter's
      brother, at Albi.
      Births of Bonnard and Maxime Dethomas.

1868 August 27, death of Richard de Toulouse-Lautrec, at Lovry.
      *Births of Jane Avril, Émile Bernard, Charles Conder, Yvette
      Guilbert and Vuillard.*

1869 Birth of Gabriel Tapié de Céleyran.
      Birth of Matisse.

1870 *Births of La Goulue and Maurice Denis.*

1871 December 23, death of Raymond-Casimir de Toulouse-Lautrec.

1872 October, Lautrec began his schooling at the Lycée Fontanes
      (today: Condorcet).

1873 Lautrec's first known drawings.
      Cézanne's La Maison du Pendu.

1874 *The first Impressionist exhibition.*

1875 Lautrec left the Lycée Fontanes.
      Birth of Marquet.

1877 *Renoir painted* Le Bal au Moulin de la Galette.

1878 May 30, Lautrec's first accident: a fracture of the left femur.
      Van Gogh in the Borinage.

1879 August, Lautrec's second accident: a fracture of the right femur.

1881 Lautrec illustrated a novel by Devismes: *Cocotte*. Having passed
the first part of his *baccalauréat* in November, he abandoned
his studies to devote himself to painting.
Salis founded Le Chat Noir *in Montmartre.*
Birth of Picasso.

1882 March, Lautrec entered Bonnat's studio.
André Gill exhibited Le Fou *in the Salon.*

1883 Lautrec working in Cormon's studio.
Death of Manet.
Birth of Utrillo, the son of Suzanne Valadon.
Gauguin abandoned stockbroking to devote himself to painting.

1884 Lautrec painted a parody of the *Bois sacré* by Puvis de Chavannes
and *La Grosse Maria.* Went to live in Montmartre.
*Émile Bernard joined Cormon's studio in October. The founding of the
Société des Artistes Indépendants in Paris, and of the Société des
'XX' in Brussels. Fénéon founded* La Revue Indépendante.

1885 Lautrec frequenting the *Élysée-Montmartre*, the *Moulin-de-la-
Galette* and the *Chat Noir;* became friendly with Suzanne
Valadon and Aristide Bruant (proprietor of the *Mirliton*).
During the summer, stayed at Villiers-sur-Morin. Began to
take an interest in La Goulue and in Valentin le Désossé.
Death of André Gill in the asylum at Charenton.

1886 Lautrec left Cormon's studio. Some of Lautrec's work hung in
the *Mirliton*. His first drawings published. Acquired his first
studio. Shared a flat with Bourges, a medical student.
Van Gogh in Paris, working at Cormon's studio.
Seurat's Le Dimanche à la Grand-Jatte. *Fénéon published* Les
Impressionistes en 1886.

1887 Lautrec influenced by Van Gogh. Exhibited with him, Bernard
and Anquetin, in Montmartre restaurants.

1888 February: Lautrec took part in the exhibition of the 'XX' in
Brussels. Relations with Suzanne Valadon came to a sudden
end. Contracted syphilis from Rosa la Rouge. Spent part of
the winter at Villiers-sur-Morin. Painted *L'Écuyère du Cirque
Fernando.*
Van Gogh in Arles.

1889 Lautrec's technique began to crystalise. Discarded the influence of Bruant. Met Degas. Exhibited for the first time at the Salon des Indépendants. Painted *Au Moulin de la Galette*.
Opening of the Moulin Rouge in October.

1890 In Brussels for the exhibition of the Société des 'XX'. Quarrelled with Henry de Groux about Van Gogh.
Painted *La Danse au Moulin Rouge*.
Death of Van Gogh. His brother, Théo, who was gravely ill, left the Boussod et Valodon gallery in the Boulevard Montmartre. Joyant succeeded him as manager.
Death of John Lewis Brown.

1891 Poster for the Moulin Rouge; the beginning of Lautrec's fame. In the autumn, Gabriel Tapié de Céleyran arrived in Paris. Lautrec attended the operations of Dr Péan. With Bernard, Anquetin, Bonnard and Maurice Denis, he exhibited at Le Barc de Boutteville's.
In October, the Natansons founded La Revue blanche.

1892 designed posters for Bruant's Le Divan Japonais. Began to lose interest in Montmartre. Frequenting brothels. The first lithographs.

1893 January to February: an exhibition at Joyant's gallery. Lautrec's mother took a flat in the Rue de Douai. Lautrec illustrated songs, published (with Ibels) an album on *Le Café-concert*, designed posters for Jane Avril. Became acquainted with the circle of *La Revue blanche*, made friends with the Natansons, Tristan Bernard and Romain Coolus. In September, developed an interest in the theatre.
Ambroise Vollard opened his gallery.

1894 Visited Brussels. In Paris, took up residence in a brothel recently opened in the Rue des Moulins. Lithographs of the theatre (*La Loge au mascaron doré*) and posters; paintings of brothels; the *Yvette Guilbert* album. Working on his big canvas: *Au Salon de la Rue des Moulins*.

1895 *Au Salon* completed; he painted *Marcelle Lender dans Chilperic dansant le boléro*. Designed posters for May Milton, May Belfort and Misia Natanson. Painted panels for La Goulue's fairground booth. Met Oscar Wilde in London. Journey to Lisbon in pursuit of the 'Passenger from No. 54'. Became interested in bicycling and went to the Vélodromes (*Tristan Bernard au Vélodrome Buffalo*). Uncle Charles ceremoniously burnt some canvases in Albi.

1896   In January, an exhibition at the gallery of Manzi and Joyant. Began to frequent Lesbian bars. Attended the trials of Arton and Lebaudy. Portraits of Cha-U-Kao. Publication of *Elles*. Lautrec's alcoholism grew worse.

1897   *La Grande Loge.* Journey to Holland with Dethomas. In May, moved to a new studio in the Avenue Frochot. Returned to work on some of his old themes.
       Deaths of Salis and Père la Pudeur.

1898   Lautrec drinking heavily and working less. In May, an exhibition at the Goupil Gallery, London. Illustrations for the *Histoires naturelles* by Jules Renard. The painter's health deteriorated during the winter.
       Death of Péan.

1899   In February, as the result of an attack of delirium tremens, Lautrec was taken to an asylum at Neuilly. He stayed there until May. To prove that his mental condition was satisfactory, he produced some fifty works during his confinement, of which thirty-nine were of the Circus. On being released in the care of a guardian, he went to Le Crotoy and Le Havre, where he stayed on to paint the barmaid at Le Star. Spent part of the summer at Taussat. Returned to Paris in the autumn. He started drinking again.

1900   May. Left Paris for Le Havre and Arcachon. Arguments about money with his family. Spent the Autumn at Malromé. In December, went to Bordeaux.

1901   Returned to Paris in May. Painted his last canvases and put his studio in order. At Taussat, on August 20, struck down with paralysis. Taken to Malromé by his mother, where he died on the morning of September 9.

1902   Retrospective exhibition at the Salon des Indépendants (fifty works) and at the Libre Esthétique in Brussels (forty-five

works), at Durand-Ruel (two hundred and one works).
Countess Adèle presented the Cabinet des Estampes at the
Bibliothèque Nationale with three hundred and seventy-one
lithographs. Léonce Bénédite, keeper of the Musée du
Luxembourg, accepted only one picture (*La Femme au boa*)
from Lautrec's works offered him by Joyant on behalf of
Countess Adèle. Death of the Countess Raymond de
Toulouse-Lautrec, the painter's paternal grandmother.

1903   April to May, an exhibition of nineteen works at the Bar-
        thélemy Gallery, Paris.
        *The first Salon d'Automne. The last number of La Revue blanche
        appeared on April 15. Death of Whistler.*

1904   Retrospective exhibition at the Salon d'Automne (twenty-eight
        works). Countess Adèle gave *Comquête de Passage* to the
        Toulouse Museum.

1905   April, at Bruant's sale, *Rosa la Rouge* sold for 4,500 francs. The
        Superior Council of Museums, presided over by Bonnat,
        refused the gift of the *Portrait de M. Delaporte au Jardin de
        Paris*, offered by the Société des Amis du Luxembourg.
        The 'Fauves' exhibited for the first time at the Salon d'Automne.

1906   At the Blot sale *La Mélinite* sold for 6,600 francs; at the Depeaux
        sale, *Intérieur de Cabaret* sold for 7,000 francs.
        Death of Cézanne.

1907   February. At the Viau sale, the decoration for La Goulue's
        booth sold for 5,200 francs. In December, an exhibition
        organised by the *Télégramme*, in Toulouse. Death of Louise
        Tapié de Céleyran, the painter's maternal grandmother.
        Picasso painted Les Demoiselles d'Avignon. *Death of Valentin le
        Désossé.*

1908   October. Twenty-three paintings exhibited at the Bernheim-
        Jeune Gallery, Paris. *The Impressionists first entered the Louvre
        (the Moreau-Nélaton bequest).*

1909   November. Retrospective exhibition at the Salon des Humoristes,
        in the Georges Petit Gallery, Paris (thirty-six works). Count
        Alphonse refused to allow a statue to be erected to his son.
        Deaths of Charles Conder and Cipa Godebski.

1910 Exhibition at the Museum of Decorative Arts, Paris (twenty-nine paintings, sixty-eight lithographs). Étienne Devismes became a monk. Before retiring from the world, he sent Countess Adèle the eight letters he had received from Lautrec. *Death of Jules Renard.*

1911 At the Masson sale, *Gueule de Bois* sold for 7,100 francs.

1912 At the Heine sale, *La Partie de Cartes au Salon* sold for 8,200 francs. Count Alphonse died in December.

1914 A portrait of the female clown, Cha-U-Kao, accepted by the Louvre. The first Lautrec to be so honoured. Pierre Goujon left to the Luxembourg *La Toilette* (transferred to the Louvre in 1947). The Kunsthalle at Bremen bought *Hélène V . . ., modèle d'atelier*. In January and February, exhibition at Paul Rosenberg, Paris (forty-six paintings); in June and July, retrospective exhibition in the Manzi-Joyant Gallery, in Paris (202 works). In May, at the Roger Marx sale, *Dans le Lit* sold for 15,000 francs. 'The drawings of Lautrec,' wrote Jean de L'Hers in *L'Express du Midi*, 'have acquired today a considerable value. While the house of Goupil (Boussod et Valadon) was selling them, some fifteen years ago, for 100 francs, they fetch today prices between 6,000 and 8,000 francs.' *Deaths of Princeteau and Charles Maurin.*

1915 *Death of Manzi. Fire destroyed part of the Moulin Rouge.*

1917 *Death of Degas.*

1919 At the first Manzi sale, *Le Premier Maillot* sold for 14,000 francs.

1920 Paul Leclercq gave the Louvre his portrait by Lautrec. In March, at the Sévadjian sale, *La Danse au Moulin Rouge* sold for 69,500 francs.

1921 *Deaths of Carabin and Footit.*

1922 On July 30, the Musée de Toulouse-Lautrec was opened at the Palais de la Berbie, Albi. In January, at the Kalekian sale in New York, the portrait of Cipa Godebski sold for 3,100 dollars. *Deaths of Bonnat and Joseph Oller.*

1923 The Kunstmuseum of Hamburg bought *La Fille du Sergent de Ville.*

1924 May to June. Exhibition at the Winterthur Museum (257
      works), and at the Barbazanges Gallery, Paris, in November.
      *Bruant's return to the stage at L'Empire. Deaths of Cormon and
      Raffaëlli.*

1925 February. Exhibition at Wildenstein's, New York (fourteen
      works).
      Deaths of Bruant, René Grenier and Félix Vallotton.

1926 In June, at the Decourcelle sale, *Danseuse en scène* sold for
      221,000 francs. A dealer cut the panels for La Goulue's booth
      into several pieces.
      *Deaths of Monet and Willette. Cormon's Cain was removed from
      the walls of the Luxembourg.*

1927 March and April, Exhibition of lithographs at the Luxembourg.
      Exhibitions at the Kraushaar Galleries, New York and at the
      MacLellan Galleries, Glasgow.
      Death of Marcelle Lender.

1928 Exhibition at the Cairo Museum and at the Kunsthalle in
      Bremen.

1929 The panels for La Goulue's booth, now restored, were bought
      by the state for the Luxembourg. Exhibitions at the Fine
      Arts Museum, Copenhagen (posters and lithographs), at the
      Berlin Museum and at the Fogg Art Museum, Cambridge
      (Massachusetts). Founding of the Société des Amis de
      Toulouse-Lautrec. At the Laurand sale, *Le Cheval de renfort*
      sold for 67,000 francs.
      Deaths of Maxime Dethomas, La Goulue and Grille d'Égout.

1930 Exhibition at the Art Institute, Chicago.
      Deaths of Countess Adèle, Maurice Joyant, Gabriel Tapié de
      Céleyran and of Renée Vert.

1931 Thirtieth anniversary of Lautrec's death marked by a retro-
      spective exhibition at the Musée des Arts Décoratifs in Paris
      (423 works). Exhibitions at the Bliss Memorial Gallery, New
      York; the Galerie Jeanne Castel, Paris; the Albright Galleries,
      New York; the Art Institute, Chicago; and the Museum of
      Modern Art, New York.
      Deaths of Forain and Nini Patte en l'Air.

1932 Exhibitions in Indianapolis, and the Cleveland Museum (Ohio).
      Deaths of Anquetin, Jules Chéret and Charles-Édouard Lucas.

1933 Exhibitions at the Art Institute, Chicago, and the Museum of
      Art, Boston (lithographs).

1934 François Gauzi bequeathed his collection of paintings by
      Lautrec to the Musée des Augustins, Toulouse.

1936 Exhibition at the Galerie Bernheim-Jeune, Paris.
      Death of Lily Grenier.

1937 November and December. Exhibition at Knoedler's, New
      York. Antonin Personnaz bequeathed to the Louvre *Le Lit,
      Jane Avril dansant, Femme de Profil (Mme Lucy)* and *Femme se
      coiffant.*

1938 Exhibitions at Knoedler's, London and Paris; at the Galerie des
      Quatre-Chemins, Paris; at the Musée de Gaillac; at the F.A.R.
      Gallery, New York (posters); at the Museum of Modern
      Art, New York; at the Mayer Gallery, New York; and at the
      Stedeljik Museum, Amsterdam.
      Deaths of Suzanne Valadon and Adolphe Albert.

1940 Exhibitions at the Musée d'Ixelles, and at the Institute of Art,
      Detroit.
      Death of Vuillard.

1941 Exhibitions at the Brooklyn Museum, and at the Allison
      Gallery, New York (lithographs).
      Death of Émile Bernard.

1942 Exhibition at the Arcade Galleries, London.

1943 Exhibitions at the Kunsthaus, Zurich; at the Nordyst Gallery,
      New York. Berthellemy bequeathed the portrait of Louis
      Bouglé to the Louvre.
      Deaths of Maurice Denis and Jane Avril.

1944 *Deaths of Henri Rachou, Félix Fénéon and Yvette Guilbert.*

1946 Exhibitions at the Galerie Bignon, Paris; the Wildenstein
      Gallery, New York, and the Cleveland Museum (Ohio).

1947 Exhibitions at the Carnegie Institute, Pittsburgh, and the
      Galeria dell'Obelisco, Rome. An exhibition went on tour to
      the Palais des Beaux-Arts, Brussels, the Stedelijk Museum,
      Amsterdam, the Kunsthalle, Basle, the Petit Palais, Zurich,

La Chaux-de-Fonds and Geneva (sixty-three paintings, fifty drawings, ninety lithographs and posters, one piece of ceramic).

Death of Tristan Bernard.

1948   Exhibition at the Galerie Bernhein-Jeune, Paris.

1949   The Louvre purchased *La Femme qui tire son bas*.
       Death of Misia, ex-wife of Thadée Natanson.

1950   Exhibition at the Kunsthaus, Zurich. Touring exhibition in the United States organised by the Knoedler Gallery (thirty paintings).

1951   Fiftieth anniversary of Lautrec's death marked by an exhibition at the Musée de l'Orangerie, Paris (122 works); an exhibition of engravings at the Bibliothèque Nationale, Paris (241 works); and an exhibition 'Toulouse-Lautrec, his friends and his masters' at the Musée d'Albi (183 works).

       Exhibitions of Lautrec's lithographs at the Arts Council Gallery, London; the Munich Museum; and the Boymans Museum, Rotterdam.

1952   Exhibitions in Frankfurt, Bremen, Mannheim, and at the Biennale in Venice.

1953   The first showing of the film *Moulin Rouge*, given at Albi on December 1. (Lautrec was portrayed by the actor José Ferrer.) The publication of Devismes' novel, *Cocotte*, illustrated by Lautrec.

       The centenary of Van Gogh's birth.

1956   Furniture from one of Lautrec's rooms in the Château de Malromé was sold for 470,000 francs.

1958   Exhibition in the Musée Jacquemart-André in Paris.

1959   A painting sold for 180,000 dollars at the Chrysler-Foy sale in New York. A collection of lithographs sold by auction for 86,000,000 francs at the Galerie Charpentier, Paris.

INDEX